Multimodal Participation and Engagement

Studies in Social Interaction
Series Editors: Steve Walsh, Paul Seedhouse and Christopher Jenks

Presenting data from a range of social contexts including education, the media, the workplace, and professional development, the *Studies in Social Interaction* series uncovers, among other things, the ways in which tasks are accomplished, identities formed and communities established. Each volume in the series places social interaction at the centre of discussion and presents a clear overview of the work which has been done in a particular context. Books in the series provide examples of how data can be approached and used to uncover social-interaction themes and issues, and explore how research in social interaction can feed into a better understanding of professional practices and develop new research agendas. Through stimulating tasks and accompanying commentaries, readers are engaged and challenged to reflect on particular themes and relate the discussion to their own context.

Series Editors
Steve Walsh is Professor of Applied Linguistics at Newcastle University

Paul Seedhouse is Professor of Educational and Applied Linguistics at Newcastle University

Christopher Jenks is Assistant Professor of English and Intensive English/TESOL Coordinator at the University of South Dakota

Titles available in the series:

Social Interaction in Second Language Chat Rooms	Christopher Jenks
Social Interaction and L2 Classroom Discourse	Olcay Sert
Social Interaction and Teacher Cognition	Li Li
Social Interaction and English Language Teacher Identity	John Gray and Tom Morton
Intercultural Transitions in Higher Education	Alina Schartner and Tony Johnstone Young

Visit the Studies in Social Interaction website at www.edinburghuniversitypress.com/series/ssint

Multimodal Participation and Engagement
Social Interaction in the Classroom

Christine M. Jacknick

Edinburgh University Press is one of the leading university presses in the UK. We publish academic books and journals in our selected subject areas across the humanities and social sciences, combining cutting-edge scholarship with high editorial and production values to produce academic works of lasting importance. For more information visit our website: edinburghuniversitypress.com

© Christine M. Jacknick, 2021, 2022

Edinburgh University Press Ltd
The Tun—Holyrood Road, 12(2f) Jackson's Entry, Edinburgh EH8 8PJ

First published in hardback by Edinburgh University Press 2021

Typeset in Minion Pro by
Servis Filmsetting Ltd, Stockport, Cheshire

A CIP record for this book is available from the British Library

ISBN 978 1 4744 5518 3 (hardback)
ISBN 978 1 4744 5519 0 (paperback)
ISBN 978 1 4744 5520 6 (webready PDF)
ISBN 978 1 4744 5521 3 (epub)

The right of Christine M. Jacknick to be identified as the author of this work has been asserted in accordance with the Copyright, Designs and Patents Act 1988, and the Copyright and Related Rights Regulations 2003 (SI No. 2498).

CONTENTS

Preface   vii
Acknowledgments   viii

1 Introduction   1
  1.1 Introduction   1
  1.2 Action, Alignment, and Participation   8
  1.3 The Significance of this Book   11
  1.4 Overview of the Book   12

2 Classroom Discourse and Multimodal Conversation Analysis   15
  2.1 Introduction   15
  2.2 Classroom Discourse   15
  2.3 Participation in Instructed-Learning Settings   21
  2.4 Multimodal Conversation Analysis   25
  2.5 The Data   34

3 The Presentation of Self as Student   41
  3.1 Introduction   41
  3.2 The Presentation of Self as Student: A Return to Goffman   41
  3.3 Reconceptualizing Participation and Engagement   47
  3.4 Summary   49

4 Student Participation and Engagement   51
  4.1 Introduction   51
  4.2 Participation and Engagement in Choral Responses   52
  4.3 Engaged Participation vs. Engaged Studenting: Teacher-to-Student Interaction   56
  4.4 Engaged Participation vs. Engaged Studenting: Student-to-Student Interactions   64
  4.5 Summary   72

5 Multimodal (Non-)participation and (Dis)engagement   74
  5.1 Introduction   74
  5.2 Multimodal Participation and Engagement   75

	5.3 Multimodal Engagement	76
	5.4 Waves of Embodied Response	93
	5.5 Summary	103
6	Multimodal Listening	106
	6.1 Introduction	106
	6.2 Doing Multimodal Listening	107
	6.3 Active Multimodal Listening	117
	6.4 Summary	129
7	Non-participation and Disengagement	131
	7.1 Introduction	131
	7.2 Embodied (Non-)participation and (Dis)engagement	132
	7.3 Self-presentation as (Dis)engagement	159
	7.4 Summary	164
8	Conclusion	166
	8.1 Introduction	166
	8.2 Contributions	166
	8.3 The Challenges of Multimodal Data	170
	8.4 Reflections on "Participation"	186

Appendix 1: Transcription Conventions	190
Appendix 2: Multimodal Transcript of Extract 6.2 Visual Writing	192
Appendix 3: Multimodal Transcript of Extract 6.4 I hope everybody's noticing	198
References	202
Index	216

PREFACE

I submitted the final manuscript of this book on February 24, 2020. Fifteen days later, I taught my class in person for the last time and left campus for the foreseeable future when all courses at my university shifted to remote learning in response to the COVID-19 pandemic. Teaching at a large public community college in New York City has often meant close contact—students sitting shoulder to shoulder in classrooms, shared faculty offices, and packed elevators. As we shifted to online learning platforms like Zoom and Blackboard, I wondered what participation and engagement would look like for students with unstable internet connections and limited data plans, to say nothing of the pressures of quarantine in the epicenter of the disease in the US. Many students chose not to share their video during Zoom sessions, which, for an instructor, means talking to black squares with students' names on them. Students could click a button to raise their (emoji) hand or they could use the chat function, but these group interactions were an enormous departure from in-person classroom interactions and from traditional approaches to online learning. Many students declined to join synchronous sessions at all. What could I reasonably conclude about my students' participation and engagement? While participation monitoring is always a complex task for teachers, synchronous online teaching brings up new questions about which student actions we attend to and "count" as participation and engagement.

Understanding how little we know about participation and engagement is a crucial step toward better pedagogy, whether in traditional face-to-face classrooms, distance learning contexts, or whatever classrooms may look like in the future. As this book highlights, students are often engaged and participating when we think they are not, and likewise, students can appear to be engaged and participating, when in fact, careful analysis of their embodied actions shows they are not. The book argues that teachers and researchers need to recognize (1) the multimodal complexity of student (non-)participation and (dis)engagement, and (2) how much of students' participation and engagement is essentially unknowable to us. Our methods for measuring participation are imperfect, and as we move into new kinds of instructed-learning contexts, it is more important than ever for us to realize these basic facts. We don't know what online, synchronous learning will look like, nor do we know how socially distant face-to-face classes might work. My hope is that this book helps teachers and researchers pay attention to how they define participation and engagement, as well as the complex, varied ways students "do" participation and engagement in instructed-learning contexts.

ACKNOWLEDGMENTS

First and foremost, I am thankful for the teachers and students who so generously allowed me and my cameras into their classrooms. I am particularly indebted to my students at Borough of Manhattan Community College for opening my eyes to the many ways of doing-being-a-student.

This research would not have been possible without generous funding from Borough of Manhattan Community College (*Faculty Development Grant 2016-2017* and *Faculty Publication Grant 2019-2020*) and the City University of New York (*PSC-CUNY Research Awards in 2016-2017* and *2019-2020; William Kelly Fellowship 2018-2019;* and *CUNY Book Completion Award 2019-2020*). These grants supported transcription of recordings, subsidized travel to the International Academy for Conversation Analysis in 2016, and secured time for writing. I am also grateful for BMCC funding that has allowed me to collaborate with (and pay!) undergraduate researchers, including the CSTEP and work-study programs. This book would not be what it is without my undergraduate research assistants, Yongfeng Liang and Christal Rodriguez, who created the line illustrations you see throughout the book, Nick Melgar, who noticed the absence of phones in my older data and suggested collecting more recent data to see how their presence might affect participation and engagement, and Nicholas Salion, who helped me compile references and the index.

This book was completed over many hours in libraries and cafes, and I would like to thank the Hendrick Hudson Free Library and the Peekskill Coffee House in particular for being my homes away from home.

Writing this book while simultaneously being the mother of two small children is the hardest thing I have ever done, and I am grateful to the many mothers in my life for commiserating with me, cheering me on, and showing me how it's done, one day at a time. Thank you particularly to all those who have cared for my children while I write, but especially thank you to Joyce, who makes my life possible. All my love to Andy, Cece, and Al, who make my life a joy.

Many, many people read early versions of analysis or talked through ideas over coffee, and though any remaining errors are mine, I could not have produced this finished product without their generosity: Sharon Avni, Sarah Creider, Jen Delfino, Spencer Hazel, Gabi Kahn, Elisa Koniski, Santoi Wagner, Hansun Waring, and Linda Wine. I can never repay Derya Duran for her assistance with data collection, and for taking over entirely when I came down with the flu! Lorenza Mondada's workshop on multimodality at the International Academy for Conversation Analysis (IACA) in 2016 started me on the path to multimodal analysis and opened my eyes to the complexity of students' multimodal actions in the classroom. Thank you to my friend Olcay Sert, for encouraging me to write this book back in 2013 and for his unwavering support along the way. The editors of this series, Steve Walsh, Paul Seedhouse, and Chris Jenks, have been generous with their feedback, and I am grateful for their guidance. Eliza Wright did an unbelievable job editing my manuscript. My thanks to Mike Olmert for his guidance on indexing, and for everything. Finally, I dedicate this book to my academic/life bestie, Maureen Matarese, my most enthusiastic cheerleader and my best reader. Tag, you're it.

1

INTRODUCTION

1.1 INTRODUCTION

Participation is colloquially understood to mean speaking, and many syllabi count "participation" toward students' grades, generally considered to be their willingness to contribute to class discussions. The push to get students to "participate" can also be found in teacher-preparation programs: edTPA, a teacher-certification assessment used by many states in the United States, requires that teachers utilize "activities, discussions, or other modes of participation that engage students" (Stanford Center for Assessment, Learning and Equity 2016: 52). However, the terms "participation" and "engage" are undefined, a common trend. In addition, students' conception of what "counts" as participation at any given moment in classroom interaction may be out of alignment with the teacher's interactional and/or pedagogical agenda. This misalignment can have serious consequences, including teachers' moral categorizations of "bad students," with differential interactional treatment leading to negative consequences for participation, engagement, and learning (see Hall 1998). This monograph presents a more complete picture of what doing-being-a-student *looks like* in classroom interaction, including consideration of not only students' verbal contributions in class but also their embodied actions. In order to do so, I propose a reconceptualization of *participation* as a hybrid phenomenon consisting of not only the interactional alignment of student actions but also their pedagogical alignment with the teacher's agenda. I also suggest a definition of *engagement* as students' close monitoring of the interaction, as evidenced by the precise temporal and sequential deployment of their multimodal resources. Finally, I hope to illustrate the limits of observable behaviors, highlighting what this means for our characterizations of student participation and engagement, for the analyst as well as the teacher, and the implications of these limitations for teacher education and evaluation, as well as for classroom discourse research more generally.

Our understanding of the complexity of teaching has been illuminated by a vast trove of research on teachers, teaching, and teachers' interactional competence in particular (see Hall and Looney 2019; Walsh 2006, 2011; Waring 2016; Wong and Waring 2010). Hall and Looney's (2019) edited volume and Waring's (2016) monograph expand our understanding of the "specialized nature" of teaching as an interactional achievement (Hall et al. 2019: 53), and I argue that doing-being-a-student deserves the same analytic treatment. Waring says that for teachers, "being responsive to the moment in part means tuning in to the simultaneous happenings of that moment and attending to such simultaneity to the best of one's abilities" (2016: 127), but the complexity of those "simultaneous happenings" has received much less attention. In her introduction, Waring recounts the experience of watching her daughter playing school and enacting the role of "teacher." In reading that, I wondered what it would look like to "play" student. Perhaps children so often want to be the teacher in imaginary play because it is clearer what that role entails and requires. To the question of "how students learn to be students within the traditional school system," Nuthall briefly refers to "the culture of studenting" (1997: 710), but the question of what "studenting" involves is one that has not yet been answered. This volume aims to shed light on the interactional work of doing-being-a-student in a classroom in all its multimodal complexity.

This extract taken from the first Harry Potter film (Columbus 2001) shows how misalignments and teacher categorizations can occur within the first few moments of the first class meeting, and underscores the relevance of multimodal analysis for classroom discourse research.

Extract 1.1 Not pay attention

```
1          (4.0)
    ss     ((speaking to one another))
2          *(2.0)
           *door bangs open, Sna walks toward front-->
3   SNA    >there will be no foolish wand-waving?
4          or silly incantations< in this *class?*
                                      -->*Sna turns to class*
5          (1.4)
6   SNA    as such, I don't expect many of you
7          to appreciate the subtle science and
8          exact art that is potion-making?=
9          =however, for <those select *few,*>
                                       *....*gaze to Mal-->
10         (0.2) *#(0.4) who possess: (0.4)*#(0.4)
                 *Mal small smile-->        *gaze to S?-->
           #fig. 1.1                  #fig. 1.2
```

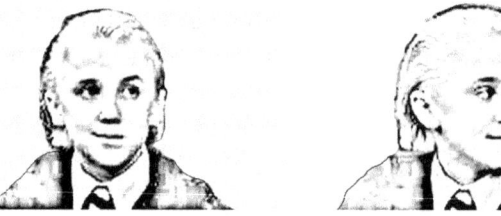

```
11         the pre*disposition,* (2.6) I can teach
                  *Mal gaze to Sna-->
                         *Sna gaze around at class-->
```

Extract 1.1 Not pay attention (continued)

```
12        you how to be↑witch the mind and ensare
13        the senses. I can tell you how to
14        bottle fame, brew glory, and <even put
15        a stopper (.) in *death.>#
                              *Mal eyebrows up, eager face-->
                              #fig. 1.3
```

```
16        (2.2)*(1.0)
              *Har audibly writing-->
17   SNA  then again, maybe some of you have
18        come to Hogwarts in possession of
19        abilities so formidable that you feel
20        confident enough to <NOT PAY ATTEN*TION.>*#
                              *......*Her gaze to Har-->
                                    -->*Har stops writing
                                       #fig. 1.4
```

```
21        (1.2)*(0.1)*(0.7)*(0.2)*#(4.2)
              *Her elbows Har/Har putting away quill
                  *Har gaze to Her
                      *Her gaze to Sna and head nod towards Sna
                          *Har gaze to Sna and posture shift-->
                              #fig. 1.5
```

Extract 1.1 Not pay attention (continued)

```
22   SNA   <mister Potter, (1.2) <our new celebrity.>*
                                          *Har furrowed brow
23         (2.1)
24   SNA   >tell me,=what would I get if I added
25         powdered root of asphodel to an
26         infusion of wormwood?<
27         *(0.8)*
     her   *.....*hand-raising
28   HER   *.hhhh
           *hand raise-->
29         (0.6)*(0.1)* (0.2)# (1.0)   *#(0.4) *
              *Har gaze to Her------*.......*head down and shake*
              *Her gaze to Har*gaze to Sna-->
                          #fig. 1.6 #fig. 1.7
```

```
30   SNA   you don't know? well let's: >try again.<
31         >where mister Potter would you look if
32         I asked you to find me a bezoar,<
```

Extract 1.1 Not pay attention (continued)

```
33         (0.1)*# (1.3)       *# (0.1)     *#(1.6)
           *Her hand raise*gaze to Har*gaze to Sna-->
           #fig. 1.8       #fig. 1.9    #fig. 1.10
```

```
34   HAR   I- I don't know sir.
35   SNA   >and what is the difference between
36         ↑monkswood< and wolfbane?
37         (1.0)
38   HER   #.hhh
           #fig. 1.11
```

Extract 1.1 Not pay attention (continued)

```
39   HAR   I don't know sir,*#
                    *Har gaze down
                    #fig. 1.12
```

```
40         (1.0)*#(0.4) *#(0.8)
               *Her gaze to Har*gaze to Sna-->
               #fig. 1.13      #fig. 1.14
```

```
41   SNA   pity. (2.2) clearly, (0.8) fame isn't
42         everything, (0.4) *#is it,  *#mister Potter,
                              *Mal smile*gaze to S?
                              #fig. 1.15 #fig. 1.16
```

This 2-minute extract highlights many of the complex, shifting, and varied ways of displaying participation and engagement that I will focus on in this volume. Malfoy, who will become a teacher's pet to Professor Snape, engages in mutual gaze with him in line 9, and smiles in affiliation in line 10. He maintains an upright posture and shows his appreciation of the teacher turn with an eyebrow flash and eager facial expression (line 15). However, even this "good" student's display of participation and engagement is marked by a brief shift in gaze and smile to a fellow student (line 10), a kind of embodied "byplay" (Goffman 1981). He does the same in line 42, smiling in appreciation of Snape's rebuke of Harry, and again engaging in mutual gaze with another student. These actions are not doing-listening-to-the-teacher, but they do not disrupt the progressivity of Snape's turn. This fact, along with Malfoy's status as "good" student, means these actions are unsanctioned by Snape.

Harry and Hermione, however, prove less adept in their displays of participation and engagement, though in different ways. During the beginning of the extended teacher turn, Harry maintains his gaze toward his paper, writing down highlights of Snape's speech; because he is using a quill, this writing is audible, particularly during the silence in line 16, and Snape orients to Harry's writing as non-participation, glossing his actions as "not pay[ing] attention" (line 20). Harry's note-taking might well be an appropriate form of participation in another classroom context, or a different kind of extended teacher turn, but this one is designed as a performance to be attended to closely by all students, and so neither his writing nor his gaze down toward his materials counts as participation, and worse, they are oriented to as non-participation and disengagement.

Snape then shifts the participation framework, directing his talk to Harry (addressing him by name in line 22), with all other students as unaddressed but ratified recipients (Goffman 1981). Harry participates in this exchange appropriately, with an embodied claim of insufficient knowledge (CIK, Sert 2011) and verbal CIK in lines 34 and 39. Harry also mostly maintains his gaze toward Snape during this sequence, with occasional glances toward Hermione, seated next to him, who is also participating inappropriately. While Snape's turns in lines 24–26, 30–32, and 35–36 are directed to Harry, Hermione eagerly displays her willingness to participate with dramatic hand-raises (i.e., bids to reply) and audible in-breaths as displays of her incipiency (lines 27–28, 33, and 38). Because Snape's turns are directed toward Harry in particular, her displays of engagement and willingness to participate are also inappropriate. Harry and Hermione are both *engaged* in demonstrable ways, but they are simultaneously participating in misalignment with the teacher's expectations.

The "participation" of these three students in this brief extract is complex, dynamic, and reflexively related to the other co-present parties and their multimodal actions. While the need for a clearer definition of participation has been noted by some (e.g., van Lier 1988), even the clearest definitions we have are vague, potentially to allow for an expansive analytic view of the phenomenon. For example, Goodwin defines participation as "actions demonstrating forms of involvement performed by parties within evolving structures of talk" (1999: 177). This includes hearers as well as speakers, and Goodwin stresses the importance not only of hearers' displays of engagement, mutual monitoring, and participation, but also of their "displays of inattention, byplay or heckling" (1999: 178). In this book, I conceive of participation as including the full range of potential student multimodal action (including non-participation), with engagement as a display of close monitoring of interaction, allowing for precisely timed multimodal actions. By broadening our focus to include students' multimodal actions, we can specify analytically what is meant by "participation" and "engagement."

1.2 ACTION, ALIGNMENT, AND PARTICIPATION

Within conversation analysis (CA), one of the first steps is "to identify the actions that participants in interaction do and describe the particular practices of conduct that they use to accomplish them" (Sidnell 2013: 78). Sidnell includes as examples of "actions" things like "asking, telling, requesting" (2013: 78), though in the same volume, Levinson (2013) acknowledges the need to include actions beyond the canonical list. Goodwin argues that actions include the "public recognition of meaningful events" (2000: 1492), suggesting that the typical list of actions seen above is but the tip of the iceberg. In advocating for including multimodal resources in the scope of our analysis, Mondada argues that what CA analysts call "next-turn proof procedure" is in fact "next-action proof procedure" (2016a: 361); participants demonstrate their understanding of the prior action in the production (or absence) of their responsive action. By proposing an expansion of our sense of "action," Mondada is in fact returning to the most basic form of what is meant by *social action*. Goffman argues for "move" as the unit of analysis rather than "utterance" or "turn," noting that the latter terms are "responsive to linguistic, not interactional, analysis" (1981: 23). Following Mondada (and Goffman), in this book I will use the term "action" in a broader sense than has been used traditionally, to include any use of the body to project/index stance or alignment (whether pedagogical or interactional), i.e., the students' understanding of, and willingness to embody, what doing-being-a-student entails at that particular moment. Here I also draw on Goffman's (1981) claim that the "moves" in interaction communicate an individual's alignment.

A word here about alignment will aid in understanding how I am conceiving of students' (non-)participation and (dis)engagement. Stivers teases apart affiliation and alignment, noting that the latter "acknowledge[s] the information provided ... and support[s] the progress of the telling" (2008: 32). As a feature of responsive actions, alignment is "omnirelevant" (Lindström and Sorjonen 2013: 353), and so students' alignment with the interaction and the lesson is apparent in their actions and their inaction. Stivers was examining storytelling sequences, and this type of activity has some relevant parallels to teacher-led classroom interaction, mainly that there is a "structural asymmetry" (2008: 34) built in, with one participant holding the floor for an extended period, and the listeners' alignment being necessary to allow the progression of the telling. Likewise, in a classroom, the students' alignment is needed in order to allow the progression of the lesson, and just as Stivers notes for tellings, "activity alignment by the recipient is not a given" (2008: 35). The key for my analysis is Stivers' note that "alignment is with respect to the activity in progress" (2008: 34). In the whole-class setting, "the activity in progress" has both an interactional and a pedagogical momentum, directed by the teacher, that can be either disrupted or facilitated by the actions of the students. Thus, I characterize student actions as being in (or out of) alignment both pedagogically and interactionally. As an example, during an extended teacher turn, a student who is writing in their notebook might be aligned interactionally by not disrupting the progressivity of the turn, but if the teacher turn calls for students to orient toward their books or to the teacher

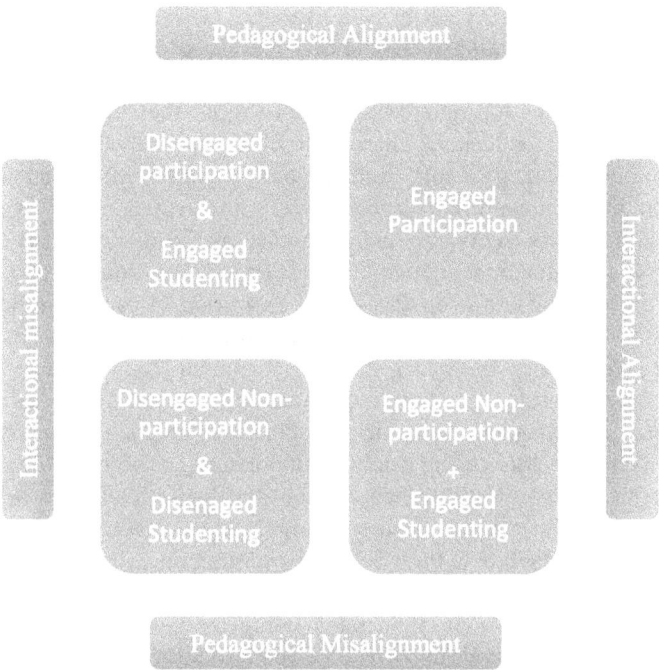

Figure 1.17   Reconceptualizing "participation" and "engagement"

directly, the activity of writing would be misaligned pedagogically. On the other hand, students who display engagement with a discussion through gaze orientation, for example, while simultaneously being unwilling to participate are pedagogically aligned, though not interactionally.

In a recent volume on the embodied work of teaching, several authors note that teachers' management of classroom interaction involves not only interactional alignment, but also pedagogical alignment (see Hall and Looney 2019; Hall et al. 2019). This conception of teaching relates directly to my reconceptualization of student (non-)participation and (dis)engagement as a function of their (mis)alignment with the ongoing interaction and the pedagogical focus. Figure 1.17 shows a matrix with my reconceptualization of (non-)participation and (dis)engagement, with the X axis representing the student actions' interactional alignment and the Y axis representing the student actions' pedagogical alignment.

The upper right quadrant is the space where we might place the role of "good student"—someone who is participating appropriately and demonstrating their engagement. However, the reality of students' participation and engagement in whole-class interaction is messier and more complex. Students display their participation and engagement differently from moment to moment, sometimes in ways that align with the teacher's interactional and pedagogical agendas, and sometimes in ways that do not. I do not suggest that a student can be placed into one of these quadrants (as a "good" or "bad" student), but that any given student action, based on its sequential and temporal placement in a specific context of classroom interaction, may be categorized according to this matrix.

You may notice that "studenting," or participating inappropriately, exists in every other quadrant but the top right, but I do not suggest that "studenting" is equivalent to being a "bad" student. Rather, studenting represents the undertaking of a category-bound action of the role "student," but in contexts where that action is out of alignment interactionally or pedagogically. It is an interactional achievement in its own right and can represent quite skillful interactional work on the part of students. In the bottom right quadrant, a situation where students are doing-listening by being silent but engaging in off-task writing or organization of papers would represent a case of studenting where there is interactional alignment (i.e., the student is not disrupting progressivity) but pedagogical misalignment (i.e., the student is observably not doing-listening). The bottom left quadrant, where there is a lack of both interactional and pedagogical alignment, would cover situations where students are overtly and covertly disengaging from the interaction (e.g., sleeping for the former, and holding a phone in front of their handout for the latter), both of which might be considered part of the role "bad student." In these cases, students sometimes orient to the accountability of these actions by putting on a show of doing-being-a-student. However, in this same quadrant, we also have cases of studenting because of students' lack of classroom interactional competence, such that they are unable to identify appropriate places to participate and also misjudge the pedagogical goal of the moment. Lastly, in the upper left quadrant, we might see interactional misalignment but pedagogical alignment when students are unwilling to participate but display engagement, or when students participate in a delayed way.

"Participation," "participate," and "participant" are terms that appear in most research on social interaction, and the "participation metaphor" is ubiquitous in educational research (Sfard 1998). However, clear definitions of these terms are few and far between. Matoesian says that "participation refers to the interactive and embodied positioning of speaker and recipient roles" (2010: 556); this definition helpfully suggests that participation is more than speaking, but it is unclear analytically what that "positioning" might entail. Kendon likewise argues that "the status of interactional participant is entered into or relinquished" (1990: 3) in embodied ways. Goodwin defines participation as "actions demonstrating forms of involvement by parties within evolving structures of talk" (1999: 177). However, this definition suggests more questions: *What kinds* of actions? *How* do they demonstrate involvement? Are there *degrees* of involvement? This monograph addresses those questions by placing the focus on different kinds of participation in classroom interaction.

Goodwin and Goodwin (2004) represents one of the clearest treatments of the concept of participation itself, drawing on Erving Goffman's foundational work (to be discussed in further detail in Section 3.2), but simultaneously highlighting the limitations of his approach. Because Goffman categorizes speakers according to production format, but all other co-present persons according to the participation framework (or participation status), speakers and hearers are separated from each other analytically, with no clear path to a holistic analysis of interaction. Goodwin and Goodwin note that this analytic separation not only privileges speakers over hearers, but it also privileges the speech of speakers as opposed to their "other forms of embodied practice that might also be constitutive of participation in talk" (2004: 225). Goodwin and Goodwin include prosody, objects, and the environment as among the multimodal resources drawn on for social action, including also the "visible bodies" of speakers and hearers (2004: 227). This distinction helps to highlight the relevance of monitoring to participation; how much access co-present persons have to each other visually can affect the forms of participation available to them (Markaki et al. 2014; Mondada 2012). By including the full range of students' multimodal actions in my analysis, I hope to realize Goodwin and Goodwin's call for an analytic framework that acknowledges that "as a set of practices for building relevant social and cultural action talk does not stand alone" (2004: 239).

1.3 THE SIGNIFICANCE OF THIS BOOK

Teachers (and analysts) sometimes think students are participating and engaged when they are not, or conversely that students are not participating and are disengaged when in fact they are. Participation is a complex and varied multimodal phenomenon. This book uniquely takes a radical focus on students' multimodal actions, including those that do not collude with the teacher's pedagogical goals (see McDermott and Tylbor 1986 for more on collusion). Along with expected ways of participating like raising hands and speaking, students also display their unwillingness to participate by, for example, avoiding eye contact with the teacher. However, they also occasionally display resistance to participation in more overt ways, such as by sleeping or wearing headphones in class. These "non-verbal" actions are not usually included in analyses of student participation because they are not seen by teachers (or researchers) as *forms of participation*. While teachers tend to conflate "participation" and "engagement," my analysis demonstrates that while students are always displaying participation (or a lack thereof) through their multimodal actions, clear *engagement* and *disengagement* are demonstrable in only a minority of cases. Engagement may be publicly evident by the precise timing of some multimodal actions, such as when students are able to anticipate opportunities for initiation or to time their contributions to fit teacher-designed spaces for participation; however, other multimodal actions which may count as public displays of participation/engagement to the teacher (e.g., student gaze to the book during individual desk work) are essentially unknowable in terms of whether there is *actual* student engagement.

A particular strength of my research is the combination of data from language classrooms and "content" classrooms, which allows me to make claims about the nature of student participation more generally. My monograph joins a movement in CA research toward greater integration of embodied behaviors (e.g., smiles, eye gaze, positioning) in analysis, and the acknowledgment of the role gesture plays in classroom learning (Jacknick 2018; Jacknick and Thornbury 2013; McCafferty and Stam 2008). For example, Jacknick (2018) found that a teacher and her students draw on a wide array of interactional resources, including gesture, eye gaze, and proxemics (i.e., physical distance between persons), as they collaboratively build understanding of a grammar point. Much of the existing research on embodied behaviors is limited in scope, drawn from experimental settings or from a limited corpus. While there has been increasing attention to multimodality within CA, to my knowledge no monographs have taken an entirely multimodal approach to examining the embodied nature of student participation and engagement.

The question of how participation and engagement relate to learning is an important one, and many researchers of classroom discourse have focused on learning specifically (e.g., Appel 2010; Hellermann 2008a, 2009; Jacknick 2018; Majlesi and Markee 2018; Markee 2015a; Markee and Kunitz 2015; Mori and Markee 2009; Seedhouse 2010; Walsh 2011), or sometimes learning through demonstrations of socially-distributed cognition (e.g., Kasper 2008; Seedhouse and Walsh 2010). Socially-distributed cognition can be seen in the pursuit of intersubjectivity through repair (Schegloff 1991), as well as through sequence and turn-taking (Seedhouse and Walsh 2010), with analysis including participants' embodied actions (Cole and Engeström 1993; Mori and Hasegawa 2009). Learning can be seen as both product and process (Seedhouse 2010); it can be demonstrated by tracking, for example, a language learner's movement toward native-like production of a particular item, or by examining how learners "contribute to the process of co-constructing meaning" (Seedhouse and Walsh 2010: 141). While the investigation of learning is a worthwhile pursuit, I wish to be clear at the outset that while my analyses relate to learning (see discussion in Chapter 8), they are not focused on learning per se. It is for this reason that I use the term "student" throughout, rather than "learner"; I am interested in the role "student," undertaken by participants as they enter the physical classroom space. My focus in this volume is on students' "co-operative action" (Goodwin 2018), i.e., how they draw on a variety of multimodal resources at the same time to create meaning and action, and do so with co-present others in classrooms. How do students display their understanding of what doing-being-a-student looks and sounds like? To answer this question, we must broaden our focus to see what students are doing with their "visible bodies" (Goodwin and Goodwin 2004).

1.4 OVERVIEW OF THE BOOK

This book presents a definition of participation in classrooms as a function of alignment with both (1) pedagogical goals and (2) interactional context. Conceptualizing participation in this way allows us to characterize student actions that collude with the teacher's pedagogical and interactional goals, but also those that do not, what I am terming *non-participation*. Importantly, this definition allows us to examine the full range of student action in the classroom, moving beyond students' verbal contributions to analyze their embodied actions as they index their (non-)participation. Finally, a major goal of this monograph is to distinguish *participation* from *engagement* in classroom interaction (more on this in Chapter 3). In so doing, I also highlight the limits of observable behavior, and by extension, of CA.

Chapter 2 presents a condensed background of classroom discourse research, particularly focused on whole-class, teacher-led interaction. Because the interactional context of participation is so crucial to my analysis, a consideration of classroom interactional organization is presented, with particular focus on Walsh's (2006, 2011) modes. In Section 2.3, I review research on the nature of participation in classrooms, including the few studies that have focused on what I am calling "non-participation" and "disengagement." The methodology for this study, multimodal conversation analysis (CA), is described in Section 2.4, and here I will provide overviews of relevant multimodal resources, and I will further explain my analytic methods. Finally, in Section 2.5, I provide an overview of the three data corpora I draw on for this study.

Chapter 3 explores the ideas of Erving Goffman, foundational for CA, and explains how they have influenced my own thinking and my definitions of (non-)participation and (dis)engagement. In particular, I discuss his views on social interactions, participation frameworks, and the performance metaphor. I also provide a brief review of classroom discourse research inspired by Goffman's ideas, and conclude with a fuller explanation of my reconceptualization of "participation" and "engagement" which will inform the analysis throughout Chapters 4 to 7.

Chapter 4 presents a range of examples of student participation in line with how participation has traditionally been conceived, i.e., as verbal contributions. However, through multimodal CA, I show how even common, familiar forms of student participation shed light on students' (dis)engagement. Through these examples, we will begin to see the ways in which we can disambiguate participation from engagement. I also illustrate a new term in this chapter, "studenting," an interactional achievement through which students deploy a category-bound action of the category "student" at inappropriate moments in the classroom interaction.

Chapter 5 turns to a consideration of students' *multimodal participation*, and particularly, *engagement*. While students' verbal contributions are included in this analysis, I focus especially on how students use their bodies to display their participation and engagement, revealing the complex temporal and sequential waves of student embodied action in the classroom. Chapter 6 likewise focuses on students' embodied actions when they are mostly silent, an activity I am calling *multimodal listening*. In this chapter, I address the question, "what does doing listening look like in instructed-learning settings?" I show the dynamic nature of students' multimodal listening displays and examine students' multimodal demonstrations of active listenership.

As will become evident through the preceding chapters, students' (non-) participation and (dis)engagement are dynamic, and in multiparty classroom talk, it is most often the case that some students are participating (and possibly engaged) while others are not. Chapter 7 explores the concept of "non-participation," examining a variety of ways of not participating that index differing levels of (dis)engagement. Following the wave metaphor introduced earlier in the book, I show how students' collective engagement with and disengagement from whole-class interaction unfolds in waves of multimodal action.

Chapter 8 presents a discussion of the conceptualizations of (non-)participation and (dis)engagement as illustrated in the preceding data analysis chapters, with focus on the new contributions made by this volume. Challenges of multimodal transcription and analysis are discussed in Section 8.3, including single-case analyses of phenomena for future study. Finally, I reflect on how participation and engagement relate to both (1) the performance of the role "student," and (2) classroom interactional competence and learning. Implications for professional practice are discussed in this final chapter, including the importance of teacher interactional awareness, critical reflection on the pedagogical effectiveness of different activities and participation structures, and the observability of teaching and learning.

2

CLASSROOM DISCOURSE AND MULTIMODAL CONVERSATION ANALYSIS

> Learners are interesting, at least as interesting as teachers, because they are the people who do whatever learning gets done, whether it is because of or in spite of the teacher.
>
> Dick Allwright (1980: 165)

2.1 INTRODUCTION

This book focuses on students' multimodal actions in whole-class, teacher-fronted interaction, a setting which is often assumed to entail predominance of teacher control and a monolithic participation structure. The literature on classroom discourse is extensive, and thus this review focuses on research on participation structures and particularly, students' place within the discourse in teacher-fronted activity. Given my conception of participation and engagement as context-sensitive phenomena, I devote a section specifically to consideration of the interactional organization of classrooms as an example of institutional talk. Special attention will also be given throughout to analysis of student participation, though I also focus in Section 2.3 on studies of participation specifically. As we will see in reviewing these studies, "participation" is often equated with verbal contributions, but following a general "embodied turn" (Nevile 2015) within the social sciences, more consideration has been given to how embodied actions work alongside (or in the absence of) verbal participation. In Section 2.4, I introduce multimodal conversation analysis, devoting sections to the multimodal resources that will be most integral to my analysis of students' displays of (non-)participation and (dis)engagement: gaze, gesture, body movement, and artifact manipulation. I also address the need to analyze the full multimodal picture by introducing "complex multimodal Gestalts" (Mondada 2014c) and the creation of multimodal collections. I address the challenges inherent in multimodal transcription in Section 2.4.6, and then I conclude by introducing the three data corpora I draw on for this study.

2.2 CLASSROOM DISCOURSE

In their seminal study, Sinclair and Coulthard (1975) examine the discourse in fairly homogenous classrooms in whole-class, teacher-led discussion, developing a classification system for teacher talk, broken down into moves, and later, into types of moves by subsequent researchers (e.g., Love 1991). The focus on teacher talk may have been born out of the scarcity of student talk in the classrooms under observation (particularly in the activity of whole-class, teacher-led interaction), and in turn, the scarcity of student talk may stem from conceptions of teaching and learning that are mostly implicit in Sinclair and Coulthard's report. Given that classrooms are places where teaching and learning occur, they seem to suggest that the teacher talk and behavior *must* be teaching. The talk of students is rarely considered, and when it is examined, it is used mostly as an indication of how the prior or subsequent teacher talk should be characterized. The resulting classification system advanced knowledge of teacher talk, and also implicitly set a standard understanding of what "traditional" teacher-fronted activity looks like. In addition to creating a catalogue of possible teacher moves, Sinclair and Coulthard (1975) demonstrated the predominance of the teacher initiation–student response–teacher evaluation (IRE) sequence in the discourse of classrooms. Learner contributions are included in their coding scheme as they relate to the coding of teacher talk, a trend followed by other researchers (e.g., Fanselow 1977; Greene et al. 1988). Notably, many subsequent studies have used the phrases "traditional" or "teacher-fronted/led/directed" as shorthand for the kind of interaction found by Sinclair and Coulthard. The current study's focus on teacher-fronted activities provides the opportunity to examine the discourse in this setting in micro-analytic detail, and to show that it does not entail such a monolithic participation structure.

In his study on the interactions taking place in an elementary school classroom over the course of a school year, Mehan (1979) highlighted the nature of turn-allocation in the classroom, including the initiation rights of students within teacher-fronted activity. In order for a contribution to be successfully incorporated into a lesson, Mehan argued that students must master "getting the floor," "holding the floor," and "introducing news" (1979: 139–40). In order to accomplish these three things, students must be effective participants in the classroom discourse, a large part of which consists of knowing "with whom, when, and where they can speak and act" (1979: 133). In this way, Mehan stressed the importance of the interactional (or communicative) competence of the students in the classroom setting, a major focus of this book as well.

McHoul's (1978, 1985) studies on primary school classrooms apply CA to the institutional setting of the classroom in order to determine how the interactional architecture of these settings (e.g., classrooms) differs from the baseline of everyday talk-in-interaction. These studies provide an important benchmark for later studies, but they have had a similar effect as Sinclair and Coulthard's (1975) descriptions. That is, the persistence of participation structures in teacher-fronted activity as described in these studies has been assumed by subsequent researchers. In particular, McHoul notes that due to the teacher control of discourse in formal classroom contexts, longer gaps are possible than in everyday conversation and the potential for overlap is minimized. In addition, he found that the pre-allocation of turns called for the teacher to hold every other turn (i.e., teacher–student–teacher), and that deviations from this pattern were subject to repair. McHoul discusses nomination as involving not only the right but the obligation to speak, arguing that no other student but the nominated student has such a right or obligation. McHoul (1978) argues that students may not self-select to initiate sequences since such an action is unaccounted for by the turn-taking mechanisms for teacher-fronted classrooms. He posits that a student selecting another student as next speaker might be an interaction a certain type of educator would want to encourage, but in the face of the foregoing (i.e., the apparatus for turn-taking), it would seem that this would involve enforcing an entirely different speech exchange system for classrooms based either on the same rules as conversational exchange or on a less modified form of them than that in use in the classrooms he studied.

The nature of talk in whole-class interaction has often been found to be teacher-focused; communication directed by the teacher represents "the deep grooves" whole-class talk runs on, as Edwards and Westgate (1994) put it. The three-part initiation–response–evaluation (IRE) structure identified by Sinclair and Coulthard (1975), with the third turn later renamed 'feedback' (IRF) by Mehan (1979), has been extensively documented and studied by researchers of classroom discourse (Candela 1999; Lemke 1990; McHoul 1985; Markee 1995; Nystrand 1997; Seedhouse 2004; Wells 1993), with many looking at pedagogical and interactional consequences of differential design and action in the third turn by the teacher (Cullen 2002; Hall 1998, 2002; Hall and Walsh 2002; Hellermann 2003, 2005; Liu 2008; Waring 2008; Wong and Waring 2009). However, the description of teacher-fronted activity advanced by McHoul (1978) and others (Mehan 1979; Sinclair and Coulthard 1975) may also be related to the age of the student participants, i.e., turn-taking in teacher-fronted activity in adult classrooms may be quite different from elementary or secondary school classrooms. In addition, as van Lier (2001) notes, no discursive structure is inherently unproductive for learning; rather, the question of whether the IRE/F sequence is appropriate depends upon the interactional and pedagogical context. Waring (2009), by tracing how one student breaks out of the initiation–response–feedback sequence, demonstrates the pervasiveness of the IRE/F, but also how participants negotiate their way out of chained IRE/F sequences. Jacknick (2011a) flips the traditional focus, looking at three-part sequences initiated by students, examining how students capitalize on the sequential opportunity of post-expansions to launch new sequences. Uncovering whether and how students are able to affect the trajectory of classroom interaction is likewise a central aim of this book.

2.2.1 INTERACTIONAL ORGANIZATION OF CLASSROOMS

Within CA, there is a foundational belief that social order is produced by participants; rather than imposing an etic perspective, categorizations of classroom talk can be seen as post hoc attempts to illustrate the order that has been co-created by the social actors in interaction. Goffman, with his "interaction order," suggests that "forms of face-to-face life are worn smooth by constant repetition" (1983: 9), though he notes these smooth grooves are also by definition actively produced and co-constructed by co-present parties. Sarangi and Roberts likewise talk about "shared habitual practices" (1999: 3) that shape interaction in institutions. Describing how people create, sustain, and change the interaction order through social interaction is the main focus of CA (Kasper 2008).

Many different analytic frameworks have been proffered by classroom discourse researchers, but there is a lack of agreement about how to categorize classroom interaction (not to mention whether such categorization is wise or in alignment with the theoretical framework of CA). In his plenary at LANSI, Sarangi (2018) discussed categorization as a method itself, arguing that everything could be categorized in a myriad of ways, so each time we categorize our data, we are picking our approach as we go, what he called "the emergence of category." Mehan (1979), for example, was looking at the structure of lessons, and included in his analysis categories like opening, instructional, and closing phases. Given my focus on students' participation and engagement as context-sensitive phenomena, two approaches to analyzing the interactional organization of classrooms are particularly relevant to the analysis here: Seedhouse (1994, 2004) and Walsh (2006, 2011). While it would be unwise to enter a conversation analytic project with too many preconceived ideas of what kind of interaction one will find, it is likewise sensible to draw on a framework of the kinds of interaction that habitually occur in classrooms, and this book references Walsh's (2006, 2011) modes throughout as shorthand for the kinds of interactional "fingerprints" found in each (more below).

Seedhouse's (1994) investigation of the interactional architecture of the language classroom argues that there is an essential characteristic which distinguishes talk in the second language classroom from other forms of communication: "the connection between the pedagogical purposes which underline different classroom activities and the linguistic forms and patterns of interaction which result from those classroom activities" (1994: 303). In line with van Lier's (1984) consideration of activity types, Seedhouse argues that it is impossible to evaluate all classroom discourse by the same criteria, since the purposes of the teacher and learners vary throughout a lesson, and thus, so does the nature of their talk. Seedhouse (2004) expands this perspective to present an all-encompassing view of second language classroom discourse from a CA perspective, examining each of the special and particular constraints on the talk that takes place in language classrooms. He examines turn-taking, sequencing, repair, and overall structural organization in three contexts: form and accuracy, meaning and fluency, and task-oriented. Seedhouse's contention that talk has a reflexive relationship with pedagogical purpose very much informs my conceptualization of participation and engagement as locally-contingent, context-sensitive phenomena.

In the service of a model of self-evaluation of teacher talk (SETT), Walsh (2006) introduces the concept of *modes* to describe what he terms "classroom microcontexts," each of which entails different participation structures related to pedagogical goals and activity types. The aim with this framework is not to create broad generalizations about classroom discourse, but rather to show the particularity of it; to identify how pedagogical goals and interactional rights and obligations are intertwined and co-constructed by teacher and students. Walsh likens modes to "fingerprints"—each is recognizable by its interactional features and pedagogic goals. Given his desire to produce a workable framework for teacher self-reflection, Walsh limits his discussion to four modes: managerial, materials, skills and system, and classroom context. These are argued to be representative of classroom discourse, though not comprehensive. I review each briefly, both as originally described by Walsh with respect to the L2 classroom, as well as through a consideration of what each mode might look like in a "content" classroom.

Managerial mode is a common type of classroom interaction, found often at the beginning and end of lessons or activities as teachers set up expectations for the activities to follow or make connections between different segments of a lesson. Interactional features common to this mode include extended teacher turns, use of transitional markers, and confirmation checks. This mode is characterized by a lack of learner involvement (i.e., verbal contributions), though as the analysis in Chapters 5, 6, and 7 will show, learners' embodied actions contribute to the success (or not) of the teacher's pedagogical goals in this mode, and their (non-)participation (i.e., their (mis)alignment with the teacher's pedagogical and interactional agenda) either aids or deters progressivity in these sequences.

Materials mode interactions center around a text or some other material which plays an outsize role in determining the nature of the ensuing interaction, i.e., the material itself may constrain "who may speak, when and what they may say" (Walsh 2006: 73). "Checking episodes" (Gourlay 2005) where the teacher is reviewing previously completed work with students are a common example of materials mode interactions, though any activity centered on a shared focal material (e.g., a list of vocabulary, a projected screen image, text written on a black/white board) could be an example of materials mode. The predominant interactional feature in this mode is the IRF sequence, though as Walsh (2006) notes, learners may have more or less interactional space depending on the type of material and/or activity. That is, while learner contributions may be limited in some ways by the constraints of the material or the use of chained IRF sequences, if, for example, the third turn is used to extend learner contributions and to scaffold learner responses, learners might contribute a great deal verbally. As Jacknick and Creider (2018) note, learners produce an array of multimodal actions in materials mode interactions, only some of which are arguably in alignment with pedagogical goals in these sequences. The analysis in Chapter 5 in particular furthers this discussion.

With some exceptions, the pedagogical goals and interactional features identified by Walsh in managerial mode and materials mode apply equally well to language classrooms and content classrooms. *Skills and system mode*, on the other hand, transfers a bit less directly. Language classrooms are often focused on sub-skills of language, including reading, writing, speaking, listening, and sometimes explicit focus on grammar (i.e., the "system"). For any given content classroom, the "sub-skills" will differ. For example, Walsh (2006) suggests that the establishment of important factual information may be a primary goal in skills and system mode in some contexts like history classes. In extracts from the Reading Data, the sub-skills of reading might include understanding vocabulary in context, skimming/scanning, identification of main idea, etc. For the College Data classrooms, it might be applying the tools of discourse analysis (forensic linguistics), examining organizational culture (communications), or analyzing arguments (philosophy). Given pedagogic goals like providing corrective feedback and providing learners with practice, common interactional features in this mode include teacher repair, extended teacher turns, teacher echo, and display questions. As in materials mode, use of chained IRF sequences often occurs. The focus in this mode is on accuracy, and as such, turn-taking and topic are tightly controlled by the teacher, who decides what counts as accurate.

The final mode identified by Walsh is *classroom context mode*, where the pedagogic focus is on fluency and teachers move into more of a facilitative role in the interaction. Classroom discussions predominate in this mode, with more local management of turn-taking than is seen in the other modes, including extended learner turns and teacher repair and feedback both centered on meaning rather than accuracy. As Walsh notes, "the defining characteristic of classroom context mode ... is interactional space" (2006: 82). Whether learners take up this space or how they use it is a focus throughout the data chapters, and I present a single-case analysis in Chapter 8 of a discussion to highlight how spatial considerations can affect participation in this mode.

The interactional features identified in each mode are ideally "mode convergent," i.e., they represent a match between pedagogical goals and interactional patterns. Walsh (2006) describes "mode divergence" as instances where the teacher's language use does not align with their pedagogical purposes. Because the teacher is the one setting the pedagogical agenda and managing the interaction in most cases, mode divergence by teachers is potentially more disruptive to progressivity than mode divergence by students. My analysis provides a more in-depth examination of student actions, both those that might be termed mode convergent, and also those that are mode divergent. Students' use of divergent interactional features may represent confusion about interactional expectations, but it may also represent resistance to the teacher's pedagogical and/or interactional agenda, as we will see particularly in Chapters 4 and 7.

Walsh's (2006, 2011) modes are chosen to present clear contrasts between different modes, but as he acknowledges, there are tensions within the framework which are inherent to the context-sensitive and context-dependent nature of classroom interaction. For example, Walsh notes that some sequences might seem not to "fit" into any of the identified modes. In addition, his framework both allows for movement between modes (which he terms "mode switching"), including "mode side sequences" (brief movements from one mode to another and back again), and also acknowledges that there are times when multiple modes appear to be occurring simultaneously.

While Walsh describes typical interactional patterns in each mode, because his framework was designed for teacher self-observation and reflective practice, there is more focus on what these modes entail for teachers than for students. To address this imbalance and provide a more comprehensive view of classroom interaction, this study draws on Walsh's modes for an examination of *student* actions in the classroom. Students' ability to determine what mode they are in and act accordingly is part of their classroom interactional competence (CIC), which Walsh defines as "teacher and learners' ability to use interaction as a tool for mediating and assisting learning" (2006: 132). Because my data includes both L2 and general education classrooms, my monograph will not only elucidate the role of students in classroom interaction, it will also expand Walsh's concepts of modes and CIC beyond second language acquisition.

2.3 PARTICIPATION IN INSTRUCTED-LEARNING SETTINGS

The question of what we mean when we say "participation" is a complicated one. In one (conversation analytic) sense, simply being co-present and engaging in perceivable social action near others might be enough to be considered a "participant." In another (pedagogical) sense, students' active contribution to ongoing discourse, particularly in the form of verbal contributions, is often what is meant by *participation*. While the first definition is perhaps so broad as to leave the phenomenon unclear, the second is problematic on several levels. The privileging of verbal contributions favors students who are comfortable speaking in front of others, while disadvantaging shy students or those lacking confidence in their abilities (whether language proficiency, grasp of concepts, etc.). However, on a more basic level, counting only students' talk as "participation" leaves out of our (i.e., teachers' and analysts') consideration the vast majority of social actions accomplished by students in classrooms. As Candela notes, "students' participation in classroom discourse is active and complex and does not always follow the teacher's attempts to control" it (1999: 156). This monograph approaches the complexity of participation by examining the full range of students' multimodal actions as they index students' displays of doing-being-a-student. To situate this new look at student action in the classroom, I provide a brief review of classroom discourse research with participation as a central focus.

Examining teacher talk can illuminate practices that create interactional space for learners, and my early research took this approach as well (Jacknick 2009). In doing so, I drew on prior research like Lerner (1995), who examines teacher utterances that provide spaces for learner participation to determine how turn design affects the interactional work being done and what sort of relevant next turn the teacher utterance projects. Lerner claims that turn design is emergent as an utterance is delivered, and that the interactional work being accomplished by an utterance can be seen only when it is complete. Lerner examined different teacher prompts and their uses as invitations to participate, but his focus was on teacher elicitation, rather than student initiation. This work contributes to an understanding of the kind of communicative competence that teachers and learners need to gain in order to communicate effectively in the classroom, and in particular how students can participate in invited ways, but he leaves student initiation largely unexamined. Van Lier emphasizes the importance of student initiative and cautions that researchers who focus on teacher behavior because they assume teacher dominance are likely to turn their research into a "self-fulfilling prophecy" (1984: 164). Several researchers have applied coding schemes (van Lier's or others), beginning with an assumption of teacher control, and not surprisingly, have found support for that assumption (Allwright 1980; Bannick 2002; Kinginger 1994). Emanuelsson and Sahlström (2008) argue that there is a tension between teacher control and the desirability for student participation; however, I argue that students are *always* participating (or not) with their bodies, not only in verbal ways, but by engaging in public displays of listening and attention during extended teacher turns, for example.

Others have looked closely at students' contributions to interaction, documenting the ways in which students participate, mostly verbally. Markee's (1995) examination of the nature of teacher responses to student questions stands in contrast to many second language acquisition studies focused on student responses to teacher prompts. He argues that rather than answering questions directly, teachers often employ referential counter-questions to regain control of the discourse, ultimately reifying the notion that teacher-led interaction leaves little room for student participation. Jacknick (2009), in contrast, focuses entirely on student initiative in teacher-led, whole-class interaction, classifying such turns in terms of difficulty of initiation with regard to sequential positioning, turn composition, and action. This context-sensitive analysis of student-initiated participation demonstrates the importance of attending to the local interactional context when characterizing student participation. That is, student actions gain their meaning by their placement within particular interactional environments and "classroom micro-contexts" (Seedhouse 2004) or "modes" (Walsh 2006, 2011).

Much research on language learning classrooms falls under the "participation metaphor" (Sfard 1998), where participation is seen *as* learning (cf. Seedhouse et al. 2010). I will return to the question of the relationship between participation and learning in Chapter 8, but here I will focus on two studies that directly address this concept because they also directly address the nature of participation itself. Appel (2010) asks how participation contributes to instructed learning, drawing on Goodwin and Goodwin's (2004) definition of participation, including the observability of actions. He raises the question of "access to interaction" (2010: 207), particularly in complex participation structures with multiple participants, noting that "non-official participation" is possible as one of the "interrelated speech exchange systems" in multiparty classroom interaction (2010: 210). This idea will have resonance to the analysis here, particularly when we consider student actions outside of the "main" interaction led by the teacher. At times, Appel conflates participation per se with participation structures, as when he suggests that participation can inhibit learning or encourage it by providing space. I argue that it is the nature of whole-class participation structures that impedes or facilitates the participation of learners, not participation itself that hampers learning. In the same volume, Leung (2010) problematizes the conflation of participation and learning, noting that while participation can provide opportunities for learning, it does not entail them. Examining the interaction between a pupil and teacher, Leung notes that while they both "did and said all the 'right' things to play themselves as teacher and pupil" (2010: 200), this performance did not automatically represent learning. How much social action in classrooms is a performance of these roles of teacher and student? This is a question I return to throughout this book.

A distinction is to be made between those few studies where "participation" is clearly defined and those where a definition is only hinted at through analysis, usually to mean verbal contributions. While there are innumerable references to participation opportunities *as* opportunities for learning, especially in the L2 classroom

(Hellermann and Cole 2009; Mondada and Pekarek Doehler 2004; van Compernolle 2015; Walsh 2011; Walsh and Li 2016; Waring 2008; Young and Miller 2004), as van Lier (2008) suggests, talking and being "active" are not necessarily conducive to learning. Van Compernolle talks about participation but also about "active reception" and "displays of engagement" (2015: 113, 114), a concept which will be crucial in my analysis here. Hellermann (2008a) makes a distinction between participation and "reification," arguing that reification is a more apt turn for student actions that are teacher-assigned or routinized, and that participation (i.e., student-initiated action) generates much more engagement, and thus more propitious circumstances for learning. He also mentions learners' ability to engage in embodied displays of participation (e.g., postural shifts, pointing) as "peripheral participation" (2008a: 153, cf. Lave and Wenger 1991). Hellermann (2008b) likewise seems to suggest that embodied action is separate from participation. For example, he refers to hand-raising by several students and just one verbal response as "student responses and participation" (2008b: 56). However, I argue that even within routinized tasks, students' complex, shifting, and embodied actions show their differential attention to the task of doing-being-a-student, and are thus expressions of their participation and engagement in the classroom.

With his consideration of the constantly shifting nature of students' participation and engagement, Koole (2007) is also an important precursor to the analysis in this book. By focusing on each individual student's actions during classroom interaction, he shows how students simultaneously monitor the ongoing "primary" activity while engaging in their own "parallel" activities (cf. Markee 2005). Koole claims that "student participation is interactionally constructed. What counts as participation and what does not is established in the interaction between teacher and student" (2007: 492). In this way, he makes the important point that student participation is a consideration not only of student action, but also of how such actions are oriented to by teachers. This relates to my conceptualization of participation and engagement as related to interactional and pedagogical *alignment*; it is the situated, locally-contingent, context-sensitive nature of any given action that gives it meaning.

In recent years, research on willingness to participate (WTP) and unwillingness to participate (UTP) has contributed to our understanding of "participation" as both an interactional and a pedagogical phenomenon (e.g., Bezemer 2008; Evnitskaya and Morton 2011; Fasel Lauzon and Berger 2015; Mortensen 2008; Sert 2015), and more will be said about WTP in particular in Chapters 4 and 5. These studies' consideration of how embodied actions index WTP and UTP underscores the relevance of multimodal analysis. Evnitskaya and Pochon-Berger make the excellent point that "the binary distinction between 'active verbal' participation and 'passive silent' non-participation" does nothing to illuminate the students' interactional competence (2012: 38). They focus on embodied participation, showing how students use their bodies to demonstrate their alignment with the ongoing pedagogical interaction, and proposing more nuanced categories of participation such as "listenership, attentiveness, coordination and engagement" (2012: 39), phenomena I will return to in Chapters 5 and 6 especially.

2.3.1 NON-PARTICIPATION AND DISENGAGEMENT IN INSTRUCTED-LEARNING SETTINGS

We turn now to an examination of the ways in which research on classroom interaction has characterized one type of student action: non-participation. As will be argued throughout this book, there are degrees of non-participation and disengagement in classroom interaction. For example, claims of insufficient knowledge (CIK, Sert 2011; Sert and Walsh 2012) orient to the relevance of an answer in the next turn, even though they do so in a dispreferred way. By providing a response (albeit a non-answer), students are aligning interactionally, if not pedagogically. As such, I argue that CIKs are one form of participation. Likewise, in discussing non-participation and disengagement, we can see degrees of misalignment with the teacher both pedagogically and interactionally. For example, Waring (2013a, 2013b, 2016) examines two different kinds of inappropriate participation: overly talkative students and silent students. In each case, students are failing to participate in officially sanctioned ways, but they are potentially still *engaged* with the interaction. My analysis shows how we can disambiguate participation from engagement by attending to students' verbal and embodied actions.

The entire enterprise of teaching rests upon an assumption of student collusion with the educational goals of the teacher and/or institution (Candela 1999; Diamondstone 2002; McDermott and Tylbor 1986). The question of whether students *decide* to be out of alignment with the teacher's pedagogical and interactional goals highlights the power students have to disrupt classroom discourse. They can do so overtly by undertaking social actions completely unrelated to the teacher's goals (e.g., sleeping), becoming "conspicuously disengaged" (Rampton 1996: 73). Importantly, Vavrus and Cole, examining disruption in the classroom, show how what counts as disruptive (i.e., non-participation) relates to "violations of the unspoken and unwritten rules of linguistic conduct" (2002: 90), but may vary depending on the classroom context. In his examination of the talk in classrooms at different schools, Rampton notes that the students with higher socioeconomic status "generally maintained a public show of willingness to participate in class" (1996: 42), while at the school with students from a lower socioeconomic status, there was less evidence of that "public show," a trend we may see reflected in my data, which include students from underserved communities.

Some of students' inapt or lacking participation may stem from their developing classroom interactional competence (CIC), which includes their ability to identify participation structures and secure interactional space. Dorr-Bremme (1990) looks at circle time in an elementary school classroom, showing how students misinterpreted the context and participated in ways that were deemed inappropriate by the teacher. These students were in danger of being characterized as "bad" students with poor manners, when in fact, they lacked the CIC to accurately assess their interactional rights and obligations. Margutti and Piirainen-Marsh show how the teacher (and other students) orient to some students' contributions as "unauthorized ways of behaving" (2011: 306), i.e., non-participation that disrupts progressivity in some way. Importantly, Margutti argues that the negotiation of what counts as disruptive is locally managed, and that the "norms might change during lessons" (2011: 311), requiring students' constant attention to shifting interactional expectations. In advocating for a context-sensitive view of engagement, Hellermann argues that disengagement can be seen in "constellations of different practices" (2008a: 115). When social actors deploy multiple multimodal resources in concert with one another, we might consider this a complex multimodal Gestalt (Mondada 2014c), which I will further explain in the next section on multimodal conversation analysis.

It is important to remember that students' participation and engagement may not always be observable, and so I will take pains in the following chapters to highlight the limits of this kind of analysis. Van Lier identifies a crucial difficulty for researchers of classroom interaction, noting that "attention, and indeed participation, need not necessarily be overt at all times. Participation may consist in 'eavesdropping', thinking about what is going on, internal repetition, etc." (1984: 93). These other forms of participation hinted at by van Lier are beyond the scope of this volume, which is focused on students' public displays of (non-)participation and (dis)engagement. While those other forms of participation are relevant, particularly to discussions of learning, the focus here is on how students show their understanding of what doing-being-a-student requires at any given moment, including not only the moments when they are engaged and participating verbally, but also those when they are not participating and disengaged, and all the various ways of doing-being-a-student that exist between those extremes.

2.4 MULTIMODAL CONVERSATION ANALYSIS

Conversation analysis (CA) is one of the dominant approaches to the analysis of discourse (Stivers and Sidnell 2013), involving crafting detailed transcripts based on recordings of naturally occurring interaction, identifying phenomena of interest, and creating collections of those phenomena. The theoretical foundations of CA rest on the belief that social interaction entails "order at all points" (Sacks 1984: 22), and it is the analyst's task to show how participants orient to these structures of social action. By grounding findings in transcripts that are available for review, conversation analysts can show how participants both create and sustain social order through their talk (Hester and Francis 2000). The analyst's claims are rooted in the recording and/or transcripts of the talk without reference to external factors unacknowledged by the participants themselves, striving for an emic understanding of the interaction (i.e., an understanding that is participant-relevant, not researcher-imposed).

As Heritage argues, "sequences of actions are a major part of what we [conversation analysts] mean by context" (1997: 162). The utterances of each participant can only be understood in terms of what was said before (i.e., talk is context-shaped) and what relevant next action is projected (i.e., talk is context-creating). Schegloff clarified the tradition of excluding aspects of context outside of the transcript by explaining that conversation analysis will allow the inclusion of aspects of context (e.g., the race or gender of the participants) only if they are "demonstrably relevant *to* the participants" (1992: 109). In this way, conversation analysis preserves the emic perspective advanced by their stringent adherence to the text by including only those contextual features that are oriented to by the participants. For this analysis, while some of the student actions are not oriented to by the teacher, my characterizations of their actions as (non-)participation and (dis)engagement relate directly to the participant-established participation frameworks and attending expectations. Similarly, with the increasing prevalence of video recordings and the subsequent inclusion of gesture and eye gaze in transcripts, some studies (cf. Markee 2008) include visual representations of the physical context in transcripts (e.g., reproduction of PowerPoint slides or frame grabs of text on blackboards). These images are included for analysis because participants orient to them through eye gaze and/or gesture.

Sacks et al. (1974) regard everyday conversation as a benchmark, and thus studies of institutional talk are to some degree the study of how talk in institutions compares with everyday conversation. Most conversation analytic studies of classroom talk can be seen as an attempt to illustrate one or another of the conditions of institutional talk in the specific case of the classroom, especially the "special and particular constraints" (Drew and Heritage 1992b: 22) on the talk of participants with regard to turn design, turn allocation, sequencing, and overall structural organization of discourse. A review of the robust sub-field of institutional conversation analysis is beyond the scope of this book, but readers are encouraged to consult Antaki (2011), Drew and Heritage (1992a), Heritage (2005), and McHoul and Rapley (2001), to name just a few.

A fundamental argument of this book is that social interactions in classrooms is necessarily an embodied phenomenon, and so special attention is given here to how multimodal analysis has become the standard in a field which began, as a matter of convenience, with analysis of audio recordings (Sacks 1992). Hazel et al. claim that "any research into human social interaction is research into embodied interaction... the categories of *multimodal* and *embodied* interaction are not necessary, as for us 'interaction' indexes all of that" (2014: 3; emphasis in original). While Sacks (1992) and Goffman (1959, 1961, 1963, 1981) repeatedly mark the relevance of embodiment in social interaction, these mentions did not immediately translate into sustained *analytic focus* on the multimodality of social interaction, with much early CA research (of classrooms and otherwise) relying on audio recordings, a natural consequence of the difficulty and expense involved with video recording in the 1960s and 1970s. While other researchers adopted video recording for data collection earlier (cf. Gregory Bateson, Ray Birdwhistell, and Kendon 1963 as reported on in Kendon 1990), Goodwin and Goodwin were among the earliest adopters of video recording technology (e.g., Goodwin 1981; cf. also Heath 1986) for micro-analytic research of social interaction. Nuthall, in his review of research on students in classrooms, commented on the "paradigm-breaking increase in the conceptual and methodological sophistication of the research" on classrooms, students, and learning with a "clear acknowledgement of the multi-layered and multi-dimensional nature of classroom processes" (1997: 760). However, it is only in the last ten years that inclusion of multimodal details in transcripts and analysis has become more common, and in fact, expected. This "embodied turn" (Nevile 2015) in the social sciences has been made possible through the ease and availability of video recording technology (see

Mondada 2013 and 2016b for a more complete history of the use of video recordings in CA).

As many have argued, "social interaction is intrinsically *multimodal*" (Mortensen 2013: 1; emphasis in original). Mondada (2016a) likewise makes the important point that temporality and sequentiality are key concerns for CA, with the analytic focus on *action*, but action is not accomplished solely through verbal turns-at-talk. Following Mondada (2014c, 2016a), by using the term "multimodal" as opposed to "non-verbal," I aim to demonstrate the importance of all resources in the display of (non-)participation and (dis)engagement, rather than to subordinate embodied resources as supplementary to verbal contributions. CA has been considered by many as particularly well suited to documenting the sequentiality and temporality of embodied actions related to talk (Fasel Lauzon and Berger 2015), but given the linearity of current transcription systems and a historical emphasis on talk, challenges still abound (see Sections 2.4.5, 2.4.6, and 8.3 for more on these challenges).

It is impossible to include all the potential resources in our transcription and analysis even if one were able to do so, and as Goodwin notes, "not all possible and relevant resources are in play at any particular moment" (2000: 1491). The problem of *which* multimodal resources to attend to when we are examining video recorded interaction is succinctly summarized by Markee: "how can we *empirically* show that participants are paying attention to *any, some,* or *all* of these different layers of context in the (usually unnoticed) micro-details of everyday talk-in-interaction?" (2013: 29; emphasis in original). For this analysis, because I am attempting to focus more broadly on social action, I tracked the multimodal actions of all visible participants. This involved a process of paring down and deciding which resources were, or could be construed as, social in nature. While this may suggest an outsider perspective, teachers are also faced with the task of filtering through the "noise" of a roomful of social actors constantly engaging in posture and gaze shifts, orientation to objects, etc., and thus this book provides a way of highlighting how students' actions work to demonstrate their performance of the role "student."

I briefly provide background below on some of the key "semiotic fields" (Goodwin 2000: 1490) of relevance to the upcoming analysis, including gaze, gesture, the body, and artifacts. While other resources, such as lexis, grammar, and prosody, are also among those deployed by participants in social action, I do not devote sections to them here because of well-established research on these aspects, particularly in the field of interactional linguistics (cf. Couper-Kuhlen and Selting 2018) and other research within conversation analysis, studies which I will reference opportunistically throughout my analysis. My contribution to the study of student participation and engagement is to present a more complete picture of students' multimodal actions, and so I touch briefly upon those that will be most relevant to my analysis. Finally, I discuss the creation of multimodal collections, and the challenges of multimodal transcription. In examining the many semiotic modalities at the disposal of students in the classroom, I aim to show how these become interactionally relevant as displays of (non-)participation and (dis)engagement.

2.4.1 GAZE

Kendon notes that gaze as a phenomenon of "social significance" (1990: 51) is well established, pointing to Goffman's (1963) work illuminating the function of gaze for "the initiation and maintenance of social encounters" (Kendon 1990: 52). Part of this maintenance concerns monitoring of interaction, one of two main functions of gaze as identified by Kendon (1990), the other being "control" of interaction (e.g., identifying recipients or selecting next speaker). The opportunities for monitoring afforded by gaze are crucial to participants' ability to adjust to shifting interactional expectations. Goodwin's (1979, 1980) work is foundational in the study of gaze in interaction, particularly his findings regarding the gaze patterns of listeners versus speakers. While I discuss the use of gaze by listeners in more detail in Chapter 6, in this brief review I will focus more generally on the functions of gaze in interaction, particularly as they relate to participation and engagement.

Mortensen (2013) shows how gaze functions to display *attention* to the speaker, and Gardner likewise argues that gaze helps establish "engagement frameworks" (2015: 28). Conversely, Goodwin notes that the lack of mutual gaze between speakers and listeners may be found "during periods of disengagement" (1980: 288). While gaze is not necessarily an indication of participation and engagement in all contexts (as with other multimodal resources, it is the context-sensitive deployment of these resources that is important), the temporality and sequentiality of gaze shifts is an important consideration in determining a student's (non-)participation and (dis)engagement in classroom interaction. I argue in Chapter 5 that students may use mutual gaze with the teacher to demonstrate continued engagement despite unwillingness to participate; conversely, in Chapter 7, we will see how students use gaze withdrawal to display unwillingness to participate simultaneously with other embodied displays of engagement. Looney and Kim underscore "the critical role that visual cues play in classroom, and more generally speaking human, interaction" (2019: 77). Gaze is what allows for mutual monitoring possibilities, giving participants the ability to attend to the vast array of multimodal actions on display in classrooms. Importantly, gaze is also an important resource for students to manage their availability for focused interaction; for example, gaze aversion or gaze toward objects might be used to indicate unwillingness to participate. While most transcription conventions related to gaze focus on how participants gaze at one another (Hepburn and Bolden 2017), my analysis of gaze orientation is expansive so as to include the many possible foci of attention in multiparty interaction in classrooms, including co-present parties but also artifacts, including books, papers, the blackboard, clocks, etc.

2.4.2 GESTURE

Gesture studies is a robust field of research, beyond the scope of this monograph to include, and for a full background on gesture, readers are encouraged to consult foundational works such as Kendon (1990) and McNeill (1992, 2005) as well as research on gesture use in classrooms and for learning (Hudson 2011; Jacknick 2018; Lantolf 2010; Macedonia et al. 2011, 2014; Macedonia and Knösche 2011; Matsumoto and

Dobs 2016; Rosborough 2010, 2014; Sert 2015; Smotrova and Lantolf 2013; Tellier 2008; van Compernolle 2015; van Compernolle and Smotrova 2014; Zhao 2007). I follow McNeill (1992, 2005) in considering speech and gesture to be parts of the same meaning-making system. Speech and gesture are semantically and pragmatically co-expressive (McNeill 1992), and thus analysis that privileges talk is missing part of the message. More background on gesture is provided in Chapter 5, where several different interactional functions of gesture for participation and engagement are analyzed, but suffice to say here that gesture, like other embodied actions, can be an integral part of students' multimodal displays of (non-)participation and (dis)engagement.

2.4.3 THE BODY: POSTURE, MOVEMENT, AND PROXEMICS

Much can be said about the movements of the body as social action, but I will restrict my comments here to three main areas: posture, movement, and proxemics. Related to the examination of gesture is the question of what our default body posture is, what Sacks and Schegloff call "home position" and describe as follows:

> A very large number of moves and sequences of moves in interaction end where they begin. That is, they end in the same place and regularly in the same position, which we are calling "home position." The moves depart from home and return to home. (Sacks and Schegloff [1975] 2002: 137)

In examining changes in posture or body movement, I am thus showing a change *from* home position or movement *back to* home position. Goodwin argues that the body helps to "display a reflexive stance toward other coparticipants, the current talk, and the actions in progress" (2000: 1519), and so examination of the body in context is crucial for an understanding of how students display their participation and engagement.

Posture is also important for the establishment of participation frameworks (Goodwin 2000; Mortensen 2009, 2013), such that bodies are mutually oriented toward each other or some shared focal point. Hellermann talks about "mutual postural orientation" (2008b: 49), and Kidwell and Zimmerman (2007) note that postural alignment shows participants' orientation to interactional engagement. Mondada (2009) shows that postural alignment occurs before verbal contact is initiated, and Mortensen and Hazel (2014) likewise show how postural alignment can contribute to the initiation of interactions, with the sequential nature of those movements affecting how the subsequent interaction unfolds. In Chapters 4 through 7, I show how students' posture, and importantly their shifts in posture, index their shifting alignment with the pedagogical enterprise.

Some body movements can be glossed as "listener responses," and Kendon (1990) talks about "interactional synchrony," a kind of precise coordination of bodily movements on the part of a listener with the speech of another. For example, Ford and Stickle (2012) show how people display "heightened recipiency" through head and torso movements, in combination with gaze (i.e., as a multimodal Gestalt). In line with the argument here that student engagement can be seen in publicly observable monitoring of the ongoing interaction, Kendon (1990) notes that this kind of synchrony is possible only if the listener is devoting a certain amount of attention to the speech of their interlocutor.

It is also important to look at the movement of bodies in space, particularly as these movements relate to the formation of participation frameworks (Mondada 2014a). Kendon (1990) suggests that in encounters, participants cluster themselves into various patterns, which may be static or fluid (e.g., a classroom organized with desks facing forward so that students then turn toward each other for small-group work). He calls these patterns "F-formations," where participants create a formation that is not accessible to those outside the group; this may be along the lines of Goffman's concept of "ecological huddle" (1961: 19) or Mondada's "common interactional space" (2009: 1977) and may be seen in cases where a discussion group of students is formed around a table (see Extract 8.3). Through this movement into a shared interactional space, we can see "the transformation from co-present persons to co-participants" (Mondada 2009: 1978). Participants demonstrate to one another their willingness to engage in social interaction in large part through the orientation of their bodies (Goodwin 1981, 2006; Goodwin and Goodwin 2004; Mondada 2014a, 2016b; Mortensen 2009). Body posture, movement, and proxemics will figure prominently in my analysis of students' *engagement* in particular, as they can show students' displayed (un)willingness to become involved or to sustain involvement in interaction.

2.4.4 ARTIFACTS

Within multimodal CA, there is increasing attention to the ecological environment, including objects. In describing multimodal resources, Mondada talks about "occasioned resources" (2018: 86) related to the ecology of the interaction, such that any object may become relevant to the ongoing interaction (e.g., in Figures 8.17–8.19, a student holds her handout in front of her phone as she surreptitiously disengages from the classroom interaction). Nevile et al. talk about "the *interactional ecology of objects*," noting that "objects are situated within and contribute to developing processes and trajectories of social action" (2014a: 17; emphasis in original). Nevile et al. (2014a) examine both the creation of objects during interaction—for example, writing (Mondada and Svinhufvud 2016)—as well as how participants "interact with objects, and use objects to interact with others" (Nevile et al. 2014a: 4). Van Lier (2002) looks specifically at the role of objects and spatial configurations (i.e., a multimodal Gestalt) in classrooms, describing the interactional consequences of different formations when teacher and student are looking together at the same document (cf. Tolins 2013). Objects may prove instrumental in the structuring of sequences, as well as delineating appropriate kinds of participation. Mikkola and Lehtinen (2014) and Nevile et al. (2014b) show how objects may play a role in ordering (cf. Matarese and Caswell 2017a, 2017b). The analysis in Chapters 4 to 8 includes consideration of how objects such as writing implements, notebooks, texts, food, etc. can become involved in students' displays of (non-)participation and (dis)engagement. Importantly, as with the other multimodal phenomena under consideration here, students' manipulation of objects is context-sensitive, and as such, can be part of a display of participation and engagement or non-participation and disengagement.

2.4.5 COMPLEX MULTIMODAL GESTALTS AND COLLECTIONS

Mortensen (2013) highlights yet another methodological challenge when dealing with multimodal CA: building collections. Mondada has argued that while CA research has provided a wealth of information about individual multimodal resources (see above), it also allows for examination of what she terms "complex multimodal Gestalts," i.e., "a web of resources formatting an action" (2014c: 139). Most analyses of these constellations of multimodal resources have tended to be single-case analyses, but here I am attempting to describe the use of an array of multimodal resources for doing (non-)participation and (dis)engagement across several cases (cf. Ford and Stickle 2012, Kääntä 2015, Mondada 2014b, and Mortensen and Hazel 2014 for examples of collections of multimodal Gestalts). Mortensen (2013) notes while participants have no observable trouble in interpreting a vast array of multimodal resources employed in the service of some action, the increasing complexity of these Gestalts proves challenging for the analyst as they attempt to find instances of the "same" social practice.

My initial transcriptions are "open transcripts" (Jenks 2011: 13) in which I attempted to transcribe "everything," not knowing which multimodal actions might become relevant to my analysis. These transcripts are unwieldy and difficult to read, but they preserve an accuracy that is essential for the kind of analysis I am undertaking. They also helped me to visualize moments where a "constellation of practices" (Hellermann 2008a: 155) came together to create social action. In order to argue whether any student action indexes (non-)participation or (dis)engagement, a full understanding of its sequential location and temporal unfolding, along with its temporal and sequential relationship with other actions, was crucial.

Along these lines, Mondada argues that "precise transcription of the timing of these phenomena is fundamental to catch the exact position, within a multimodal Gestalt, of emerging resources" (2016a: 346). More will be said below in Section 2.4.6 about transcription methods for the current study, but first a brief explanation of my collection building is offered here. For each phenomenon identified in this book, I collected 5–10 instances from across the data corpora. For many phenomena, many more instances than this were found in the data; for example, multimodal responses to teacher directives (hand-raises) were ubiquitous across all three corpora. However, I capped each initial collection at 10 instances to make transcription and analysis more feasible. These initial extracts were transcribed using Mondada's ([2001] 2019) conventions for multimodal transcription, and then focal extracts were chosen for inclusion. These decisions were made based on clarity, conciseness, and an effort to show a full range of possibilities. I do not claim that these categories of doing (non-)participation and (dis)engagement are exhaustive; rather, through their variety, I hope to convey the complex interactional work involved in the presentation of self as student.

2.4.6 TRANSCRIPTION AS ANALYSIS

Transcription involves deciding what to write down, and the care taken to preserve the details of the interaction reflects the analyst's lens in more ways than one. Mondada notes that the creation of multimodal transcripts in particular makes this evident:

> multimodal transcripts remind one that transcribing is always a selective activity ... depending on the objectives of the analysis, the granularity of the transcript, the private in-progress versus publicly edited status of the version, the recipient oriented/reader-friendly character of the final version, and so on. (Mondada 2018: 88)

As van Compernolle says, "different transcription practices render different things visible while obscuring (or even effacing) others" (2015: 25). A variety of approaches to multimodal transcription have been adopted by researchers to achieve different ends or in response to different transcription challenges (cf. Kendon 1990; Kidwell 2017 in Hepburn and Bolden 2017; Koole 2007; McNeill 1992, 2005). For this study, following Mondada's ([2001] 2019) conventions, multimodal transcripts were created detailing the temporality and sequentiality of all participants' visible embodied actions (see Appendices 2 and 3 for examples). After verbatim transcriptions were created, this involved watching the extracts multiple times for each modality for each participant; for example, for one student, this meant several viewings to transcribe gaze, then several more for posture, then several more for gesture, etc. Once I had transcribed several students' actions for one sequence, I began to see patterns in the coordination of multimodal resources, which informed my continuing transcription as well as my analysis. The process of creating these first in-depth multimodal transcriptions made me intimately familiar with the complexity of the phenomena under study here, and these fully elaborated multimodal transcripts following Mondada ([2001] 2016) are the basis for my analysis.

Once analyses were written up, transcripts were simplified for presentation in this monograph, in line with Mondada's (2018) urging to focus on the relevance of resources. Thus, my simplification of transcripts to improve readability involved the removal of some multimodal details if they were irrelevant to the analysis of that particular extract. For example, some extracts focus on particular students, and so the detailed transcription of other, non-focal students has been removed from the transcripts. Conversely, for some extracts, my aim was to show how the multimodal actions of the individual students within the class related to one another, necessitating the inclusion of more detail. Rather than assigning each participant a unique symbol, I began to use just one symbol to indicate the sequential location of embodied actions (*), and several actions by different participants are often included in one line to improve readability. While Mondada's ([2001] 2016) conventions call for the bolding of verbal lines, this had the tendency to mark those lines as more salient for the reader than the embodied actions transcribed below them (another hierarchical problem to be discussed later). I have instead italicized embodied actions to distinguish them from talk and time (silence), and I have chosen to use bold to highlight focal lines, whether they be verbal or embodied. In some cases, I present a transcript of the teacher's talk (Extract 6.2), but rather than transcribing students' embodied actions in the transcript itself, I follow Koole's (2007) practice of presenting prose paragraphs describing student action student by student due to the complexity of student action involved (more on this in Chapter 6). Finally, in order to show the complex sequential and temporal unfolding of students' actions, I have experimented with some new transcription conventions. In some cases, I have created boxes on the sides of transcripts to show a "zoomed" view of a particular line (Extract 4.1). In others, I have used icons to show the wave-like unfolding of students' embodied actions (Figures 4.1, 4.2, 4.3, 5.19, 5.20, 5.22). This latter development allows us not just to see the temporal and sequential unfolding, but also to see some version of what the teacher saw: a chorus of embodied action that builds to a peak and then falls away again. These visual wave transcripts are designed like a musical score, with icons representing each student's action or orientation, such that reading the visual from left to right shows how individual student actions build to a chorus, or how an individual student continues on their trajectory despite an interactional shift from their peers.

Screenshots were also added to help tell the story of each interaction, and these screenshots were transformed into line illustrations by my diligent undergraduate research assistants. As with the simplification of the transcripts themselves, the creation of the line drawings allowed us to focus on the most relevant actions in a given screen capture; for example, removing non-essential background and non-focal participants. The selection and editing of screenshots is thus itself another layer of analysis, involving choices made with the reader in mind, rather than the emic perspective of the participants. While screenshots are useful for freezing a moment in time—for example, to show where students' gaze is oriented at a particular moment in the interaction—they are also of limited use for showing the wave-like embodied actions of several students in time, or of showing that embodied actions gain their meaning from motion; that is, in some cases, freezing the video to take a screenshot obscures the very embodied action I am attempting to highlight. For this reason, videos for several extracts (Extracts 5.2, 5.9, 5.10a, 5.10b, 5.11, and 6.2) have been made available on the Edinburgh University Press website (edinburghuniversitypress.com/multimodal), and whenever you see this icon 🎬, I invite you to view the data directly to see the phenomena I describe "in flight."

In general, I have tended toward standardization (Jenks 2011) of the verbatim transcription, preserving some idiosyncrasies of delivery when relevant to analysis. For example, given that many of the students involved in my research are second language or second dialect speakers of Standard American English, I have in some cases transcribed their non-native pronunciations, most particularly when those pronunciations are oriented to as problematic by speakers or by other co-present parties, but mostly I use standard orthography to represent speech.

In short, multimodal transcriptions, particularly of large multiparty interaction like that found in classrooms, represent a series of choices for the analyst. My intent was to start with as full a catalogue of multimodal action for each visible participant as possible, and then allow sequential analysis to guide the paring down of transcripts so that each provides *enough* detail to highlight my analytic arguments without overwhelming the reader with *too much* detail. As Hepburn and Bolden (2017) note in their monograph on transcription, the complexity of conversation analytic transcripts reflects the complexity of social interaction, and orthographic representations inevitably fall short. I return to the issue of transcription in Chapter 8, with a discussion of future directions for multimodal transcription and analysis of video recorded data.

2.5 THE DATA

This book represents a unique perspective on classroom interaction drawing from recordings of language classrooms, developmental skills-based classrooms, and content classrooms; while I do not claim that these findings are generalizable to all classrooms everywhere, they do highlight the immensely complex work of doing-being-a-student in classrooms in general. The data analyzed here come from three separate corpora of classroom interactions: 45 hours of video recordings from an adult English as a Second Language (ESL) classroom (henceforth ESL Data), 20 hours of video recorded classroom interaction from a developmental reading course at an urban community college (henceforth Reading Data), and 10 hours of video recordings from mostly introductory-level classrooms at the same urban community college (henceforth College Data). Names have been changed in all cases. For the ESL Data and the Reading Data, I attempted to choose pseudonyms that matched participants' names in terms of ethnicity, number of syllables, etc. However, because I did not have access to students' real names for the College Data, I was unable to assign pseudonyms in this manner. I felt it was imperative to assign participants names rather than anonymous identifiers like "S1," following Jenks's (2011) suggestion that large multiparty interactions are easier to follow in transcripts where names are used. Since I could not match ethnicities in assigning names, there is a possibility that I am "white-washing" the data by using "English" names. However, acknowledging this potential seems the better option rather than imposing my own impressions of students' ethnicities on them from the outside.

2.5.1 ESL DATA

The first corpus was collected in 2008 as part of a larger study on the nature of discourse in adult English as a Second Language (ESL) classrooms (Jacknick 2009), and consists of video recordings of class sessions of a summer intensive ESL course for adults in a community language program in New York City. The program functioned as a lab school for the Teaching English to Speakers of Other Languages (TESOL) program at a major graduate school of education. This advanced-level ESL class had 17 students from a variety of language backgrounds (i.e., Japanese, Spanish, French, Slovak, Mandarin, Korean), ranging in age from 20 to 60 years. Their teacher was a student in a TESOL Master's program at the time and was teaching the course as part of a practicum. Her first language was Korean, but she had immigrated to the United

States at the age of 3 years and she considered herself a native speaker of English. This summer session course met 10:00am–12:30pm each day, Monday through Thursday for four weeks.

Each class session was video recorded with either two or three video cameras, as well as one audio recorder, and I was present in the classroom for all meetings, taking field notes and changing tapes in the video recorders. The camcorders for this study recorded onto 60-minute mini DV tapes, and so three tapes were used for each 150-minute class session (i.e., two tape changes). I endeavored to change tapes at times when the class was not in teacher-led interaction. Two video cameras were initially used, and I sat behind one of them and moved it as needed to capture the interaction. However, it quickly became clear that (1) the camera movement itself was a distraction to students, and (2) in moving the camera, I was instinctively reacting to actions that were not being captured by the camera. Thus, a third camera was added to better capture the participation framework of whole-class, teacher-led interaction, and ultimately, three unmanned cameras proved to be less intrusive in this case than two cameras, one of which had a researcher stationed behind it. Figure 2.1 shows the camera placement for most days, with Camera 1 and Camera 2 present for all sessions, and Camera 3 present from the second week on. Students most often sat around the tables arranged in a U-shape, with the teacher desk in the middle in front of the board. On days when all students were present, some students also sat at a small table behind the U-shape. The class met in a different classroom for the first meeting and used a different configuration of desks (small clusters of four desks each) on one day later in the semester. However, no excerpts in this text were selected from these days. Note: R designates the usual location of the researcher (in this case, me).

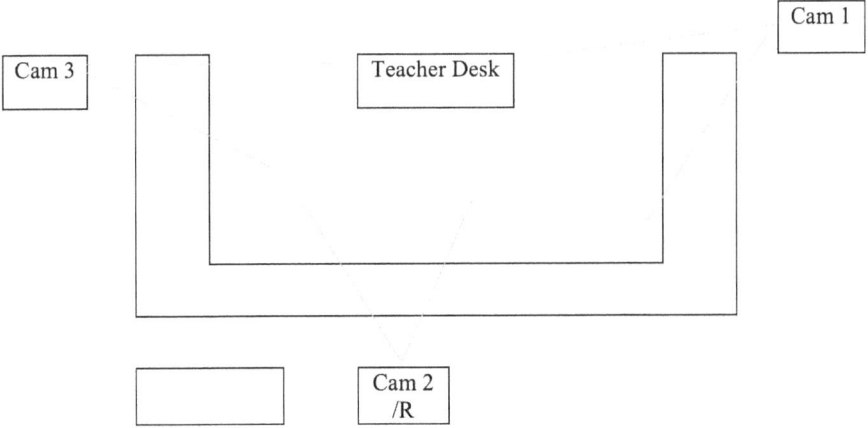

Figure 2.1   ESL Data camera setup

2.5.2 READING DATA

The second corpus was collected in 2012 as part of an interactional ethnography of a remedial reading course at an urban community college in the Northeast United States and consists of video recordings of one class session per week for 11 weeks of a 15-week semester. This class, taught by an experienced native-English-speaking educator in his 50s, was comprised of 21 matriculated community college students who had placed into this remedial reading course as a result of either their incoming reading scores, or by passing out of a lower-level remedial reading course. The class met 8:00am–9:40am three times per week. This course is not credit-bearing but is required for students who place into it; it functions as a "gatekeeping" course, i.e., students must pass in order to take freshman composition, as well as most of their upper-level major courses.

A team of three researchers coordinated data collection for this project, with one present at each recorded session to record field notes and switch tapes. The cameras used for this study recorded to 60-minute DV tapes, and so two tapes were used for each 100-minute session (i.e., one tape change). As with the ESL Data collection, we endeavored to change tapes at times when the class was not in teacher-led interaction. Three cameras were placed around the classroom in order to capture as many participants as possible, and these were not moved during class. Eleven class sessions were recorded beginning in the fourth week of the semester and continuing once per week with the exception of spring break and finals week. Figure 2.2 shows the

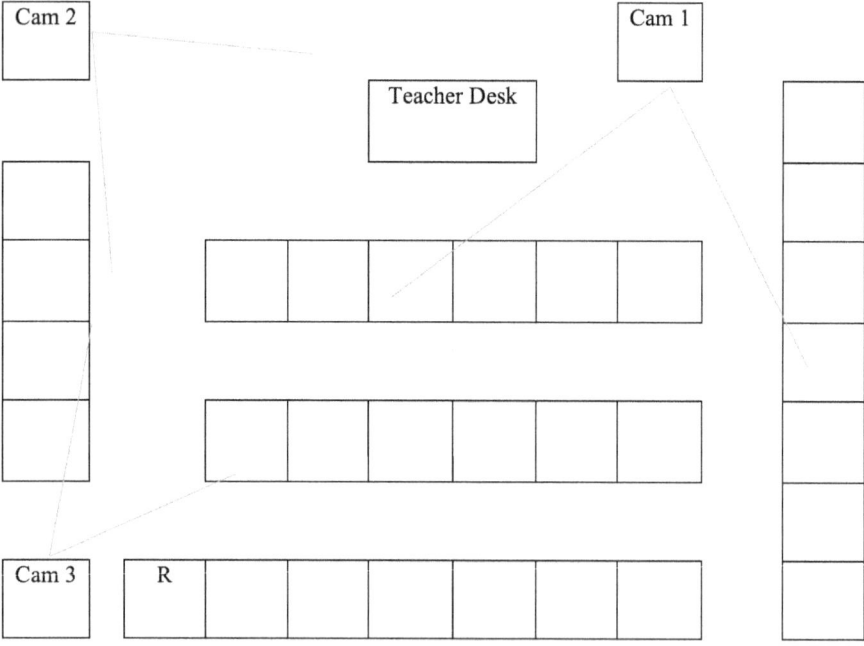

Figure 2.2   Reading Data camera setup

camera setup for this classroom; students were seated in small chairs with attached desks, and the researcher was always seated next to Camera 3 in the back corner. The configuration of the room led to these camera placements, so as to present as little obstruction to the teacher or students as possible. A consequence of this, however, is that the students seated near the window (along the same side as the researcher) are not adequately captured by any of the cameras. Note: R designates the usual location of the researcher.

2.5.3 COLLEGE DATA

The third corpus was collected in 2019 at the same urban community college as the Reading Data, to supplement the other two corpora with more recent data (particularly to account for the ubiquitous use of cell phones in college classrooms in recent years) *and* to include content area classrooms in the analysis. Eight separate classes, involving a total of 98 students and 5 faculty members, were each recorded once using from one to three iPhones mounted on tripods. iPhones were used to minimize intrusion (i.e., because of their small size), and also because they would allow for continuous recording for over 2 hours without needing to change tapes. A member of the research team was present at each meeting to monitor the recording devices, but no field notes were taken.

Securing informed consent was a delicate process that involved multiple visits to potential classrooms, and discussions with the students in those classrooms about the research, and about participation more generally. Several were interested in the research but understandably hesitant to be filmed. When several students in a class agreed to participate but declined to be video recorded, we limited the number of cameras we used and placed those we did use to capture only those students who consented to recording. The disciplines covered in these mostly freshman-level, introductory classes included philosophy, language and culture, and communications. An upper-level elective, forensic linguistics, was also recorded. The smallest class had just 6 students, and the largest class had 20. The classes had different schedules; some met twice weekly for 1 hour and 15 minutes, others had one short session per week (50 minutes) in addition to a longer session (1 hour and 40 minutes), and one class met just once per week for 2 hours and 45 minutes. These classes all met during the late morning and early afternoon hours, i.e., no evening or weekend classes were recorded. While examples were drawn from all the recorded classes, extracts or screenshots are only taken from five classrooms: an introductory Communications classrooms (COM), three different introductory philosophy courses (CRT 1–3), and an upper-level forensic linguistics (LIN). Camera setups for these five classrooms are below in Figures 2.3–2.7; these indicate the location of only consenting, filmed students (i.e., students who consented to participate but not to be filmed are not included in these figures). Note: "R" designates the usual location of the researcher.

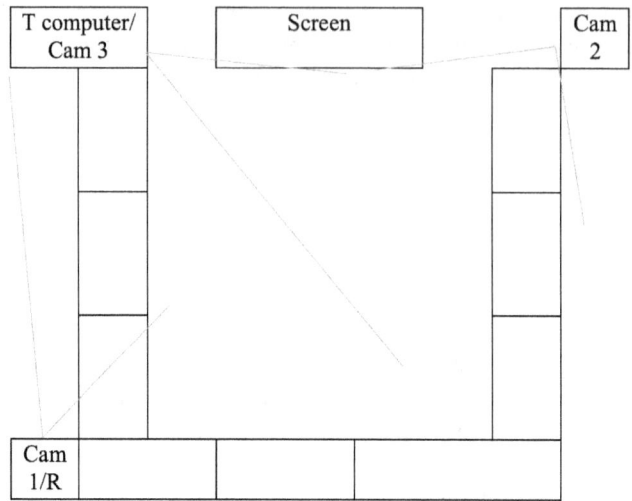

Figure 2.3   COM camera setup

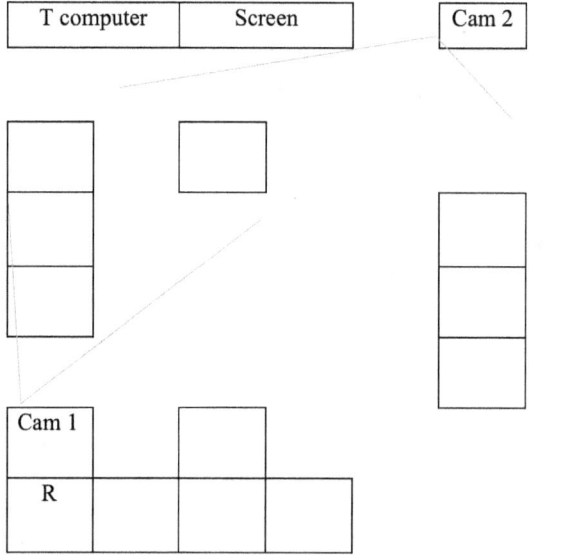

Figure 2.4   LIN camera setup

CLASSROOM DISCOURSE AND MULTIMODAL CONVERSATION ANALYSIS 39

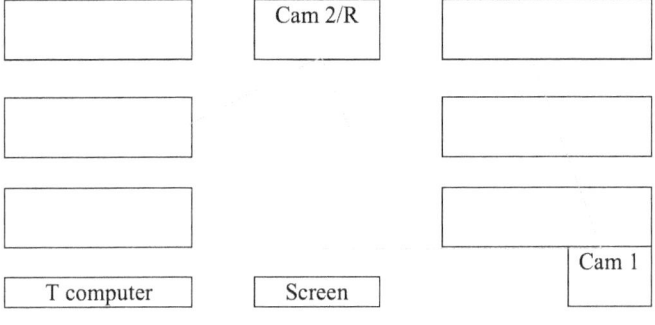

Figure 2.5   CRT 1 camera setup

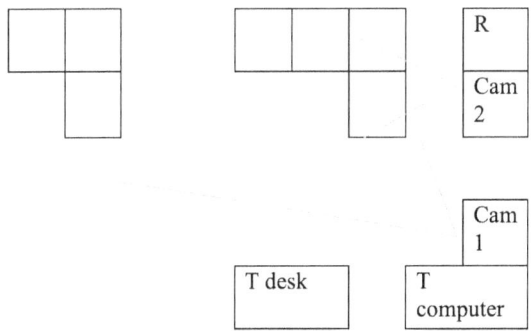

Figure 2.6   CRT 2 camera setup

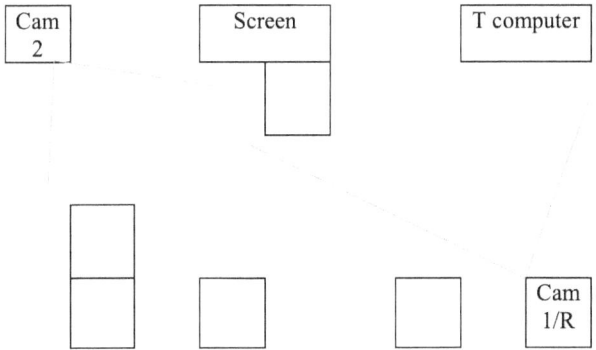

Figure 2.7   CRT 3 camera setup

2.5.4 SUMMARY

One key element that connects the three corpora is that most of the participants are not "expert" students. Many of the students in the Reading Data and College Data are in their first year of college, and many of them are first-generation college students. There are students in the ESL Data who will not pursue higher education; this is not English for Academic Purposes. All three corpora include students from diverse racial, linguistic, and socioeconomic backgrounds, though the Reading Data and College Data include many more students who are first-generation college students, i.e., "authentic beginners" (Gee 2004: 14) who come to formal instructed-learning settings unfamiliar with (or resistant to) displays of classroom interactional competence.

In particular, the fact that the Reading Data and the College Data were collected from community college classrooms adds to our current body of classroom discourse research, because these students (i.e., first-generation college students, people of color, speakers of non-standard dialects) are not often the focus of this research. While community college students, and particularly students in remedial classes (like the Reading class), are often the focus of research on developmental education, the focus in much of this research has been on quantitative metrics. That is, learning has been defined as "success" (i.e., persistence, grades, graduation or completion rates) in much of this research, despite the fact that these measures are not necessarily reflective of student learning. Thus, while we in some ways know quite a lot about the quantitative measures of this kind of success, we know very little about what developmental education looks like on the ground (cf. Levin et al. 2006; Matarese in preparation; Sullivan 2017). Because my focus is on what doing-being-a-student looks like, it is crucial that these kinds of students be included in our analysis; otherwise, we will see only students who have perfected the performance of being a student, and our picture of student participation and engagement will not reflect the realities of many students and teachers.

3

THE PRESENTATION OF SELF AS STUDENT

> The attentive pupil, who wishes to *be* attentive, his eyes riveted on the teacher, his ears open wide, so exhausts himself in playing the attentive role that he ends up by no longer hearing anything.
>
> Jean-Paul Sartre (1956: 60, as cited in Goffman 1959: 33)

3.1 INTRODUCTION

One of the main arguments of this book is that teasing apart the performance of participation and engagement from the real observable thing is a complex task, for analyst and teacher. An understanding of social interaction as entailing "the presentation of self" (Goffman 1959) helps us to understand the role(s) students are given to play in classroom interaction, and to see their actions as embracing or rejecting those roles to differing degrees. Goffman (1981) offers an understanding of participation as a constantly shifting phenomenon which may be revealed multimodally (cf. Box 2011; Goodwin 1999; C. Goodwin 2000, 2007; Wells 2000). As van Lier (1988) notes, if we are interested in actions in the classroom, we must pay attention to more than what is said. Students' multimodal actions, deployed precisely to coordinate sequentially and temporally with the teacher's actions, show us their engagement in the lesson; in order to build to my reconceptualization of participation and engagement, this chapter begins with a consideration of "action" and "participation" in conversation analytic research, and I argue for the value of returning to the work of Erving Goffman in conceiving of these concepts. Finally, I present my reconceptualization of "participation" and "engagement" which will guide the analysis for the rest of this volume.

3.2 THE PRESENTATION OF SELF AS STUDENT: A RETURN TO GOFFMAN

Along with Harold Garfinkel's ethnomethodology (Heritage 1984b), Erving Goffman's sociological consideration of interaction serves as one of the main intellectual and theoretical foundations for the field of conversation analysis (Maynard 2013). His global view of social interaction accounts for much of the micro-analytic detail that the field of CA has elucidated over the past half century, and it is still useful to return to his broader concepts in conceptualizing the focus of conversation analytic research today. In this book, Goffman's ideas about the nature of social situations and participation frameworks provide a solid foundation for understanding participants' interactional and pedagogical alignment, i.e., their sense of what they and others are doing in interaction at any given moment. In particular, his performance metaphor, including the concepts of roles and role distance, has greatly influenced my own thinking on (non-)participation and (dis)engagement. Here, I will briefly discuss each of these concepts, followed by a review of classroom discourse research influenced by Goffman's ideas. I conclude with a return to my reconceptualization of (non-)participation and (dis)engagement, including elaborated definitions of each term.

3.2.1 THE SOCIAL SITUATION

Any social interaction will have boundaries that show co-present parties negotiating the initiation and closure of that interaction (see Mondada 2009 for an example of how such openings are negotiated between strangers in public places). Goffman (1963) offers several different terms for the incidence of social interaction, but in *Forms of Talk*, he more broadly defines a "social situation" as "any physical area . . . within which two or more persons find themselves in visual and aural range of one another" (1981: 84). Co-presence is thus a fundamental element of participation, though he goes on to note that among those co-present persons, only some may be "definable as together in terms of social participation, that is in a 'with'" (1981: 84). In whole-class, teacher-led interaction, I argue that the boundedness of the classroom space itself helps to create the "with" Goffman describes. While there are certainly moments in whole-class interaction where the target of some bit of talk or embodied action might be a small sub-set of those present, for the most part, being in the classroom together while the teacher leads the activity means that all those co-present have access to the same social situation.

In defining encounters, Goffman (1959) notes that these entail co-presence (either in person or auditorily on the phone, and I would extend this definition to online co-presence as well in things like video chat). Co-presence allows monitoring capabilities, and thus its importance to establishing an "interactional space" (Mondada 2009) cannot be overstated. In classrooms, the bounded nature of the room creates an interactional space of one kind, but smaller interactional spaces are often created within the larger group, as when two or more students talk amongst themselves, or when a teacher engages directly with a student in an extended exchange. Goffman further elucidates the properties of an encounter, describing it as "an eye-to-eye ecological huddle that maximizes each participant's opportunity to perceive the other participants' monitoring of him" (1961: 18). C. Goodwin's (2007, 2018) concept of "participation framework" likewise focuses on participants' "embodied mutual orientation towards each other" (2018: para. 41), which is only possible given mutual monitoring capabilities.

The spatial organization of classrooms has consequences for the kinds of monitoring students and teachers can do in classrooms, with teachers generally having much greater ability for monitoring by virtue of their positioning and free movement within the classroom. Many "traditional" classrooms are spatially organized with students facing the teacher at the front of the room, with the teacher able to monitor the students and vice versa. If whole-class interaction is a dyad between a teacher and "the Student" (Sahlström 2002), then the participants' ability to monitor one another is not generally impeded by the traditional spatial orientation of classrooms, with small desks or tables facing the teacher at the front of the room. However, these kinds of configurations mean that students' monitoring of each other is difficult, if not impossible. In some of the classrooms included in analysis here, a U-shape is adopted, which shows the teacher's orientation to the need for mutual monitoring, not only between teacher and student, but between all co-present parties, for the encounter to function as an "ecological huddle." We will also see an example in Chapter 8 (Extract 8.3) where the teacher creates an encounter by having students form a small discussion circle, with the teacher and other students seated outside the inner circle as ratified, though potentially unaddressed, listeners (more on this later). Goffman (1961) notes that spatial orientation is important in the establishment of encounters, and we will see in the extracts throughout the book that monitoring is a crucial element of participation and engagement.

3.2.2 PARTICIPATION FRAMEWORKS

The complex possibilities inherent in the roles of "hearer" and "speaker" are highlighted by Goffman (1981), where he discusses whether speakers/listeners are ratified and whether listeners are addressed or unaddressed, etc. In whole-group interaction in a classroom, we might consider the teacher to be a ratified speaker and listener potentially at all times, with the possible exception of "byplay," when a subset of participants engages in "subordinate communication" (1981: 134), as when students speak quietly to one another during an extended teacher turn or teacher interaction with some other student. However, even instances like these are always open to reinterpretation by co-present parties. Consider this example from Jacknick and Duran (under review), where student byplay in their native language is attended to by the teacher, an unaddressed recipient, and transformed into information for which all those present are ratified listeners. Just before this, the teacher asked the students to identify activities they spent a lot of time on, and in line 18 she is reformulating a prior student contribution.

Extract 3.1 Gossiping
```
18   TEA   meets social get togethers,
19   DAM   $yes$
20   TEA   o↑kay,
21         (0.8)
22   MER   °dedikodu.°
           gossiping
23         (3.6)
24   TEA   $gossiping, (.) huh?$
25   Ss    ((laughter))
```

Extract 3.1 Gossiping (continued)
```
26    TEA   $o↓kay (0.3) ni:ce,$
27          (1.8)
28    TEA   it's a ca↑tharsism, °we call° it.
29          gossiping is (.) nice thing,
```

In line 22, Mer mentions gossiping at low volume and in her L1 (Turkish); that is, it is marked as byplay or private speech (note: it is not possible to tell from the camera angle whether her utterance is directed toward another student). The teacher, an unaddressed recipient, takes up this offstage talk and brings it centerstage, producing a translation into the language of instruction (English) with smiley voice in line 24, followed by an explicit positive assessment (EPA, Waring 2008) in line 26, also with smiley voice. She then explicitly ties the example to course concepts, classifying it in subject-specific terminology as 'a catharsism,' speaking on behalf of an unnamed expert community with 'we call it' (line 28). We see here a student who is engaged in the discussion, though not participating in projected ways. However, through her unsanctioned participation, she introduces an important point to the whole-class interaction.

While this example highlights the shifting participation status of the teacher, it also shows how students shift in their roles as well. If we follow Goffman in seeing perceptual range as an important metric of participation, the teacher's ability to hear Mer's byplay here allowed her shift in footing. Part of what makes classroom interaction unique as a setting for exploring participation is how physical space allows for particular perceptual opportunities. While byplay is certainly possible in many classrooms depending on spatial configurations, I argue that the bounded nature of most classroom spaces means that by entering into the room, one is agreeing to be a part of the encounter (though to potentially differing degrees of commitment). As Goffman suggests in *Forms of Talk*, when we find ourselves in an encounter, we owe our fellow co-present parties "evidence that we are reasonably alive to what is already in it, and furthermore to what might arise, whether on schedule or unexpectedly" (1981: 85). It is certainly not the case that all students (or teachers) display evidence of their attention to the unfolding interaction *at all times*, but in arguing that these are the default expectations, I will show also that *not* attending (or not putting on a convincing enough show of doing so) can become accountable.

"When a word is spoken, all those who happen to be in perceptual range of the event will have some sort of participation status relative to it" (Goffman 1981: 3), though speaking rights are often restricted within a group of co-present persons. Though Goffman uses the example of a word, he would likely say the same about an embodied action; throughout his published works, Goffman continually argued for the relevance of multimodal resources for an understanding of social action (cf. Goffman 1959, 1961, 1963, 1981). Thus, those within perceptual range of a verbal or embodied action will have some kind of participation status relative to that action. Talking about large multiparty encounters (e.g., dinner parties of eight or more), Goffman suggests that participation statuses are relatively unstable, and I likewise show that the same holds true for whole-class interaction. While "teacher-led" classroom interaction is sometimes treated as a monolithic participation structure, in fact, students constantly shift in their participation statuses, as does the teacher, a phenomenon we will see often in the analysis to come.

3.2.3 THE PERFORMANCE METAPHOR: ROLES AND ROLE DISTANCE

Just as I noted before that co-presence in the classroom plays a role in the establishment of what we call "classroom discourse," I argue here that entering into the classroom entails a relationship with the roles "teacher" and "student" and all their historical associations. Participants can embrace or reject these roles, but either way, their actions in the classroom show their orientation to them. Goffman's performance metaphor can thus inform our understanding of (non-)participation and (dis)engagement as we see participants' display of the role "student" in all its varied possibilities.

In defining performance, Goffman argues that a social role or position involves a display of appropriate behavior: "Performed with ease or clumsiness, awareness or not, guile or good faith, it is none the less something that must be enacted and portrayed, something that must be realized" (1959: 75). I argue that the role of student is likewise something that is *displayed* and *performed* (to differing degrees) at all times, with more or less commitment, by students in classrooms. We can see their displays of doing-being-a-student through their engagement in interaction. Goffman defines engagement as "a visible investment of attention and muscular effort" (1961: 106), arguing importantly that it indicates a mutuality: when persons are engaged with one another, they demonstrate that engagement in embodied and publicly-displayed ways (Goffman 1963).

As Goffman later says, "roles may not only be *played* but also *played at*" (1961: 99). Thus, while students often seem to display their engagement or disengagement with the interaction in observable ways, they also pretend to be engaged when they are not (e.g., holding one's phone in front of a book to appear as though one's gaze is oriented to the materials). Importantly, however, they also often demonstrate their engagement despite their lack of participation. As Goffman (1963) notes, one might be "unengaged" from one particular interaction but simultaneously be engaged in some other task (i.e., one is not "disengaged"). This question of shifting engagement, which Goffman (1981) likens to a shift in footing, will be further elucidated below, and we will see examples throughout the book.

One of the analytic foci in this book is the incidence of observable non-participation and disengagement in classrooms, concepts that relate directly to Goffman's notion of *role distance*, which he describes as behaviors that demonstrate a person's "disaffection from, and resistance against, the role" (1961: 108) they might be expected to inhabit in social interaction. It is possible that displays of non-participation and disengagement reflect students' disaffection or resistance against the role of "engaged student" (or possibly "good student," which for racialized minorities may also be seen as "acting white," Gay 2018). As noted before, the students in the Reading and College Data sets in particular are "authentic beginners" (Gee 2004: 14). They may never have developed the classroom interactional competence to display "doing being a good student," but they might just as likely not be invested in such a display, having found it to be a difficult performance to maintain, or one which they have not been given a full opportunity to play.

An important note about Goffman's performance metaphor is his inclusion of multimodal resources in the development of "impressions" (1959: 2); he notes that such impressions are a function of the words we say in combination with everything else about a performance, including embodied actions, but also our clothes, hair, etc. He goes on to suggest that in interaction, we give more credence to the impression created by these non-verbal means, because we think those are less easily manipulated than our words. If this is so, the full range of student actions in the classroom will give us a more complete picture of what kind of student they are presenting themselves to be.

3.2.4 GOFFMAN-INSPIRED CLASSROOM DISCOURSE RESEARCH

While Goffman did not focus specifically on classroom interaction in his writing, his ideas have been drawn upon by many classroom discourse researchers. Schwab (2011) draws inspiration from Goffman in his introduction of the term "multilogue" to more accurately describe whole-class interaction; he argues that all members of the class have access to contributions and could potentially contribute themselves. This importantly means that all participants' (teacher's and students') multimodal actions "have reference to more than one addressee" (2011: 7–8). Also drawing on Goffman (1981), Evnitskaya and Berger (2017) complicate the notion of willingness to participate (WTP), showing how displays of WTP function moment by moment in classroom interaction, revealing information about students' engagement, attentiveness, and participant roles. They paraphrase Goffman (1981) as follows: "participation can be accomplished to varying degrees and modalities of speakership and listenership which are oriented to by participants" (2017: 4). Mortensen (2009) likewise looks at "participation roles" including "speaker" and "hearer," noting that first actions set up expectations about what appropriate participation in the next turn will be. Mori and Hasegawa similarly argue that students' identities *as* students are "reflexively indexed by the ways in which they participate in interaction" (2009: 66). Piirainen-Marsh defines participation and participation framework as "the detailed ways in which participants ... signal to each other not only their role as speaker or hearer, but also their position in discourse ... and stance towards each other as well as the activity under way" (2011: 368). Tadic (2018) likewise argues that students' taking on different participant roles can be a way of understanding the range of student participation opportunities in a classroom. I argue that student actions within participation frameworks (whether as speakers or hearers) show their public displays of their own version of doing-being-a-student.

Van Compernolle's (2015) monograph pairs sociocultural theories of mind with micro-analytic discourse methods to trace learners' language development through interaction, and his discussions of participation draw heavily from Goffman (1981), noting that participant roles are "multi-faceted and dynamic" (2015: 10). Van Compernolle's work also serves as an important inspiration for this volume, particularly in his expansive view of participation and understanding of the intertwined nature of verbal and embodied resources. Overall, van Compernolle's book, in addition to the studies described above, shows how Goffman's grand ideas can find application in the examination of the micro-analytic detail of classroom interaction. Crucially, my analysis not only complicates our notion of the participation framework in classrooms but also expands concepts like participation and engagement beyond prior research to include things like role distance and "playing at" being a student.

3.3 RECONCEPTUALIZING PARTICIPATION AND ENGAGEMENT

I conceive of participation as an accountable, participant-relevant consideration, i.e., participants hold one another accountable for knowing what counts as participation at any given moment. For example, in one classroom context, a student writing may be treated as actively participating, while in another, that same student might be sanctioned for "not paying attention" (see Extract 1.1). I argue that participation can be conceived on a matrix, with students' alignment with pedagogical goals and with the interaction itself (i.e., students' ability to contribute appropriately, at just the right moment) influencing whether any student action is considered (non-)participation or (dis)engagement at any given moment. In addition to students' verbal contributions, "listenership" (McCarthy 2003), as evidenced by eye gaze, posture, etc., is one publicly-available type of student participation, but there are many other forms of participation (and non-participation) in the classroom that this monograph examines. Waring notes that students invest an enormous amount in "defending, maintaining, and asserting their competence," calling such efforts "competence displays" (2016: 61, 149), and these displays tell us about their participation and engagement. However, I also note that students, because of role distance or lacking classroom interactional competence, do not always make such efforts.

"Appropriate" participation is locally contingent and context-sensitive, i.e., it depends on the classroom context. Both Seedhouse (2004) and Walsh (2006, 2011) have argued that there is a reflexive relationship between language use and pedagogical goals, i.e., productive classroom interaction results when the teacher's and students' use of language aligns with their pedagogical goals. We cannot assume that any one way of interacting in the classroom will always work; rather, we must fit our contributions with the interactional patterns specific to the pedagogical purposes at any given moment. For instance, in the case of silent, individual reading, students' gaze to their books and the lack of verbal contributions is appropriate. However, these same actions might be considered inappropriate, or might not "count" as participation at all, in a small group discussion. Likewise, student-initiated questions are appropriate forms of participation during classroom-context mode, and in some classrooms, even more so if they are not preceded by a multimodal bid for a turn. However, it is easy to imagine a variety of classroom contexts where a student's self-initiated question would be considered "out of turn." When student actions are in alignment with the pedagogical purposes and interactional trajectory set by the teacher, they are considered to be appropriate participation. This emic analysis is thus informed by the individual teacher's orientation to different kinds of (non-) participation.

While students can overtly align with the teacher's goals, they can also contribute to progressivity by simply appearing to align. As Edwards and Westgate note, "appropriate participation requires of pupils that they listen *or appear to listen*" (1994: 40; emphasis added). How can we conceptualize the difference between participation and engagement? Certainly, sometimes students who participate are engaged, and sometimes students who are engaged do not participate (verbally at least). In particular, however, there also seem to be times when students appear to be engaged, but when called upon to demonstrate their engagement with verbal participation, are unable to do so. It is thus in the breach that we see what kinds of student actions might contribute to the *appearance* or *display* of engagement (i.e., studenting). It is important to note, however, that these cases are the exception, and more often than not, it is not possible to say with certainty whether a student is engaged or simply performing the role of student. Observable behavior can tell us only so much, but in this volume, I argue that it tells us much more than we have seen in prior accounts.

3.3.1 DEFINING PARTICIPATION AND NON-PARTICIPATION

This analysis shows that students are always displaying (non-)participation through their multimodal actions, and **participation** entails *students undertaking multimodal social actions in alignment with both the ongoing interaction and the pedagogical goals of the moment*. This is not to suggest that the students must align with the teacher's stance (i.e., challenging student turns are forms of participation, cf. Rampton 1996); rather, that for student action to "count" as participation, it must be in alignment with the interactional and pedagogical context. The difference between student actions in and out of alignment can be illustrated with a simple example. In some contexts, the teacher will ask students a question, expecting them to self-select as next speaker. In this context, speaking without first bidding for a turn (i.e., raising one's hand or establishing mutual gaze with the teacher) counts as participation because this action aligns with the teacher's pedagogical goals of *that moment*. In the same classroom, possibly moments later, the teacher may again ask a question, but if students speak without bidding for a turn, may sanction them for doing so, saying, "Raise your hands." In this context, self-selecting without bidding does not count *as* participation in an interactional or pedagogical sense. Attending to the teacher's cues for appropriate participation is a complex skill, particularly because in large multiparty interaction like that found in classrooms, participation structures are constantly shifting, entailing moment-by-moment shifts in expectations for the students.

Non-participation is conceptualized as *the absence of projected student action, or student actions that are out of alignment with the teacher's pedagogical goals and/or the student's current interactional rights and obligations*. The case of a lack of student participation is more clear-cut, though it must be noted that non-participation does not necessarily indicate disengagement. Students can indicate their continued engagement in embodied ways, even when they are unwilling or unable to participate as expected (see Extracts 5.3 and 5.4). In cases where students might be said to be performing category-bound actions of "students" (e.g., gaze orientation to the board or a book, writing, gaze orientation to the teacher, etc.), but whether by design (i.e., in cases of disengagement) or because of their lacking CIC, these actions are not in alignment with the teacher pedagogically or interactionally, I consider this category of actions "studenting," an interactional achievement that demonstrates students' understanding of, and/or willingness to comply with, interactional and pedagogical expectations. Hellermann (2008a) notes that after disengaging from tasks, students must engage in category-bound actions if they are to maintain their display of engagement; as an example, he says a "student may work independently (writing, reading) or wait (without overtly 'working') for the teacher to announce the next activity" (2008a: 114). By looking more closely at students' actions when they are not "overtly 'working,'" I aim to present a fuller picture of doing-being-a-student in classrooms. The difference between engaged studenting and disengaged studenting will be highlighted in examples throughout the book.

3.3.2 DEFINING (DIS)ENGAGEMENT

Engagement is primarily observable through *the timing (or lack) of student actions*. M. H. Goodwin proposes that "collaborative production of utterances, format tying, and sound play" all provide evidence of "involvement" (2007: 93), and these are good examples of the kinds of practices that I argue demonstrate *engagement* through students' careful monitoring of interaction. Students' precisely-timed actions show that they are carefully attending to their evolving interactional rights and obligations, i.e., that they are *engaging with the interaction*. As Kunitz (2018) argues, (joint) *attention* can be specified in interactional terms, and the actions that index attention are publicly available to co-present participants; the analysis here shows how students do or do not attend to the ongoing interaction in public ways.

Students can participate with more or less engagement, and likewise their non-participation can evidence more or less engagement. Engagement is not a continuous state, but rather fluctuates for all students (and the teacher) throughout the course of a lesson. Sahlström talks about "the impossibility of everyone's individual engagement" in whole-class interaction (2002: 48), and this is a key point in our consideration of what doing-being-a-student looks like. As the Sartre (1956) quote that opened this chapter suggests, creating a continuous display of engagement would be exhausting, and would in fact make true engagement an impossibility. I return to the question of what the display of engagement means for the performance of doing-being-a-student in the discussion in Chapter 8, again highlighting the limits of observable behavior for an interactional analysis of learning. Figure 3.1 reproduces the matrix introduced in Chapter 1 as a reminder of how these new definitions relate to student actions' alignment both pedagogically and interactionally.

3.4 SUMMARY

As noted above, students can demonstrate their engagement with the interaction in embodied ways, while simultaneously displaying their unwillingness to participate

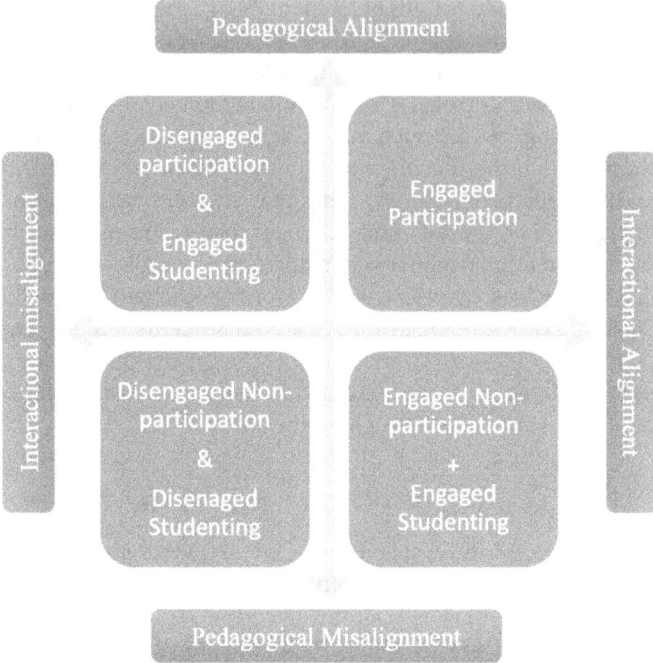

Figure 3.1   Reconceptualizing "participation" and "engagement"

(cf. Mortensen 2008). Much research on classroom interaction, particularly in language learning classrooms, has focused on students' engaged (especially verbal) participation. This book shifts the focus by presenting a multimodal analysis of a range of student action in classrooms. The focus on multimodality allows us to see the differences between (non-)participation and (dis)engagement, and to see their moment-by-moment unfolding. Most radically, my focus on the totality of student actions in classrooms means that we can see the full range of what it means to do doing-being-a-student, whether that means answering teacher questions, initiating a new sequence, sleeping, or texting a friend.

4

STUDENT PARTICIPATION AND ENGAGEMENT

> Involvement in interaction . . . is rarely explicitly addressed; if it were it would shift the focus of attention from the topic at hand to the problems of being involved in it.
>
> Christian Heath (1984: 247)

4.1 INTRODUCTION

As Heath's quote above suggests, the terms of involvement in interaction are rarely made explicit, though in the classroom, what "counts" as participation is a member's problem that becomes salient when students participate in the "wrong" ways. *Participation* refers to student turns in pedagogical and interactional alignment, while *non-participation* refers to student turns that are out of alignment in one or both ways, including missing student responses. The sequentiality and temporality of students' contributions allows us to see their attention (or not) to the unfolding interaction. That is, students can demonstrate their careful monitoring of, their *engagement* with, classroom interaction by the precise timing of aligned actions. The term "participation" has traditionally referred to verbal contributions, and in this chapter, I too focus on students' verbal contributions to demonstrate how we can characterize their participation and engagement, and in so doing, disambiguate these terms.

I introduce a new term, "studenting," to refer to student actions that fall outside our idealized sense of doing-being-a-student. *Studenting* refers to student actions that can be considered category-bound actions of the role "student in a classroom" but either (1) they are not undertaken at the "right" time, or (2) students are engaging in those actions as a *performance* of participation and/or engagement. These two possibilities represent an important distinction that will also aid in differentiating between participation and engagement. While I characterize studenting as non-participation because of its lack of alignment interactionally or pedagogically, I want to underscore that it is an interactional accomplishment in its own right. Students may undertake an action at the "wrong" time because they have not been monitoring the interaction closely (i.e., they have been disengaged), because they are engaged in some other activity, or because they have misunderstood the current interactional and pedagogical context. In any of these instances, their category-bound action conveys their understanding of doing-being-a-student, albeit inexpertly or in misalignment with the teacher. When studenting actions are undertaken as students engage in other tasks unrelated to the teacher's plan, they are skillfully finding a way to follow their own agenda without disrupting the progressivity of the lesson by putting on a show of doing-being-a-student that will pass muster. This latter case shows an advanced kind of classroom interactional competence, albeit one that may not align pedagogically with the teacher's aims.

In order to show the complexity of students' displays of participation and engagement, as well as the variability among students in these displays, I begin Section 4.2 with analysis of a mundane classroom activity: a "checking episode" (Gourlay 2005) where students are expected to produce choral responses. In Section 4.3, I will examine instances of teacher–student interaction on the open floor to contrast aligned student actions (*engaged participation*) with examples that might at first glance seem similar but are in fact instances of *engaged studenting*. Finally, in Section 4.4, I focus on student-to-student interactions to contrast examples of *engaged participation* with examples of *engaged studenting*. This final section will continue to show how participation and engagement can be disambiguated from one another, and importantly, how these characterizations might relate to learning.

4.2 PARTICIPATION AND ENGAGEMENT IN CHORAL RESPONSES

A ubiquitous classroom activity where students are expected to contribute verbally is a checking episode, where students are prompted for choral responses with multiple students saying the "same" thing at the "same" time. By tracking students' (non-)participation in this activity, I argue that we can characterize their (dis) engagement from the interaction. While Sacks et al. (1974) note in their seminal paper that overwhelmingly, one speaker speaks at a time in so-called "ordinary" interaction, in institutional multiparty interaction, other participation structures are possible. Van Lier allows for the possibility of multiple students speaking simultaneously, noting that such instances can happen only when students "say (roughly) the same thing" (1988: 139). Teasing out what "roughly" means can reveal differential participation and engagement on the part of different students, as well as changes over the course of an episode in the participation and engagement of individual students.

Choral responses are more complex than is indicated by a single transcript line attributed to "Ss" (students) or "Ll" (learners) (see Dobs 2019, and Jacknick and Creider 2018 for exceptions to this transcription practice). In fact, students (do or do not) participate in choral responses in complex ways. In this example from the Reading Data, the class is going over a vocabulary exercise they had just completed individually. My analysis focuses on differences in student responses, as well as how students' participation in this exercise changes as it proceeds. The simplified transcription shows how I initially transcribed the episode on my first pass, with choral responses represented in one line labeled "Ss" for "students." The lines on the right expand these "choral" lines, showing the complexity such transcription practices obscure. Focal lines are bolded below (see also Appendix 1 for full transcription conventions).

Extract 4.1 Utopia

```
1   TEA    so down below? just- you can
2          call them out here, an ideal or a
3          perfect place- (0.2) or state?
4   Ss     utopia.
5   TEA    utopi[a?]
6   MAH         [ut]opia. [heheh ]
7   TEA                   [$noisy$]
8          $and disorderly$? Or [bois ]terous?
9   SAR?                        [ruck-]
10  Ss     raucous.
11  TEA    raucous? okay? a source of help,
12         a strength, something to turn to,
13  Ss     recourse.
14  TEA    recourse? right? or a choice?
```

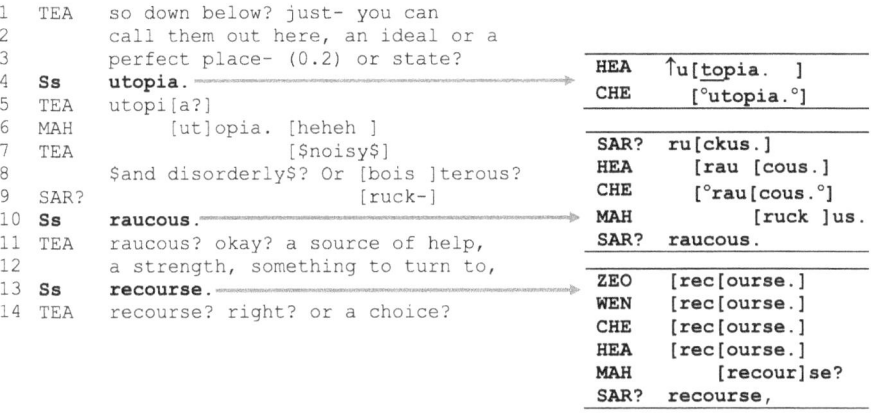

```
HEA    ↑u[topia.   ]
CHE      [°utopia.°]

SAR?   ru[ckus.]
HEA      [rau [cous.]
CHE           [°rau[cous.°]
MAH                [ruck ]us.
SAR?   raucous.

ZEO    [rec[ourse.]
WEN    [rec[ourse.]
CHE    [rec[ourse.]
HEA    [rec[ourse.]
MAH        [recour]se?
SAR?   recourse,
```

The teacher explicitly outlines the participation structure as requiring choral response as he begins this activity, directing students to 'call them out here' (line 2). Following his reading of the first item in lines 2–3, we see what might be transcribed as a choral response from students in line 4. However, the zoomed view to the right shows that this chorus contains just two students as first Heather and then Chen provide the answer ('utopia'). The teacher repeats the correct answer as positive evaluation in line 5, overlapped by Mahmoud repeating the same word. With the very first item, then, we can see that students are not really responding "in chorus." Heather and Chen, by their precisely-timed participation, have demonstrated their engagement with this task. However, even with these two, there are also differences in delivery that are masked by a choral response line in the transcript, with Chen responding very softly and Heather using marked intonation. Mahmoud also contributes, but in a delayed way, showing that he may not be attending to the unfolding interaction as carefully. He is, however, participating in the prescribed manner, which is more than can be said for the other fourteen students present who have not joined the verbal chorus (for more on the embodied actions of the students who decline to participate verbally, see Extract 5.8). As a second language user of English, Mahmoud's delayed response may be due to language processing, rather than inattention. However, Heather and Chen are both also second language users of English, but they are clearly engaged with the unfolding interaction.

As the teacher moves on to the next item, more students join in the response. In line 10, we see at least four students respond to the teacher's prompt. Sara responds first in overlap with the teacher as he reads both phrases from the book (line 9), and then repairs her cut-off turn just after the teacher finishes reading. The timing of her overlapped answer shows that she is carefully attending to the teacher's delivery as it arrives just after the possible end of a turn (i.e., after 'disorderly'), though it also shows some lack of attention to the structure of the items in the book, as this item includes two alternate definitions. Her repair, however, comes just after the teacher

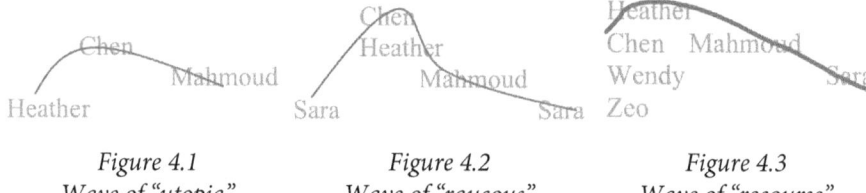

Figure 4.1
Wave of "utopia"

Figure 4.2
Wave of "raucous"

Figure 4.3
Wave of "recourse"

finishes, again demonstrating her engagement with the interaction and the exercise. Heather and Chen also precisely time their contributions, starting a moment after Sara's self-repair. Mahmoud again is a moment behind, saying the word in overlap with the end of his classmates' contribution, and echoing Sara's inaccurate pronunciation. Another student repeats the word as well, demonstrating participation if not engagement with a delayed response. If this student is Sara (as is possible though not certain given camera angles), rather than showing disengagement, this delay would instead show her engagement. Given her initially inaccurate pronunciation, her self-correction here would demonstrate her careful attention to the different pronunciation used by her classmates.

With the next item, "recourse," we see much more precise timing on the part of a group of students, with Zeo, Wendy, Chen, and Heather saying the word simultaneously (line 13). These students are attending carefully to, i.e., *engaged with* the unfolding interaction, timing their responses with the teacher's prompt and also with each other. Mahmoud's participation is delayed again, followed by Sara's contribution a moment later. These latter two students are participating, though are perhaps not as engaged as their peers. The students' participation in the choral responses here appear as a wave rather than a truly simultaneous action. Additionally, we can see that the shape of the wave changes as the checking episode progresses, with more students joining the initial crest of participation for these first three items. Compare Figures 4.1, 4.2, and 4.3 above.

Although seven more items follow "recourse" in this checking episode, this item is the peak of verbal participation, with 6 students contributing verbally to one answer. Notably, no single student participates verbally in response to every item in the exercise. At most 9 of the 17 students present contribute verbally at some point. Chen and another student speak so quietly in subsequent lines that their voices are barely distinguishable, and in some cases, they may be actually mouthing the words rather than voicing them, though it is impossible to say for certain given the quality of video recordings. This "choral" response is thus seen to involve only half of the students, and even for those students, their verbal participation is not constant. Rather, we see through the timing of their participation how engaged they are with the interaction, and importantly, how this engagement shifts over time as the parameters for participation become clearer. The decreasing verbal participation over the course of the checking episode also shows us how students' engagement with the interaction, or at least their interest in displaying their attention, wanes from its peak in line 13. The teacher does not orient to this state of affairs, nor does he orient to the differential responses from those few students who are verbally contributing. While in other

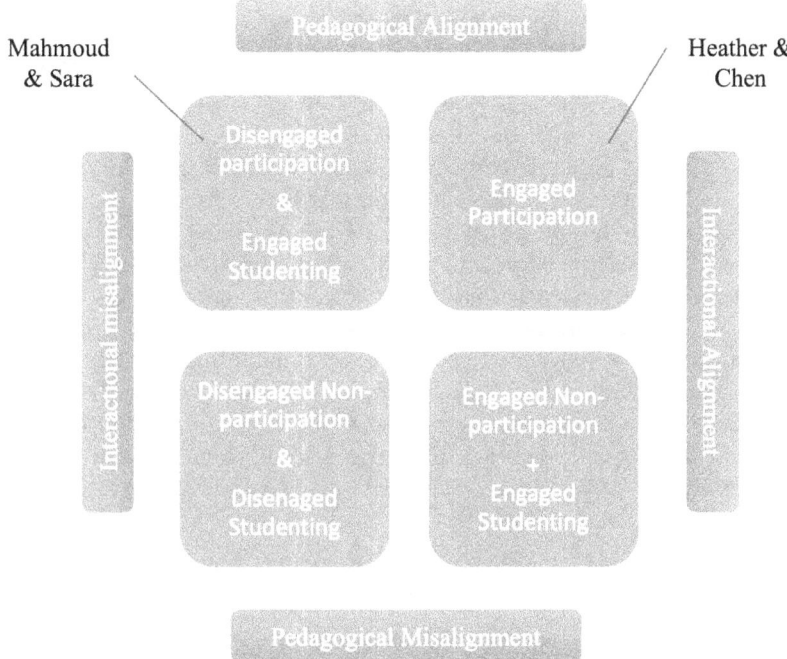

Figure 4.4 Students' participation and engagement in Extract 4.1

checking episodes, this teacher does sanction the students as a whole when only a few students participate verbally, here, this display of participation and engagement is oriented to as enough.

This one example shows us student actions that potentially fall across all four quadrants of the matrix of participation and engagement, reproduced here as Figure 4.4. In the first three items included in this extract, Heather and Chen contribute verbally for each one, with comparatively precise timing, demonstrating their *engaged participation*. Mahmoud also contributes verbally, though with delays, showing his *disengaged participation*; Sara likewise shows through her inapt timing her comparative disengagement, speaking too soon for "raucous" and late for "recourse." However, even these students do not contribute verbally to each item in the checking episode, and so some of their (lack of) actions later would fall in the bottom half of the matrix, as *non-participation*. By limiting our analysis in this chapter to students' verbal contributions, we are unable to further characterize their actions as (dis) engaged, though we will return to this example again in Chapter 5 (Extract 5.8). In the rest of this chapter, we will see how similar-seeming student actions can in fact represent different quadrants of the matrix.

4.3 ENGAGED PARTICIPATION VS. ENGAGED STUDENTING: TEACHER-TO-STUDENT INTERACTION

Having seen differences in displays of participation and engagement, we can turn to more subtle nuances in student action: differentiating engaged participation from engaged studenting. An important consideration when deciding whether a student contribution "counts" as participation is how that contribution aligns (or not) with the interactional context and pedagogical goals of the moment. Walsh's (2006, 2011) modes are important here because they help set the stage for what the class is doing as a whole, what the teacher's pedagogical purposes are, and what the participation structure is in any given moment. Consideration of these aspects of modes helps make clear whether any given student action is or is not in alignment interactionally and pedagogically. Student turns which appear discursively similar in some ways can represent vastly different kinds of displays of participation and/or engagement because of their sequential location. In Section 4.3.1, I include two extracts to illustrate *engaged participation*, contrasting them with a similar example in Section 4.3.2 showing *engaged studenting*.

4.3.1 ENGAGED PARTICIPATION

Researchers of classroom discourse have documented the predominance of teacher control of turn-taking procedures (Green et al. 1988; Mehan 1979; Sinclair and Coulthard 1975), a fact of life in "traditional" classrooms that allows little room for student talk. In particular, classroom activities involving all students and the teacher—teacher-fronted or whole-group activity—may inherently limit the ability of students to participate, as the teacher has the "right" to hold the floor and to designate speakers. Student participation in this setting was argued to be severely restricted in the original accounts of classroom discourse (McHoul 1978; Mehan 1979; Sinclair and Coulthard 1975). In these early studies, students were found to initiate in response to teacher prompts (i.e., solicited participation), and student initiation outside of the initiation–response–feedback script was infrequent. When unsolicited participation surfaced in these accounts, it appeared only in restricted sequential environments (Mehan 1979) or was oriented to by participants as a deviation from the turn-taking apparatus (McHoul 1978).

Mehan's (1979) description of elicitation techniques in the classroom provides a solid foundation for the term *student-initiated actions* as used here. In his seminal study of classroom interactions, three turn-taking procedures were described: (1) *nomination*, in which the teacher calls on a student or indicates that they may have a turn in an embodied way (e.g., by pointing or nodding); (2) *invitation to bid*, where the teacher indicates that students may raise their hands to be called on; and (3) *invitation to reply*, where the teacher indicates that any student (or several students simultaneously) may respond. Here we are concerned with turns that students self-initiate, including those that act as bids or replies to teacher prompts (cf. Jacknick 2009 for more on student initiation). By examining student questions, declaratives, and challenges in their interactional and pedagogical contexts, we can characterize students' engagement, while simultaneously answering the difficult question of what counts as participation.

Students, predictably, often ask questions during teacher-fronted activity, though the sequential location of these questions differs depending on the interactional space provided by the teacher. Jacknick (2011b) specifically examined student initiations "at the seams" of activities, i.e., during transitions, or what Walsh (2006, 2011) calls managerial mode. This mode is characterized by confirmation checks (which we will see below) and a lack of learner involvement. However, as I have argued elsewhere (Jacknick 2011b), these transitional moments can be exploited by students for interactional space, and Extract 4.2 (from the ESL Data) is an example of such a student initiation, coming just at the end of a textbook review (a materials mode activity). After reading the final sentence of the exercise, the teacher returned the student book she had been borrowing, and with her back turned to most students as she walked toward the board, uttered the understanding check 'any $questions$.' (line 1).

Extract 4.2 I don't understand
```
1    TEA   any $questions$.=
2    FLO   =yeah, the number five, I don't
3          understand why you chose "will
4          have worked out." because we
5          don't have the, this kind of
6          expression, like uh, "by" or
7          "by this time,"
8          *#(2.0)      *#(0.2)
           *Flo gaze to T*to book-->
           #fig. 4.5 #fig. 4.6
```

```
9    FLO   just "eventually," is that
10         expression? a time *expression?
                             *Flo gaze to T-->
11   TEA   kind of. "eventually" means,
```

This prompt for questions is potentially designed not to invite responses at all; the polarity of the question (using "any") prefers a "no" type response (Heritage and Robinson 2011; Waring 2012a, 2012b) and it is uttered with falling intonation (i.e., not "questioning" upward intonation) as well as smiley voice targeted toward the students seated on the side, with whom she had just established mutual gaze as she returned the book. Finally, given that the teacher has her back to most students and thus is not available for mutual gaze, she does not seem to be inviting responses. However, Florence answers immediately in the affirmative, proceeding with her problem in understanding without waiting for a go-ahead from the teacher. Notably, Florence has her gaze oriented toward her book during the teacher's prompt, a gaze orientation she maintains during her own turn: she is not pursuing mutual gaze with the teacher. During materials mode contexts (Walsh 2006, 2011), Mortensen (2009) shows that students often maintain orientation toward the materials while answering questions, and Florence's continued gaze to the book demonstrates her persistence in the materials mode activity, and resistance to the activity shift projected by the teacher. In this case, the teacher does not orient toward students because she is moving back toward the blackboard during her prompt for questions; she is also unavailable for mutual gaze.

As Jacknick (2011b) notes, students take strategic advantage of the incremental nature of activity shifts in the classroom to initiate new sequences, and this example shows just that. While Florence's gaze orientation to her book throughout the checking episode is inscrutable with regard to her engagement in the activity, her careful attention to the teacher's initiation of closing, along with her precisely timed initiation, demonstrates her engagement with the unfolding interaction and with the topic of the lesson itself. She skillfully uses her awareness of the structure of classroom talk to secure space for her question; that is, her engagement allows her to find interactional space. We can see that Florence's turn aligns interactionally; that is, the teacher prompt just prior does project a student response (if only a "no"-type response). How though does Florence's turn align pedagogically? The teacher is projecting activity transition in embodied ways (returning the student book she had been borrowing and physically moving around the classroom), but also through the formulaic prompt "any questions," a phrase which functions more as a boundary marker than an invitation in most cases (Waring 2012a). Florence's initiation could straddle the line of engaged participation and studenting, because it could be seen as pedagogically misaligned. However, the teacher's immediate abandonment of activity transition by moving away from her desk and toward Florence shows her willingness to treat her understanding check as a last chance to air problems in understanding, rather than simply as a boundary marker.

Student-initiated questions often place the teacher in a superior position with regard to epistemic rights, aligning the student role of "novice" with an unknowing position and the teacher role of "expert" with a knowing position. However, students also contribute from a knowing position to demonstrate their understanding, and sometimes to challenge the teacher, though this is a phenomenon that few studies have focused on (cf. Jacknick 2013; Margutti and Piirainen-Marsh 2011). When these contributions are precisely timed and relevant to the ongoing topic of interaction, they serve as demonstrations of student engagement, not only in an interactional sense by showing students attending carefully to interactional rights and obligations, but in a more ineffable sense of engagement as coming together around some idea or enterprise. In particular, challenging student-initiated turns demonstrate engagement by showing students grappling with teacher explanations and making their own understandings public in whole-class interaction.

In Extract 4.3 below from the ESL Data, the teacher is reviewing answers to a grammar activity where students had to identify grammatical and ungrammatical sentences. In the ensuing discussion, many students initiate verbal contributions, but I want to focus on the post-expansions (Schegloff 2007) of Rodrigo, Nobu, and Yoro, and my analysis centers on the different actions these sequentially-similar contributions represent.

Extract 4.3 It sounds so weird
```
1    TEA   kay. nine? i:s (.) correct,=
2    ROD   =do we need, (.) like "Yoro su-
3          suggests, (0.4) you to take?" No?
4          (0.8)
5    TEA   >°say that one more time?°<
6          "suggest you,"
7    ROD   "to: take."
8    TEA   "to take." no:.
9    AME   it's a gerund?
10   TEA   yeah, remember um,
11   ROD   it sounds so weird.
12   TEA   $no, c'mon guys$, we learned this
13         like, hh at the beginning. okay.
[10 lines omitted]
24   TEA   okay, so. um, that's where
25         that ↑comes from. kay.
26         (1.2)
27   NOB   so we don't use, all the time "that."
28         I mean, "Yoro suggests (.) that."
29   TEA   no you [can drop that. yeah.]
30   NOB          [unnecessary. okay. ] how
31         bout ge↑rund? "Yoro suggests? ↑your
32         taking (.) painting classes."
33   TEA   ↑yeah.[yeah- ]we went over that.
34   NOB         [yeah. ]
35   TEA   but it's a little different, remember.=
36   NOB   =ah.=
37   TEA   =then you're emphasizing the action.
38   NOB   oh.
39   YOR   so how bout the, "Yoro suggests (0.4)
40         you ↑taking, painting classes" Because
41         "suggest" to take uh, a gerund, right?
42   TEA   "Yoro suggests you taking:,"
43         (1.0)
44   TEA   [painting::]
45   MIZ   [(painting)] classes.
46   YOR   no.
```

Extract 4.3 It sounds so weird (continued)
```
47   TEA   yeah I don't-, no it's "your taking"
48         or "you-" or "take" or "take."
49   YOR   when [ do you ] omit the "that."
50   TEA        [it's not-]
51         (1.2)
52   TEA   tsk ↑usually, um: when
53         you talk fast? people drop things.
54         just to say it faster,=
55   YOR   =but this is writing.
56         (2.0)
57   TEA   ↑ye:↓s. uh huh huh. um, but people
58         drop it >in writing too,<
```

In line 1, the teacher announces that sentence number nine ("Yoro suggests you take painting classes because it is a wonderful activity.") is correct, and so Rodrigo's question in lines 2–3 can be seen as targeting the possible inclusion of "to" in the sentence. As Jacknick (2011a) argues, given that this is a student-initiated three-part sequence, Rodrigo's comment in line 11 ('it sounds so weird') acts as a non-minimal post-expansion (Schegloff 2007). While Schegloff identifies several different types of post-expansion, the action of this post-expansion is rejection/challenge/disagreement with the second pair part (line 8). In this case, Rodrigo makes his stance on the grammatical form evident. This stance is out of alignment with the teacher's position that the form is correct, and so this functions as a challenge. Rodrigo doesn't claim epistemic primacy here, though by this contribution demonstrates his willingness to comment on the form and make his stance public. The teacher responds to his challenge with a rejection, 'no', uttered with smiley voice and followed by the cajoling 'c'mon guys' and a reminder that this is a grammar point they covered at the start of the semester.

The teacher directs students' attention to a chart in their textbook that identifies which verbs take infinitive versus gerund forms and closes her explanation in lines 24–25. Nobu initiates a new sequence in line 27 with a so-preface, a turn that acts as an understanding check in the form of a declarative rather than a question (Beun 2000). As Bolden (2009) notes, such so-prefaced turns can also serve to project sequence-initiating questions, and indeed, Nobu does follow up with a question in lines 30–32. Nobu's turn here acts as a summary, aligning with the teacher's explanation but also making it more concise, while simultaneously serving as a preface for his upcoming sequence-initiating question. He then also includes a post-expansion 'unnecessary. okay.' and exploits this follow-up to initiate another new sequence, similar to the way a teacher's third turn is often used to evaluate the prior turn and start a new sequence (McHoul 1985). In contrast to Rodrigo's post-expansion challenging comment, Nobu's post-expansion is minimal, but is strategically used to secure an additional turn.

As the discussion continues, the student turns become more and more pointed, with Rodrigo asking about including "that," Nobu summarizing the teacher's explanation, and Yoro asking specifically in which environments "that" is omitted (line 49). Where Rodrigo's post-expansion in line 11 indexed his disagreement and Nobu's in line 30 demonstrated his understanding of the teacher's explanation to preface a new initiation, Yoro's post-expansion in line 55 directly challenges the teacher's most recent explanation. Her turn begins with a disagreement-implicative "but" that marks this turn as a contrastive action (Schiffrin 1987). She baldly challenges the premise of the teacher's explanation that fast speech can account for the grammatical difference by pointing out that they are talking about writing.

This extract shows student-initiated turns that demonstrate not only the students' verbal participation, but also their engagement on an interactional level. Rodrigo's question directly addresses the sentence just mentioned by the teacher, and his turn is precisely timed to latch with the teacher's. Nobu's turn overlaps the teacher's turn and exploits the sequential location of a post-expansion to initiate a new sequence. Finally, Yoro's disagreement-implicative challenge is also latched to the teacher's explanation. The precise timing we see here, along with the content of these student turns, demonstrates these students' careful monitoring of the interaction and of the discussion itself. Rampton (1996) claims that students who challenge the teacher's authority (epistemic or otherwise) are not necessarily disengaged, a situation we see clearly here with these three students' willingness to go on record with turns that challenge the teacher's epistemic primacy, i.e., to *engage* with the teacher about this grammar point. These student turns, which capitalize on opportunities for self-initiation, show students' classroom interactional competence as they align interactionally and pedagogically while challenging the teacher.

4.3.2 ENGAGED STUDENTING

The student-initiated turns in the extracts in the prior section are appropriately placed in sequential locations that allow for their inclusion (e.g., post-expansions), and when students are able to capitalize on sequential opportunities for participation, they are able to pursue explanations and resolve problems of understanding (Waring 2009). However, student-initiated contributions are not always appropriate to the mode or participation structure as established by the teacher, and they are unlikely to be taken up by the teacher if they are out of sync with the current interaction (Mehan 1979). Although such "inappropriate" contributions are potentially more likely in classroom interactions involving children (as in Mehan's data), they also occur in adult classrooms, as seen in the following example of engaged studenting from the Reading Data.

Here, the teacher is reading the first twenty pages of *Fahrenheit 451* (Bradbury 1953) aloud, stopping occasionally to talk to students about vocabulary, etc. This read aloud and teacher-led discussion had been going for over 30 minutes when the teacher paused his reading to talk about the presence of televisions in the first twenty pages of the novel. The teacher notes the prevalence of televisions in American homes beginning around the publication date in lines 1–3 and is about to launch into a personal anecdote when Greg tries to contribute in line 5.

Extract 4.4 Peter Pan

```
1    TEA   so nineteen fifty three?
2          televisions are starting to go into
3          everybody's houses in nineteen fifty three,
4          (2.0)
5    GRE   tsk Peter Pan,
6    TEA   I think my family we got our first T-V in
7          about nineteen: fifty (.) [fou::r? *#or five? ]
8    GRE                             [Peter Pan first premier-]
                                          *T chin to Gre-->
                                          #fig. 4.7
```

```
9    GRE   Peter Pan first premiered [for Disney,]
10   TEA                             [Peter Pa::n?]
11         *#oka:y? * but, if you go back and
           *Gre smile..*
           #fig. 4.8
```

```
12   TEA   look at what was on T-V in nineteen fifty
13         three? *#other than people having all their
                  *Gre gaze down-->
                  #fig. 4.9
```

Extract 4.4 Peter Pan (continued)
```
14    TEA    clothes on it was *#basically the same as what's
                     *Gre gaze to T-->
                     #fig. 4.10
```

```
15           on T-V now.
```

Greg maintains eye gaze toward the teacher throughout lines 1–4. However, as in Extract 4.1, the teacher's back was to most students just before the student contribution in question, and so he was not available for mutual gaze. The teacher thus cannot be argued to nominate Greg to speak in any way, and there is no open floor because the teacher's turn in lines 1–3 does not project a student response; Greg is speaking "out of turn" here. The pause in line 4 seems to have been intended as an intra-turn pause, as evidenced by the teacher's continuing intonation in line 3 and his ongoing turn in line 6. Greg, meanwhile, interprets the silence as an opportunity to self-select.

The teacher mentions the publication year of the novel twice in lines 1–3, and one of the students' tasks prior to this class was to research the year *Fahrenheit 451* was published, 1953. Greg seems to have taken these mentions as a cue to bring in his research, saying 'Peter Pan' in line 5, and receiving no response from the teacher, repeating it again in line 8. Greg is participating, but his participation does not align with the interactional or pedagogical goals of the moment. Finding no uptake for his contribution, Greg repeats his turn in line 8, delivered just after a micro-pause in the teacher's turn in line 7, though this micro-pause does not occur at a transition-relevance place (Clayman 2013) where a change of speakership becomes possible. Again, Greg seems to be monitoring the teacher's delivery for spaces for initiation but doing so inexpertly.

Following the overlap, the teacher makes a deictic point toward Greg with his chin which functions as an embodied "open-class" repair initiation (Drew 1997; Mortensen 2012; Seo and Koshik 2010), and Greg repeats the information a third time in line 9. The teacher repeats 'Peter Pan' in overlap in line 10 and includes a confirming 'Okay?' but continues along the lines of his prior turn without integrating Greg's contribution in any other way. Greg smiles in affiliation with the teacher's confirmation, but then withdraws momentarily from the interaction, looking down in line 13 before returning his gaze to the teacher.

Greg's contributions here are timed such that they appear as though they might fit, but they are delivered in silences that are not actually gaps. His turns in lines 5 and 8 do come after pauses in the teacher's talk. However, there are other cues to indicate that the teacher is planning to continue, including intonation, but more importantly, that the teacher has not yet delivered a relevant point. In addition, the information Greg has to add is only tangentially related to the discussion. While the teacher does topicalize the year 1953 in line 1, he quickly moves the focus of his talk to televisions, the topic of the just prior discussion about the beginning of the novel. As a second language user of English, and in particular as one who has tested into this remedial reading course, Greg may lack the ability to identify both the topic of the discussion (causing pedagogical misalignment) as well as appropriate junctions for initiation (causing interactional misalignment).

What then can we say about Greg's participation and engagement here? Greg *is* participating, but in several "wrong" ways. He *is* attending to the unfolding interaction as evidenced by the timing of his initiations (i.e., he is engaged), but he is incorrectly interpreting silences as inter-speaker gaps rather than intra-speaker pauses. Greg's interpretations are identified as "incorrect" here because of next-turn proof procedure. The teacher's continued turn in line 6 and multi-word overlap in line 7 demonstrate that he believes the turn is his. In particular, his move to continue in line 6 shows that he either does not hear Greg's contribution in line 5 or does not interpret it as intended for the open floor (i.e., he may hear it but consider it private speech). Student-initiated actions, when they are not sequentially projected or relevant to the topic or content of the talk, show students' lack of awareness of the structure of teacher-led classroom talk. It is for these reasons that I argue Greg is studenting; he is attending, though inexpertly or carelessly rather than carefully, and he is participating, though inappropriately. Greg is engaged, but he is not able to contribute substantively to the interaction, and in fact, his actions disrupt the progressivity of the teacher's turn-in-progress.

4.4 ENGAGED PARTICIPATION VS. ENGAGED STUDENTING: STUDENT-TO-STUDENT INTERACTIONS

While teacher-led interaction often represents a dyad between the teacher and "the Student" (Sahlström 2002), students also demonstrate their engagement and participation with the ongoing interaction by engaging *with each other* on the open floor. Waring, referring to Lemke's (1990) term "side-talk," marks the importance of "talking to someone else other than the teacher about what is going on in the classroom" (2016: 17). As Sahlström (2002) notes, such demonstrations of engagement with other students are made difficult by the spatial organization of classrooms in whole-class interaction, where most students' enduring focus is the teacher, making it difficult for them to direct their talk, nods, smiles, and gaze to each other. In the ESL Data, students are organized in a U-shape for most days, which facilitates students' ability to monitor and engage with each other, but the default organization for whole-class participation structure in that classroom, as in all three corpora, has students filtering their contributions through a dyadic interaction with the teacher on one side, and one or another student on the other. Student-to-student interaction is thus a marked change from the predominating interactional structure and instances where students interact with one another can help highlight differences between *engaged participation*, as seen in collaborative constructions (Section 4.4.1), and *engaged studenting*, as seen in on-task byplay (Sections 4.4.2 and 4.4.3).

4.4.1 ENGAGED PARTICIPATION: COLLABORATIVE CONSTRUCTION

"Collaborative completion" (Lerner 1987), where speakers finish one another's turns, is often seen in classrooms, and as Lerner shows, in everyday conversation. He argues that pre-emptive completion of another's turn can be a way of accomplishing agreement, when such an action is projected in the next turn. He similarly notes that such sequences are affiliative in nature; with their collaborative completion, the listener-turned-speaker is able to demonstrate their careful attention to, and alignment with, the current speaker's current turn. By completing the turn-in-progress, a second student is necessarily participating in the interaction, but it is this last aspect of collaborative completion, their affiliative nature, that I argue demonstrates the listening student's engagement.

There is a robust literature on teachers' use of unfinished turns as a method for eliciting knowledge display on the part of students (Koshik 2002; Lerner 1995), and these turns are seen as encouraging student participation. Notably, there has been little research on the use of collaborative constructions by students on turn-in-progress *by other students*. Jacknick (2018) describes a case where one student provides an embodied completion to another student's unfinished turn; embodied completions occur when a speaker uses an embodied action to bring a turn to "a kind of pragmatic completion" (Olsher 2004). The example from Jacknick (2018) is reproduced below as Extract 4.5, but here we focus on the verbal contributions of the students. This extract from the ESL Data shows Rodrigo in the process of explaining the meaning of the sentence "I stopped to smoke."

Extract 4.5 I stopped smoking

```
253  ROD   in the first one, you were walking?=
254  TEA   =mm-hmm?=
255  ROD   =and then you stopped,
256        (0.2)
257  ROD   and then *#you,=
                    *light gesture
                    #fig. 4.11
```

Extract 4.5 I stopped smoking (continued)
```
258  NOB   =*#stopped to *#[light] and then,
259  ROD                     [light]
     rod   *lighting    *lighting
           #fig. 4.12   #fig. 4.13
```

Rodrigo explains the sentence with 'In the first one, you were walking? and then you stopped and then you', providing his own embodied completion simultaneously with the word *you*, miming lighting a cigarette with his right hand. Nobu, seated next to Rodrigo, had originally introduced the sentence into the whole-class discussion. While the current interaction is a dyad between Rodrigo and the teacher (with the other students as ratified listeners), Nobu is the just prior student speaker in this open-floor discussion in skills and system mode, and so his involvement here is not out of bounds of his interactional rights. Indeed, Nobu has been monitoring Rodrigo's explanation closely, a fact made evident when he latches on to the end of Rodrigo's unfinished (but projectable) turn in line 257, adding 'stopped to light and then' (line 258). Note that Nobu's completion is syntactically designed to fit as a continuation of Rodrigo's turn.

Nobu's own turn, being projectable itself, allows for Rodrigo to join in the collaborative completion, overlapping the word 'light' with Nobu's delivery of the same word, and producing his mime of lighting a cigarette at precisely the same moment as well. This short extract shows both Rodrigo and Nobu attending closely to each other's verbal and embodied contributions, i.e., we see them *engaged* with the discussion and each other. As Lerner (1996) describes, Nobu's anticipatory completion of Rodrigo's turn from line 257 and Rodrigo's anticipatory completion in overlap with Nobu (line 259) are collaborative in nature as the two of them describe something to a third participant, in this case, the teacher. Collaborative completions show students carefully monitoring not only the teacher's speech, but their peers' multimodal contributions as well.

4.4.2 ENGAGED STUDENTING: BYPLAY

Whereas the collaborative completion in Extract 4.5 showed students engaged with and participating in the teacher-led interaction, in Extract 4.6 we see students engaging in byplay (Goffman 1981), a subordinate form of communication that might be seen as in competition with the main interaction. This brief extract from the Reading Data shows this kind of byplay as the teacher is talking about the setting for the novel

Fahrenheit 451, noting that there are television screens on three of the four living room walls in the main character's house, and his wife wants one on the fourth wall as well. Karina, seated in the back, produces an assessment in line 1.

Extract 4.6 Too many

```
1     KAR   *°too many°*#
            *shakes head-->
                        *Kar makes skeptical face-->
                        *Hea starts to turn to Kar
                        #fig. 4.14
```

2   (0.6)*#(0.4)
            -->*
                *Kar and Hea mutual gaze + smile
            #fig. 4.15

After the teacher brings up the idea of four walls of TVs, Karina comments that this is *too many* in a quiet voice, making a skeptical face (line 1). As Ruusuvuori and Peräkylä (2009) note, facial expressions such as these can not only convey the stance of the one making the face, but also pursue intersubjectivity and affiliation. Just as Karina finishes saying this, Heather begins to turn her head toward her. They briefly establish mutual gaze and smile before both turning their gaze back to the teacher. This example shows that while Heather was orienting to the teacher during his extended turn prior to this example, she is also attending to the contributions of her peers. Heather's peculiar bodily orientation, facing a side wall when most students are facing forward, puts her in a position to make such engagement with another student easier. She, more than any other student present, can easily turn her gaze to Karina to show her appreciation of her comment. These small moments of student-to-student engagement occur often throughout all the corpora, but this example shows particularly how spatial arrangements can make affordances for such interactions. While students are engaged here, and these kinds of interactions may be crucial for developing rapport among students, they are participating in the "wrong" way for the whole-class interaction; they are doing *engaged studenting*.

4.4.3 ENGAGED STUDENTING-CUM-LEARNING

Particularly in language teaching, there is a persistent belief in the value of student talk, and in the cases to be examined here, representative of all three corpora, we see students talking with one another in on-task (though potentially unsanctioned) ways. This might seem at first glance to be a clear example of engaged student participation, and when the participation structure in a classroom is set up for pair or group interaction, that is true. However, the cases below show instances where students' engagement with each other represents an "inappropriate" form of participation in whole-class interaction. While they are engaging in a category-bound action of a student (i.e., talking with a peer about the topic of the lesson), they are doing so at the wrong time, and so they are studenting. Mortensen (2008) and Koole (2007) talk about this as engagement in parallel activities. This kind of "subordinated communication" (Goffman 1981: 134), even when centered on the pedagogical focus, creates interactional and pedagogical misalignment, but also shows students as agents of their own learning, and thus I am calling these instances *engaged studenting-cum-learning*. This kind of student-to-student interaction often occurs at participation structure transitions, when the teacher attempts to shift from pair work back into whole-class interaction but is met by resistance (i.e., continued discussion) from the students, but also during whole-class interaction when students initiate new interactions with their neighbors. In both of these cases, students are argued to be studenting, i.e., undertaking category-bound actions of the role "student" in ways that are out of alignment with the pedagogical and interactional goals of the teacher. Notably, this engaged studenting indicates intense engagement *with each other* and *the task*, but shows students disengaged from the "main" interaction. Extract 4.4 showed an example of engaged studenting with Greg attempting to contribute in relevant and interactionally-projected ways but misinterpreting the topic and sequential context; he was participating in the "wrong" way at the "wrong" time. There are, however, also examples of students undertaking category-bound actions at the "wrong" time because of their resistance to the teacher's interactional and pedagogical agenda in the pursuit of learning. While these actions are also glossed as studenting, their disruption to the progressivity of the interaction is related to the students' engagement in other, pedagogically-relevant activities.

This first example from the ESL Data comes during whole-class interaction when a student is asking the teacher a question. In parallel to that interaction, which occurs on the open floor for all to hear, Amelie and Fleur also talk quietly about on-task matters.

Extract 4.7 I'll have been earning
```
1    TEA   I'll have been earning or I will
2          have earned,
3          (1.0)
```

Extract 4.7 I'll have been earning (continued)

```
4    ROD   I'll have been earning?
5          (1.0)
6    TEA   yeah.
7    ROD   [which is *#better? (to say?)]
8          [((Amelie and Fleur talk ))  ]
                    *Ame leans towards Fle, points to book
                    #fig. 4.16
```

```
9    TEA   [it depends. o:n what the person]
10         [((Amelie and Fleur talk ))     ]
11   TEA   m[e- wants to say. (.)          ]
12         [((Amelie and Fleur talk ))]
13   ROD   mmhm,
14   TEA   so if that *#earning #uh you know is
                    *Ame/Fle start to disengage from dyad
                    #fig. 4.17 #fig. 4.18
```

Amelie and Fleur's actions, talking quietly to one another, eye gaze oriented toward materials, deictic points toward materials, all would "count" as participation in another mode/context. Here, however, their actions are considered non-participation (i.e., studenting), as their talk could impede the progressivity of the front stage activity between Rodrigo and the teacher. However, their awareness of the effect of their schism (Egbert 1997) can be seen in Amelie's disengagement from the dyad and gaze orientation toward the teacher in line 14. As Schwab notes, such side conversations exist outside the participation framework of the whole-class setting, and "students are obliged to remain part of the ongoing interaction" (2011: 6). Waring et al. likewise consider instances like this to be "sideplay," and argue that students are "abandon[ing] their roles as ratified participants" (2016: 32) in such cases. However, in line with Koole (2007), I argue that we can see the students simultaneously (1)

engaging in the side conversation, (2) doing so in a manner that indicates their awareness of its potential for disruption, and (3) ultimately continuing to monitor the frontstage interaction as well. The side conversation between the two lasts only a few moments and ends before it is oriented to as disruptive by the teacher. Amelie and Fleur are engaged—with each other, the task, the grammatical point, *and* the whole-class interaction, though to differing degrees at different moments.

In the final example of engaged studenting from the ESL Data, several pairs of students resist a shift in participation structure from dyadic to whole-group interaction by continuing their engagement in dyadic interaction. Students had been working in pairs to find a number of mistakes in a text, and the teacher attempts to bring the class back together in line 1, but as the transcript shows, the student pairs instead persist in their dyadic interactions.

Extract 4.8 Let's talk about it together

```
1    TEA    oka:y. let's talk about it together:?
2           *#{(4.0) - Ss talking in pairs}
            *Ss gaze to materials
            #fig. 4.19, fig. 4.20, fig. 4.21, fig. 4.22
```

```
3    TEA    okay?*#
            *Rod and Yor point to text, gaze to text
            #fig. 4.23
```

Extract 4.8 Let's talk about it together (continued)

```
4         {(2.4)*#( 2.6) - students still talking in pairs}
           *Sac and Cla change an answer
           #fig. 4.24
```

```
5   TEA  so the first *#mistake is already
           *Rod and Yor point to text
           *Fle points to text, Ame/Fle gaze to text
           #fig. 4.25  fig. 4.26
```

```
6         *#done for us?
           *Sac and Cla orient to T
           #fig. 4.27
```

The teacher first signals an activity shift with a drawn-out 'Oka:y' in line 1, followed by an explicit shift to whole-group participation structure with 'Let's talk about it together:', also delivered with an elongated last syllable. With these stretches and delays, the teacher may be orienting to the lack of movement on the part of the students; that is, by lengthening out her boundary markers, she is providing them more time to comply. However, during the 4.0 seconds that follow, students continue talking with one another at low volume, and four dyads in particular are seen to continue their gaze orientation toward the materials (Figures 4.19–4.22). The teacher again provides a cue for activity shift with 'okay?' uttered with rising intonation (line 3), but Rodrigo and Yoro, in fact, become more engrossed in their task, with both leaning over more markedly and pointing to the same place on the paper (Figure 4.23). Again, during the 5.0 seconds that follow, students continue their dyadic interactions, and Sachiko and Clara are seen changing an answer on the paper.

The teacher persists with her shift in lines 5–6, saying 'so the first mistake is already done for us'; in this way, she is using the text as a way of ordering the activity (Jacknick and Creider 2018; Matarese and Caswell 2017a, 2017b; Mikkola and Lehtinen 2014; Nevile et al. 2014b). While some dyads (e.g., Nobu and Kazumi) begin to orient to the teacher following this shift, others persist in their engagement with the prior task. Rodrigo and Yoro point to another item on the paper and maintain their gaze orientations and postures as they continue talking. Likewise, Amelie and Fleur lean over Fleur's paper and point to items as they talk. Such intense engagement with a task and with each other would be a marker of participation and engagement in other settings and modes, but here, in a whole-class, materials mode checking episode, these students' unwillingness to shift participation structures creates a problem of progressivity for the teacher, and so I characterize their actions as *engaged studenting*. Because the students are creating this progressivity issue as they engage with the pedagogical focus, in the pursuit of understanding, I call these actions *engaged studenting-cum-learning*.

4.5 SUMMARY

This chapter has shown how students can demonstrate their (dis)engagement through their verbal (non-)participation. In line with my conception of participation and engagement as locally-contingent and context-sensitive phenomena, we can see how forms of participation that might be expected or even desired in one context might instead be oriented to as inappropriate (see Chapter 7 for more on disengaged non-participation and disengaged studenting). Extract 4.1 showed examples of different kinds of (non-)participation and (dis)engagement within one episode. The lack of verbal participation from half the class might be considered disengagement, but as we will see in Chapter 5, students' unwillingness to participate in verbal ways may co-exist with their embodied displays of engagement.

The matrix is reproduced here for reference as we review how participation and engagement have been disambiguated in students' verbal contributions. Beginning with the upper right quadrant, we have seen examples of engaged participation when students ask questions (Extract 4.2), challenge the teacher (Extract 4.3), and join in collaborative turn construction with their peers (Extract 4.5). We have also seen several examples where students are engaged, but not participating in the "right" way. In Extract 4.4, we saw a student attempt to find sequentially- and pedagogically-relevant slots for initiation, but being unable to do so, representing *engaged studenting*. This example contrasts with Extracts 4.2 and 4.3, where students self-selected in interactionally and pedagogically appropriate places. This example of engaged studenting also contrasts with the engaged studenting we saw in Extracts 4.6, 4.7, and 4.8. Particularly the last two excerpts show students doing this as they engage in other, pedagogically-relevant interactions with each other.

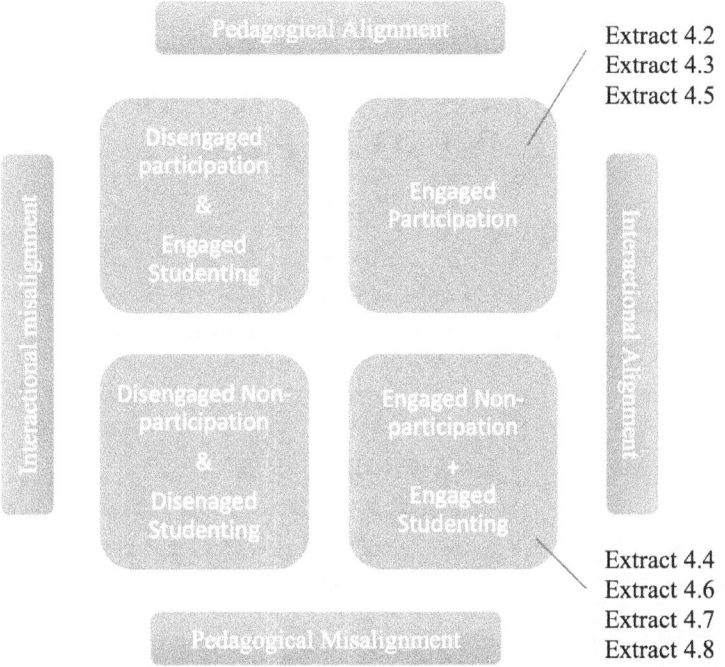

Figure 4.28 Engaged participation vs. engaged studenting in Chapter 4

Students' engagement can be at odds with the interactional context, as was seen in Extracts 4.6, 4.7, and 4.8, where students engaged in "parallel activities" (Koole 2007), engaging with peers at low volume despite the prevailing participation structure of whole-class interaction. Within these three, we see differences as well, with a brief embodied byplay in Extract 4.6, two students creating an "ecological huddle" (Goffman 1961) during whole-class interaction in Extract 4.7, but several student dyads resisting the teacher's shift back to a whole-class participation structure in Extract 4.8. These last two examples show students acting as agents of their own learning in small ways by engaging with pedagogical tasks in non-sanctioned ways. Thus, I describe these examples as *engaged studenting-cum-learning*.

Notably, we can make claims about engagement when participation is precisely-timed, but when it is delayed, the reasons for the delay are essentially unknowable in most cases. It's possible that students in such instances are disengaged, but they also might be engaged but unwilling to participate or engaged but unsure how to participate. Attending more carefully to their embodied actions can help tease apart some of these differences, as we will see in the next chapter.

5
MULTIMODAL (NON-)PARTICIPATION AND (DIS)ENGAGEMENT

How does a glance become an action?

Harvey Sacks (1992: 84)

5.1 INTRODUCTION

To put Sacks's question another way, when does a glance count as participation? For teachers, it is often the case that while subtler forms of engagement exist, the ones that "count" most are verbal, because we notice those contributions more readily and they seem to have greater potential to affect the trajectory of classroom interaction. This chapter prompts researchers and teachers to examine the full range of students' multimodal actions to characterize their participation and engagement. Goodwin and Goodwin aptly state that "most simply, many of the phenomena relevant to the study of participation as action will be rendered invisible or lost if analysis focuses exclusively on the talk or texts of speakers" (2004: 227). In addition to all the expected ways in which students respond verbally to prompts or questions from the teacher, they also accomplish many actions in the classroom with their bodies, drawing on a variety of multimodal resources in concert with one another, i.e., in complex multimodal Gestalts (Mondada 2014c). This means that students create meaning with their bodies while also speaking, but given the constraints of multiparty interaction, students often display their engagement with the ongoing interaction *primarily* in an embodied way. While Chapter 4 showed how we might disambiguate participation and engagement by analyzing students' verbal contributions, students' embodied actions in the classroom are often constitutive of their participation and engagement, and this chapter will show how a combined multimodal analysis of verbal and embodied actions gives us a fuller picture.

In operationalizing the concept of "engagement" as an embodied phenomenon, I will show the crucial importance of the *alignment, temporality*, and *sequentiality* of students' multimodal actions. Alignment allows us to contextualize student actions as "appropriate" or not within the pedagogical and interactional goals and expectations of the moment. Timing and sequence of actions are likewise crucial for a contextualized understanding of student action as (non-)participation or (dis) engagement. As Fasel Lauzon and Berger note, "it is not so much the embodied behavior as such (e.g., gazing at the teacher, stretching one's arms, yawning) that the participants rely on to organize their own participation, but the exact timing when they are produced" (2015: 28). I argue that we can see students' engagement with interaction in the precise timing of their multimodal actions in relation to the teacher's just prior actions and the expectations for student response they engender (i.e., next-action-proof procedure).

This chapter examines students' participation as instantiated in (mostly) embodied ways in order to answer the question, "what do multimodal (non-)participation and (dis)engagement look like?" I begin with a short extract to highlight the challenges of differentiating participation and engagement, and the crucial role of multimodal analysis in this effort. To continue this argument, Section 5.3 shows examples where students' embodied actions demonstrate their engagement in the absence of full verbal participation. Finally, in Section 5.4, I uncover the moment-by-moment nature of students' embodied responses, showing how these actions often occur in a wave, potentially obscuring the teacher's (and analyst's) sense of how any individual student is participating in classroom interaction.

5.2 MULTIMODAL PARTICIPATION AND ENGAGEMENT

When the teacher asks a question such as "How many people think X?," she is, in effect, asking the students to display their answer with their bodies (i.e., raised hands). Likewise, directives for multimodal action make the expected student response clear. In contrast, sometimes students produce embodied responses to open-floor questions, i.e., those that do not designate a next speaker and often do not designate a "correct" response. Extract 5.1 from the ESL Data is a prototypical example of this and is representative of this phenomenon throughout all three corpora. The teacher asks a polar question of the format "Does anyone know X?" (which prefers a "no"-type response), and students respond in a variety of multimodal ways, including verbally, with head nods or shakes, as well as actions that may index an unwillingness to participate, and thus potentially a lack of epistemic standing (e.g., gaze aversion).

In this lesson, the class had been going over the instruction sheet for their upcoming oral presentations. Prior to reading it, the teacher had identified a number of lexical items that might be unfamiliar and written them on the board. This extract begins just as she moves on to the next identified word, "rubric." Most of the visible students have their gaze down toward the handout, and some are writing. Only one student, Yasuko, is oriented toward the teacher as this extract begins.

Extract 5.1 Rubric

```
1    TEA  okay, ↑rubric.
2         *(0.6)
          *Eik writing-->
3    TEA  does every- does anybody know
4         that word? °rubric?°
5    SAC  *°no°         *
          *head shake*
6         *(0.8)        *
     yas  *head shake*
```

In line 1, the teacher looks to the board to locate the next item, and then turns her gaze back toward the students just before delivering the unfamiliar word 'rubric' with emphasis and pronounced upward intonation. Eiko, who has had her gaze down toward her materials, begins writing just after the word is announced.

Following a brief silence, the teacher begins to ask a question 'Does every-' but cuts herself off and repairs her question to change its polarity, saying 'does **anybody** know that word?' and then repeating the word softly. Sachiko, who has been writing with her gaze down, answers multimodally, saying 'no' softly simultaneously with a small head shake. Her professed lack of understanding is not specifically directed toward the teacher (i.e., she has not established mutual gaze with the teacher prior to responding and her head movement is so slight that it can easily be missed), but it is clear that she is engaged with the teacher's question, as her answer is delivered without delay. Following Sachiko's response, Yasuko also minimally shakes her head while maintaining her gaze toward the teacher. Both Sachiko and Yasuko are engaged with the teacher's query. Interestingly, Sachiko's engagement takes a form that potentially "looks" disengaged; her continued gaze toward her materials, the soft delivery of her verbal response, and the minimal nature of her head shake all act to minimize her display of engagement. This mismatch between perceived and actual displays highlights the need to examine the totality of student actions, as well as the limits of real-time observation. Only looking or only listening once would not give us, as teachers or analysts, a full picture. Without focusing specifically on Sachiko, it would be difficult for a teacher or a co-present observer to identify the speaker, if they were even able to hear her contribution at all. The other students' continued gaze toward their materials, some writing, appears to indicate their unwillingness to participate, though there is in fact no way of knowing whether they have been monitoring the ongoing interaction or not, or are disengaged from the interaction and are oriented toward their materials as a display of participation, i.e., whether they are studenting. Notably, Eiko's precisely-timed initiation of writing seems to be an indication of her engagement in the interaction, a phenomenon we will return to in Extract 5.8.

5.3 MULTIMODAL ENGAGEMENT

Where in Extract 5.1, the students displayed their participation and engagement in verbal and embodied ways, we turn now to examples where students' embodied actions are the primary indicator of their participation and engagement. First, we will examine cases where students' embodied participation is delayed, but they demonstrate their continued engagement through gaze. Next, we turn to cases where students convey meaning primarily in embodied ways, looking at their use of gestures. Finally, we turn to cases of engaged studenting, where students' embodied actions show their engagement in category-bound activities that are out of step with their current interactional rights and obligations. These examples show how crucial consideration of multimodal resources is to an analysis of students' participation and engagement.

5.3.1 ENGAGEMENT WITH DELAYED PARTICIPATION

Sometimes when students are called upon to participate in either verbal or embodied ways, they decline to do so, while simultaneously engaging in other embodied actions to demonstrate their continued engagement. In the first instance, I will show how a teacher's prompt for multimodal response on the open floor (an informal poll asking "How many people think X?") is followed by a display of engagement by one student as he simultaneously shows delayed willingness to participate in the embodied choral response called for by the question. I then include two examples of students who, after being nominated to respond by the teacher, demonstrate their continued engagement in embodied ways despite their unwillingness or inability to participate verbally.

Taking an informal poll through a show of hands is commonplace in teaching, and we can see the complexity of participation and engagement in such a poll through careful attention to the sequentiality of responses: who responds first, later, or not at all? The expectation that students will respond multimodally with raised hands to such a question is made explicit when students fail to produce the expected response (or not enough students do so), and teachers explicitly sanction this lack of participation (see Extract 7.2 for an example of this). However, other embodied actions beyond hand-raising are relevant displays of participation and engagement in such environments, as we will see by following Nobu's embodied actions. Video of this extract is available online (edinburghuniversitypress.com/multimodal), and I encourage readers to watch as they read to see the unfolding of these multimodal actions. Again, focal lines are bolded, and embodied actions are italicized; see Appendix 1 for full transcription conventions.

Extract 5.2 Take over
```
1    TEA   okay? >he's demanding that my *boyfriend<
                                         *Nob hand opens-->
2          take over the business,
3          (0.4)*(1.0)   *(0.4)                   *
     noG        *gaze up*gaze/head down-->
     nob                 -->*hand closes and down*
4    TEA   how *many people say that's correct.*
               *T gaze up-->
                                         *Nob gaze up-->
5          (0.4)*(1.0)
               -->*Nob gaze at classmates-->
6    S?    °take over-°
7    TEA   take*over.          *Good.        *
               *Tea big nod----*
                                         *Nob hand up*
8          okay.*
               *Nob hand down
```

As the teacher repeats the answer just given by Florence (not in the transcript) in lines 1–2, Nobu begins to open his hand in a bid for a turn. However, the teacher's gaze is oriented toward the material, and during a silence (line 3) following her repetition, Nobu looks up, sees that he has not established mutual gaze, and turns his gaze down to his book as he closes and lowers his hand. Nobu's pursuit of a turn here is relevant as we see that his response to the teacher's prompt for multimodal responses is delayed.

The teacher raises her gaze to the students during her prompt (line 4), indicating that she expects to see the student response to her question. Immediately following the completion of her turn in line 4, Nobu raises his gaze toward her, demonstrating his engagement through the precision timing of this embodied action. Very quickly (0.4 seconds) after the prompt is completed (line 5), three students raise their hands, while Nobu gazes around at his classmates but does not raise his hand. He is *engaged* but is not yet participating in the embodied response.

Other students join the chorus by raising hands or saying the word, and the teacher repeats the form again with an exaggerated nod in line 7; it is only once the correctness of the focal phrase "take over" becomes clear that Nobu belatedly raises his hand. The teacher produces an explicit positive assessment (EPA, Waring 2008) 'good' in line 7, and then after her boundary marking 'okay', Nobu puts his hand down, having just raised it a moment before. He is participating in the embodied response, though in a delayed way.

Nobu had begun to pursue a turn prior to the teacher's prompt for multimodal action, and though he does not immediately participate by raising a hand, his careful monitoring of his peers' responses and the timing of his own participation following the teacher's marking of the form as correct show his *engagement* in the interaction. His actions index his uncertainty around this answer (or unwillingness to publicly display his understanding), but not his disengagement. Notably, for other students who may not be carefully monitoring the interaction in (observable) embodied ways, we can't make strong claims about their engagement. Multimodal actions can demonstrate (non-)participation and (dis)engagement, but a lack of student response does not necessarily index disengagement.

The next two examples show students who have been nominated by the teacher for a turn-at-talk and are unwilling (or unable) to participate verbally (cf. Evnitskaya and Berger 2017). While Hall and Looney (2019) highlight research on the embodied resources teachers use to deal with interactional trouble, there has been less research about how *students* draw on embodied resources in these moments. In the cases we look at here, rather than withdrawing from the interaction entirely (i.e., disengaging), the students use embodied actions to demonstrate their continued engagement in the interaction, despite their inability or unwillingness to participate. In this first example from the Reading Data, Chen is nominated to read aloud a set of sentences from a vocabulary exercise.

Extract 5.3 Hypnotic

```
1    TEA   number fi::ve.
2          *(0.4)       *(1.2)
           *............*Tea point to Che
           *Che gaze to T*to book-->
```

Extract 5.3 Hypnotic (continued)

```
3    TEA   Chen?
4    CHE   "the intense eyes of the woman in
5          the photograph mesmerized me. I
6          couldn't take my eyes off the
7          picture." "when driving at night
8          you can become mesmerized by the
9          lines on the road or by other cars'
10         head- headlights or taillights.
11         to avoid a (.) hi-"
12   TEA   *hyp,          *
             *Che book mvmt*
13         (0.4)*
                *Che gaze to T-->
14   TEA   hypnotic.=
15   CHE   *="hypnotic state keep your eyes
             *Che gaze to book-->
16         moving from front to side to
17         rearview mirror."
```

The teacher produces the next item number with extended delivery, potentially drawing it out to allow time as he seeks a willing next speaker. By orienting her gaze toward the teacher during the silence in line 2, Chen makes an embodied bid for a turn, and the teacher simultaneously moves to make a deictic point toward her (line 2). Her orientation to her book just after the teacher's embodied nomination indicates her acceptance. Chen reads the first two sentences without trouble, but when she reaches the word "hypnotic," she indicates pronunciation trouble with a pause before the word and a cut-off. She had pronounced the first syllable with a diphthong /ai/ rather than a high-mid front vowel /I/. The teacher other-corrects this self-repair by pronouncing the first syllable of the word, a correction designed to target the repairable as identified by Chen's repair-initiation. During the teacher's correction, Chen simultaneously moves her book page in what appears to be an embodied self-repair (i.e., as though to look at the word again). That Chen is unable or unwilling to proceed with the sentence with this degree of assistance, however, is evidenced by the brief pause following the teacher's other-correction. Her head movement and gaze orientation toward the teacher (line 13) act as repair on his correction, but also show that she is engaged in the task despite her inability or unwillingness to proceed. The teacher does other-correction once again, this time producing the entire word with stress on the trouble syllable, and Chen then immediately reorients to the book, utters the trouble source, and continues reading.

Where the prior example showed a brief disruption in the progressivity of the activity, in the next example from the Reading Data, we will see an extended sequence where the teacher problematizes a student response. The class is going over a vocabulary exercise, and Larry provides an incorrect answer. During the evaluation and repair that follow, Larry demonstrates his continued engagement with the interaction through his embodied actions, though his verbal contributions are minimal.

Extract 5.4 Does that make sense

```
1    TEA   okay? uhh Larry? are you ready?
2          *#(0.4)     *#(0.6)
           *Lar G to T*to book-->
           #fig. 5.1 #fig. 5.2
```

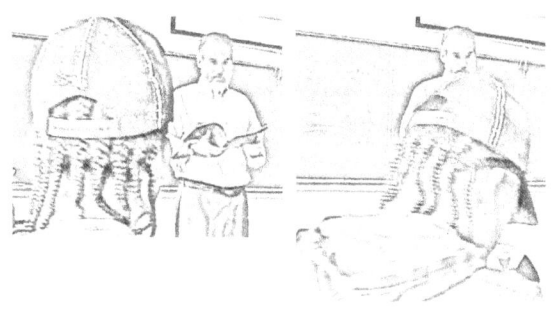

```
3    TEA   do number two and then we'll come back to,
4          (.)
5    LAR   "the instruction man[uals ] that come with
6    TEA                       [Dave.]
7    LAR   computer software often use such (.) es::oteric?=
8    TEA   =goo:d.
9    LAR   terms that they seem to be written
10         in a foreign language. the poetry
11         of (.) Ezra Pound filled with reference
12         to ancient Greek culture is so- is
13         too esoteric for most readers."
14         (0.8) unfavorable.
15   TEA   *say that *#again?
           *.........*Tea hand to ear-->
                     #fig. 5.3
```

```
16   LAR   (I had) C?
17   TEA   for unfavorable?=
```

Extract 5.4 Does that make sense (continued)

```
18   LAR   =unfavorable.
19   TEA   let's *see if that works if we plug it in.
               -->*Tea releases gesture
20         "the instruction manuals that come with computer
21         software often use such unfavorable terms?"
22         *#(1.0)*(0.8)
           *Tea gaze to Lar with smirk-->
                 *Lar gaze to Tea-->
           #fig. 5.4
```

```
23   TEA   (does) that make *#sense?
                         *Lar gaze to book-->
                         #fig. 5.5
```

```
24         (0.6)*(1.0)           *
                 *Lar gaze to T*gaze to book-->
                               *Tea gaze to book-->
25         *(1.0)         *(0.4)*(0.2)
           *Lar gaze to tea*Lar gaze to book/Tea gaze to Lar-->
                         *Lar nodding-->
26   TEA   *what do you *think.*
           *............*Tea gaze to book-->
                         *Lar gaze to Tea and stops nodding-->
27   LAR   yeah?
28   TEA   yeah makes sen[se    ]to you?*
29   S?                  [yeah.]
                                *Lar gaze to S?-->
30   TEA   "the poetry of Ezra Pound filled with
31         *references to ancient Greek culture is too
           *Lar gaze to book-->
```

Extract 5.4 Does that make sense (continued)

```
32    TEA    un*favorable? for *most? *readers?"      *#
             *...............*T gaze up-->
                                    *Tea turns to Lar*
                                    *Lar shaking head-->
                                                      #fig. 5.6
```

```
33    Ss¹    no
34    TEA    something that you read is un*favorable?*
                                         *Lar gaze up-->
                                         -->*Lar stops shaking
                                            head
35    LAR    nah,
36           *(1.0)             *
             *Tea head shakes*
             *Tea gaze to book-->
             *...............*Lar gaze to book-->
37    TEA    no. which one makes more sense.
38    LAR    [dif]fi*cult to# understand? *
39    Ss     [A. ]
                       *Tea gaze up-->
                       *eyebrows up---------*
                          #fig. 5.7
```

---

[1] Several students respond with "No" here and are represented in this transcript with "Ss." The nature of this one line is likely much more complex than this transcript shows, but the response of other students in this moment is not the focus of this analysis. The same holds true for the "choral responses" in lines 39 and 40.

Extract 5.4 Does that make sense (continued)
```
40   Ss    (A.)
41   TEA   yea*:::::h. difficult to under*stand. *okay?
           *Lar gaze to Tea-----------*to book-->
                                                *Tea turns away from
                                                 Lar-->
```

Larry's pronunciation while reading aloud is less than fluent in several noticeable ways, including his delivery of the answer (with five syllables compared with a more "native-like" four, eliding the "o"), and it may be this that causes the teacher to initiate repair in line 15. However, the answer Larry produces ('unfavorable') is also the wrong answer, uttered at reduced volume (line 14), so the teacher's repair may be targeting any of these issues: pronunciation, accuracy, or volume. Notably, the teacher is also facing away from Larry, and so there may be an issue of a break in the embodied participation framework (Mortensen 2016). The teacher's repair is an "open class" repair initiation (Drew 1997) in which he verbally requests a repetition of the line along with his iconic hand-to-ear gesture (an embodied "open class" repair initiation, following Seo and Koshik 2010 and Mortensen 2012). Following Larry's confirmation of his response by identifying the letter of the answer he chose in line 16, the teacher repeats the (incorrect) answer with stress and questioning intonation. Larry latches onto this repetition, also repeating the answer, this time with more target-like pronunciation.

Rather than providing an overt evaluation, the teacher indirectly indicates that the answer is incorrect by suggesting a test and reading the sentence from the exercise with "unfavorable" substituted in for "esoteric" (lines 19–21). If the lack of positive evaluation was not enough indication to Larry that he had the wrong answer, the teacher's smirk during their mutual gaze in line 22 serves as another clue. Ruusuvuori and Peräkylä (2009) find that facial expressions precede verbal stance-taking, and here too we can see that the teacher is communicating his stance (i.e., skepticism about this being the answer) before he provides negative evaluation, and in fact, such negative evaluation only comes in line 37 after the teacher has prompted Larry himself to reject his original answer. The teacher asks more directly, gaze still oriented toward Larry, 'does that make sense?' in line 23, while Larry turns his gaze back to his book. In the silence that follows, Larry orients his gaze back and forth between the teacher and his book (line 24). Larry looks back up toward the teacher and they establish mutual gaze again briefly in line 26 just before Larry turns his head back toward his book and begins nodding. All of his embodied actions thus far, including his nods and shifting gaze orientation between the book and the teacher, serve to indicate his continued engagement in the interaction despite his delay in responding verbally.

The teacher prompts again in line 26 ('what do you think.'); just after the prompt, Larry orients his gaze toward the teacher again and answers 'yeah', the delayed second pair part to the teacher's question in line 23. The teacher confirms in line 28, asking 'makes sense to you?', and is overlapped by a different student who also responds 'yeah' in line 29. Larry turns his gaze toward this student, and then the teacher reads the second sentence in the pair with "unfavorable" substituting in for "esoteric" (lines 30–32). During this reading, Larry returns his gaze to the book, and following the teacher's rising intonation on the word in question ("unfavorable"), Larry beings to shake his head, gaze still oriented toward his book. Several students respond to this new reading with 'no' (line 33). Larry does provide a verbal response here (line 27); he is *participating* in the question–answer sequence initiated by the teacher in line 23, but he communicates much more about his *engagement* through his multimodal actions.

The teacher produces a formulation of what he has just read, asking 'something that you read is unfavorable?' (line 34). Just at the end of this utterance, Larry stops shaking his head and looks up, and responds 'nah' in line 35. The teacher confirms his response with 'no' in line 37 and asks for a new answer. Larry offers the correct answer in line 38 (in overlap with several students giving the letter of the correct answer); once the production of this answer is recognizable, the teacher orients his gaze to Larry and flashes his eyebrows up to mark change of state or surprise (Peräkylä and Ruusuvuori 2006). The teacher provides a positive assessment in line 41, during which Larry orients his gaze to the teacher. This assessment is followed by repetition of the answer and a transitional 'okay?' (line 41). During the repetition, Larry turns his gaze back to his book, and just after it, the teacher turns away from Larry, breaking their "ecological huddle" (Goffman 1961) to continue with the exercise.

Most interesting here are Larry's gaze movements and embodied responses, which serve to demonstrate ongoing engagement in the task despite limited verbal involvement. In lines 22–26, Larry looks back and forth between his book and the teacher multiple times, showing not only that he is paying attention to the teacher, but that he is grappling with the question the teacher has asked about his answer. While he turns his gaze toward another student briefly in line 29, Larry again goes back and forth between looking at the book and the teacher in the remainder of the excerpt, with his gaze movements helping to negotiate the closing of the "ecological huddle" with the teacher.

Larry's embodied responses in lines 25–26 (nodding) and 32–34 (head shakes) indicate his answers to the teacher without having to verbalize them, and so the teacher is able to design his interventions to target Larry's (lack of) understanding. Larry and the teacher shift their orientation continually between the book and each other, with the teacher also pursuing mutual gaze with other members of the class as he makes clear with his gaze shifts and movement through space that he is directing his speech toward the whole class, not just Larry, with the other students as ratified listeners to this interaction. Most importantly, even when he is unsure of what the correct response is, and thus momentarily unwilling to participate verbally, Larry's sustained mutual gaze with the teacher, paired with his shifting orientation to the materials, demonstrates his engagement with the ongoing interaction.

In both these cases, the focal students have been nominated by the teacher, and their inability to continue (in Chen's case as seen in Extract 5.3) or delay in responding (in Larry's case as seen in Extract 5.4) could indicate an unwillingness to participate. However, through their multimodal actions, they are able to demonstrate their continued engagement and to solicit additional assistance from the teacher before continuing.

5.3.2 ENGAGEMENT WITH EMBODIED PARTICIPATION

We have seen that students' embodied actions can index their engagement despite their unwillingness or inability to participate, but it is also the case that students are engaged and participating, but their participation takes *primarily* an embodied form, and I focus here specifically on students' gestures in classroom interaction. Gestures most often involve movements of the hands and arms, but other body movements may also be considered gestures (e.g., nods, pointing with a foot). Also worth noting is Schegloff's observation that "gesturing is largely, if not entirely, a speaker's phenomenon" (1984: 271). Here, I am looking at gestures of students who are also speakers, but we will see in Extracts 5.7 and 8.3 that listeners can gesture too. While a full discussion of gesture studies is beyond the scope of this chapter, readers are encouraged to consult Kendon (1990, 2004) and McNeill (1992, 2005, 2016) for a full background on gesture, as well as McCafferty (2002, 2004) and McCafferty and Stam (2008) for considerations of the role of gesture in second language acquisition. The analysis in this section focuses on how students' gesture with or without accompanying speech can indicate their *engagement* with interaction, including during sequences of interactional trouble. To do so, I include examples of students' verbal turns accompanied by gestures, embodied completions, catchments, and monitoring gestures.

Gesture use can provide a window onto students' understanding by introducing or emphasizing meaning that may be lacking from a student's verbal output (Goldin-Meadow 2010). Such gestures can complement co-occurring speech, adding shades of meaning to the verbal output, or in some cases, supplanting the verbal mode entirely as in the case of embodied completions (i.e., where a gesture is used *in place of* the lexical affiliate). We turn first to co-occurring speech/gesture use, and in particular, to an examination of the temporality of gestures. In this example from the Reading Data, the class is about to discuss the comprehension questions related to a passage they had just read. The teacher has identified several vocabulary items for review before doing so and prompts the students to explain their meaning, which Mahmoud does in multimodal fashion below. Note: the overhead projector is obscuring Mahmoud's face, but his hands are clearly visible.

Extract 5.5a Broad

```
3     TEA    what does "extensive"  *mean?*=
                                    *.....*Mah hands up-->
4     MAH    =broad.
```

Extract 5.5a Broad (continued)

```
5        *#(0.4) *#(0.2) *
         *.........*Mah hands spread*
         #fig. 5.8 #fig. 5.9
```

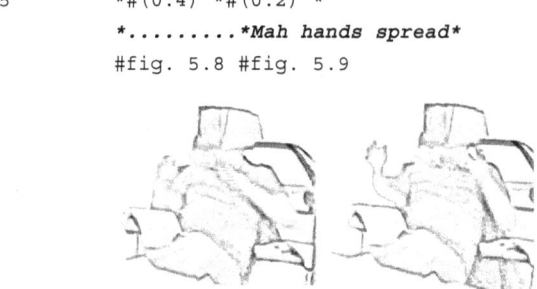

We can often see the preparation for a gesture well before the gesture itself is clear, and before the teacher has even finished his question in line 3, we see that Mahmoud is bringing his hands up toward chest height. He had begun with both hands down to his sides, and as the teacher utters 'mean', his hands come up and move slightly toward one another. He delivers his synonym for "extensive" in line 4 ('broad') and produces a metaphorical gesture with a similar meaning in the brief silence just following, holding his hands out for 0.2 seconds before dropping them back to his "home position" (Sacks and Schegloff [1975] 2002). Mahmoud's gesture is complementary in nature, meant to reinforce the meaning of the synonym he has just provided, and the timing shows his careful attention to the teacher's unfolding turn in line 3, i.e., his *engagement*.

Whereas Mahmoud produced a synonym for "extensive" along with his gesture, in this example from Jacknick (2018) drawing on the ESL Data, the student's gesture does the work of providing the synonym. This is from the same lesson as Extract 4.5, where the teacher has been discussing the meanings associated with gerund vs. infinitive grammatical forms (this interaction occurs approximately 30 minutes prior to Extract 4.5). She asks Yoro to explain the meaning difference in a pair of sentences in lines 11–14, and Yoro responds in line 15.

Extract 5.6a Sarah quit

```
11   TEA   Yoro, what's- what's the first and
12         the °second- sentence.° 'Sarah quit
13         going to- quit to go to school.'
14         'Sarah quit going to school.'
15   YOR   second one is Sarah has (.) quit.
16         *#(0.4)      #            *
           *Yor 'finished' gesture*
           #fig. 5.10 #fig. 5.11
```

Yoro's verbal explanation fails to provide a synonym for the word "quit," and so is not an adequate paraphrase. However, her "finished" gesture, produced just after her verbal contribution, clearly demonstrates her understanding (line 16), and is a crucial measure of her *engagement* in the interaction.

While Yoro includes a lexical affiliate ('quit') just prior to producing her gesture, another way that gestures can function for meaning-making is as *embodied completions* (Olsher 2004). In this case, gestures and speech contribute semantically, pragmatically, and syntactically to express an idea that would be incomplete without both. In this extract from the same interaction over 200 lines later, Nobu has introduced a new example, and is providing a gloss of the sentence "I quit smoking." He produces 'I' in line 242, but rather than verbally completing the sentence, he finishes his turn in an embodied way, producing a similar "finished" gesture to the one introduced by Yoro earlier, hands coming together at midline, palms down, before sweeping out to the sides.

Extract 5.6b Sarah quit
```
242  NOB    *I- *#(0.2) *
            *...*'finished'*
            #fig. 5.12
```

While embodied completions can be utilized by the speaker to bring their own utterance to pragmatic completion (i.e., to make meaning), they can also demonstrate cohesion when the embodied completion itself entails the recycling of a gesture from earlier in the interaction. That is, not only is Nobu communicating his meaning, he is also demonstrating his engagement in the interaction by imitating a gesture made by another participant in the discussion, a phenomenon we turn to next.

Students' careful attention to ongoing interaction (i.e., their *engagement*) is on display in their imitation of the teacher's and their classmates' gestures; only by monitoring the gestures of co-present participants could students so closely mirror the form or movement of their gestures. Different terms have been used to describe this phenomenon, with De Fornel (1992) calling it a "return gesture," Arnold (2012) describing a "gesture lead" produced by an expert with the novice's "gesture follow" demonstrating their understanding, and Majlesi (2015) calling these "matching gestures" when they are repeated by a teacher after a student has first introduced them. McNeill (2005) uses the term *catchment* to describe the reoccurrence of gestural features (e.g., handedness, shape, movement, etc.) in at least two gestures in connected discourse. Whatever terminology is utilized, students' recycling of gestures demonstrates their engagement with the ongoing interaction.

In the "Sarah quit" lesson, during pair work interaction with Nobu, Rodrigo was seen to imitate Yoro's "finished" gesture (Extract 5.6a) just minutes after she had introduced it. More than 30 minutes later in the lesson, in Extract 5.6c below (the same interaction seen earlier in Extract 4.5), Rodrigo produces a new version of this gesture, as well as another gesture for lighting a cigarette adapted from Nobu's earlier smoking gesture.

Extract 5.6c Sarah quit

```
255 ROD   =an*d then you *#stopped,*
               *...........*beat down*holds-->
                         #fig. 5.13
```

```
256       (0.2)*
               -->*Rod releases gesture
257 ROD   *and then *#you, *=
          *.........*lights*
                    #fig. 5.14
```

```
258 NOB   =*#stopped* to *#[light]* and then,
259 ROD                    [light]
rod        *lights  *     *lights  *
           #fig. 5.15     #fig. 5.16
```

Rodrigo produces a version of Yoro's "finished" gesture simultaneously with the word *stopped* (line 255), and then in lines 257 and 259, he adapts Nobu's gesture for smoking, miming lighting his gestural cigarette three times (by holding an imaginary lighter in his right hand, moving his thumb down to "light" the imaginary cigarette held in his left hand). This adaptation of the smoking gesture produced by Nobu more accurately fits the meaning of the sentence. Rodrigo's gestures here not only help make his meaning clear, but they also make clear that he has been carefully attending to the unfolding interaction throughout this over 30-minute discussion, despite limited verbal involvement until the very end.

I return now to Extract 5.5a, where Mahmoud introduced a gesture for "broad" or "extensive." In Extract 5.5b below, we will see the teacher repeat Mahmoud's gesture.

Extract 5.5b Broad
```
6     TEA    *broa:d.*#
             *gesture*
                    #fig. 5.17
```

```
7     S?     a l[ot.]
8     TEA    [*#a ]lot.*
             *gesture *
                 #fig. 5.18
```

The teacher repeats *broad* in line 6 and simultaneously produces a similar gesture (a "matching gesture," per Majlesi 2015), bringing his hands up and then spreading them out. His repetition of both the verbal and gestural contributions of Mahmoud confirm them both as appropriate glosses of the meaning of "extensive." Another student offers a different synonym, saying 'a lot' in line 7, and the teacher overlaps this suggestion by repeating 'a lot' and simultaneously producing the gesture introduced by Mahmoud again. The teacher's repetition of the verbal contribution similarly confirms this student's contribution, but the fact that he again uses the same gesture creates cohesion among the various answers so far, suggesting that "broad" and "a lot" have similar meanings which can be gleaned from this gesture (cf. Majlesi 2015). The teacher makes the "broad" gesture several more times during the rest of the class session, referring not only to this vocabulary word but also to identification of topics, etc. The teacher's gesture calls back to Mahmoud's, showing how crucial it is to include students' embodied actions in an account of their participation in classroom interaction.

How gesture is deployed in unfolding interaction is also an important indication of its social action. Students often hold a gesture to suggest unresolved interactional trouble (Groeber and Pochon-Berger 2014; Sikveland and Ogden 2012; Smotrova 2014), and the retraction of a held gesture can indicate that the trouble has been resolved. The example below from the ESL Data (Jacknick 2018) likewise shows how gestural holds can show students' monitoring of interaction.

Extract 5.6d Sarah quit
```
253  ROD   in the *first one, *you were walking?=*
                 *...........*walking right hand*
254  TEA   =*mm-hmm?=
             *Rod holds walking fingers-->
255  ROD   =an*d then you stopped,
             -->*
```

Rodrigo holds the gesture for walking (two fingers held pointing downward, moving as "legs") until after the teacher confirms her understanding in line 254, releasing it only when he continues with his explanation. His gestural hold shows his engagement through his careful attention to the teacher's understanding and the pending success (or not) of his explanation.

Finally, in addition to conveying semantic or pragmatic meaning, gestures, particularly beat gestures, can also be used to indicate that a participant is carefully monitoring (their own or others') speech (Lantolf and Thorne 2006), i.e., that they are *engaged*. Beat gestures are quick movements that co-occur with speech, most often manifesting as head nods, chin movements, or hand/arm movements. McNeill (1992) argues that beat gestures work to identify some aspect of speech as particularly salient. In these two examples from the ESL Data lesson on gerunds and infinitive verb forms, we can see Yoro (in Extract 5.6e) and Nobu (in Extract 5.6f) producing beat gestures along with their verbal output.

Extract 5.6e Sarah quit
```
15   YOR   second one is *Sarah has (.) quit.*
                         *beat on each word  *
```

Extract 5.6f Sarah quit
```
232  NOB   *say, if eh, 'I stopped to, smoke,'*
           *pointing, beats with each word    *
```

Lantolf and Thorne (2006) have argued that for language learners in particular, such beat gestures indicate that the speaker is monitoring their own production, and Smotrova (2014) notes that both teachers and students use beats to emphasize stretches of talk. Thus, while Yoro and Nobu are participating verbally in the extracts, their beat gestures additionally convey their careful attention to their speech output.

Small beat gestures from listening students may also serve as indications that they are monitoring another's speech, particularly when they are precisely timed. Nods may also indicate affiliation with the speaker's stance (Stivers 2008). In this case, student nods during an extended teacher turn may indicate monitoring of the turn (particularly the portion overlapped by the nods), but also affiliation with the teacher's point. In this example from the Reading Data, the teacher is talking to students about the importance of asking questions as they read.

Extract 5.7 Questions
```
1    TEA   on the second day of class,
2          what did I fill the board with?
3    ALI   questions.
4    TEA   who, what, *when, where,* why.
                     *Zeo two nods*
```

Alice contributes verbally, indicating her participation, and also, through the precise timing of her response, her engagement. Although she is the only one who responds to the teacher's query, other students are also engaged with the interaction. As the teacher continues, Zeo demonstrates her engagement by nodding along with him (line 4). This small extract shows that students use gesture to display their participation and engagement in classroom interaction, but we will see much more detail about the nature of multimodal listening in the next chapter.

5.3.3 ENGAGEMENT WITH EMBODIED STUDENTING

Whereas students' gestures in the prior section were argued to be a crucial indication of their participation and engagement in the activity, this next section shows how students' embodied actions show their engagement, despite the fact that they are participating in the "wrong" way for the participation structure of the activity. Extract 5.8 is the same workbook checking interaction presented in Extract 4.1, with multimodal details added to the transcript. Here, the participation framework established by the teacher involves students providing the answer in chorus as he makes clear in lines 6–7 with 'you can call them out here'. As this activity proceeds, several students write in their books as some, but certainly not all, of the students verbally contribute to the checking episode.

Extract 5.8 Utopia
```
6    TEA   so down below? just-*you can          *
                              *Ali pencil to book*
7    TEA   call them out here, an ideal *or a
                                        *........-->
```

Extract 5.8 Utopia (continued)

```
8    TEA   perfect place-*(0.2) or
                 .............*Rob pencil to paper-->
9    TEA   state?
10   HEA   ↑u[topia. ]
11   CHE      [°utopia.°]*
                           *Rob writing-->
12   TEA   utopi[a? ]
13   MAH        [uto]pia. e[heheh ]
14   TEA                   [*$noisy$]
                            *Kar/Ali writing-->
15   TEA   $and disorderly$? Or [bois ]terous?
16                                [rauc-]
17   S?    ru[ckus.]
18   SS      [ rau ][cous.]
19   MAH           [ruckus.]
20   SS    raucous.
21   TEA   raucous? okay?* a source of help,*
                 -->*Kar stops writing
                             -->*Rob/Ali stop writing
22   TEA   a strength, something to turn to,
23   TEA   an option"?
24   OLI   [recourse. ]
25   Ss    [rec[ourse.]
26   MAH       [recour]se?
27   S?    recourse,*
                 *Rob writing-->
```

Throughout this review, several students respond verbally, and these speaking students' gaze orientation shifts in expected ways between their materials and the teacher. Other students remain oriented toward their books or notebooks throughout the extract, and many do not contribute verbally either here or in the remainder of the activity. Rather, some of these students write as the checking episode progresses, precisely timing their actions with the unfolding review, demonstrating their engagement as they simultaneously do *not* participate in projected ways. As the teacher begins, both Alice and Robert bring pen or pencil to paper in preparation for writing, and in fact, following Heather and Chen's production of the correct response in lines 10–11, Robert does begin writing. Alice and Karina likewise start to write after the teacher has confirmed the correct response and begins to move on to the next item (line 14). All three students continue writing until after the teacher confirms the correct response for the next item and moves on with 'Okay?' (line 21). Robert begins writing again just after the correct answer to the next item has been made public (lines 24–27). These student-initiated writing episodes are distinct from the kind of "covert participation" that Gourlay (2005) discusses. Through their precision timing, they are demonstrating their engagement with the checking episode. Without access to the artifacts (i.e., their notebooks), we can't say for certain what they are writing, but that they are able to so skillfully time their writing episodes with the unfolding interaction suggests that they are attending to it quite closely. However, the lack of verbal contributions from these students marks their actions as *studenting* given the constraints of the current participation framework. This multimodal analysis, in addition to the detailed transcription of the choral responses themselves (Extract 4.1), shows the complexity of student actions during mundane classroom activities.

5.4 WAVES OF EMBODIED RESPONSE

The examples seen throughout this chapter have demonstrated the varied and complex ways in which students use their bodies to display their participation and engagement in classroom interaction. However, the focus on individual students also obscures another important element of this multimodal analysis: the fact that participation and engagement happen in *waves*. In using the metaphor of a wave to describe this phenomenon, I draw the reader's attention to the way such group responses begin slowly and small with just a few students participating, and then build to a crest, the peak of participation, before the movement recedes as students return to their home position. These embodied responses thus mirror the shape of an ocean wave, but they also unfold similarly to the stadium wave, a sequence of actions by individuals (standing, raising arms, and then sitting again) that build to create a wave of action around a large stadium. Teachers attend to a dizzying array of multimodal actions in the classrooms, but as we saw in the analysis of choral responses (Extract 4.1), even when students seem to be doing "the same thing" at "the same time," in fact, the reality is much more complex. For teachers, it can sometimes be difficult to differentiate individual students within a wave of multimodal activity, and this will have implications for their pursuit of responses as they monitor participation. We will look here at teacher requests for multimodal responses and directives for multimodal action, showing how careful analytic attention to the temporality and sequentiality of multimodal actions can inform our understanding of individual and collective participation and engagement in the classroom.

Although teacher requests for embodied responses are often made indirectly with a formulation like "How many people think X?" (e.g., see Extract 5.2), teachers' expectation that students should respond with their bodies can be seen in the breach, i.e., when students do not respond as expected, or not enough of them do so (see Extract 7.2 for an example of explicit teacher sanction of inadequate embodied participation). Note that these embodied responses are to be distinguished from what Gardner (2015) calls "summons turns." Students are not bidding for a next turn here; rather, their hand-raises *are* the action; however, my analysis extends beyond gaze and hand-raising to include other multimodal resources like posture and interaction with objects that may be relevant for our consideration of participation and engagement.

Let us return to Extract 5.2, reproduced below as Extract 5.9, and presented first with a simplified transcription of embodied choral response from students. Rather than focusing on the participation and engagement of Nobu in particular, this time through we will turn our attention to the complex wave of embodied response to the teacher's request that comes from the students individually and as a group, focusing specifically on the temporality and sequentiality of the students' responses, particularly gaze and hand-raising.

Extract 5.9 Take over

```
4    TEA   how many people say that's
5          correct.*(0.4)
                 *Ss gaze up
6          *(1.0)
           *Ss hands up
7    S?    *°take over-°*
8    TEA   take*over.          *good.           *
              *Tea big nod----*
                               *Ss hands up/down*Ss hands down
9          okay.*
           *Ss hands down
```

While the simplified transcription in Extract 5.9 includes multimodal detail, by showing students' embodied response in a "choral response" (Ss), the complexity of this response is obscured. Figure 5.19 shows the waves of embodied response unfolding left to right with the stretch of talk and time from lines 5–9. Orientation toward the teacher is represented by eyes (with the absence of eyes indicating a gaze shift down or away), and raised hands are indicated by the hand icon. This figure shows

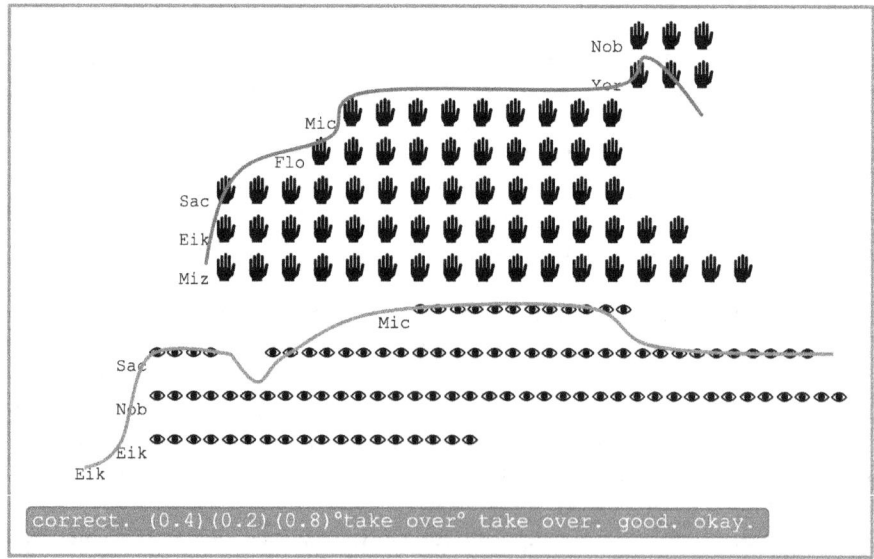

Figure 5.19 Waves of embodied response to teacher question

the sequentiality of the waves of embodied response, with students first orienting gaze toward the teacher, and then beginning to join the chorus of raised hands. Interestingly, the wave drops off just at the moment that two other students belatedly join in the chorus.

The teacher raises her gaze to the students during her prompt (line 4), indicating that she expects to see, not hear, the student response to her question. Immediately following the completion of her turn in line 5 ('correct'), Eiko, Sachiko, and Nobu raise their gaze toward her, demonstrating their engagement through the timing of this embodied action (note that Eiko begins this gaze movement before the teacher's turn is completed in anticipatory recognition). Sachiko looks briefly away before returning her gaze to the teacher, and Michiko looks up as another student echoes the form ("°take over°").

Very quickly (0.4 seconds) after the prompt is completed, three students (Eiko, Sachiko, and Mizuki) raise their hands, while Nobu gazes around at his classmates but does not raise his hand and Rodrigo shifts his gaze toward Sachiko's book, potentially checking her answer against his own. Eiko, Sachiko, and Mizuki have made their understanding public, and done so without hesitation, participating in the embodied response and doing so *with engagement.* While Sahlström (2002) notes that students' gaze patterns generally follow their hand-raising, with their gaze directed toward the teacher at the peak of their hand-raising gesture, and gaze lowering as they lower their hand, this wave of gaze shift toward the teacher clearly precedes the raising of hands. Sahlström was examining embodied bids for turns (i.e., displays of willingness to participate or incipiency), and the interplay of gaze and hand-raising here is different in this embodied response. Some students raise their hands before raising their gaze, and others shift their gaze between the book and the teacher (e.g., Sachiko) or gaze to the book before the embodied response is over (e.g., Eiko and Rodrigo). Establishing and maintaining mutual gaze may be relevant for displaying incipiency or willingness to participate, but here students' participation requires only their display of hands.

Following this initial wave of multimodal responses, other students join the "chorus" of raised hands, first Florence and then Michiko. A student quietly repeats the correct form, and just after the student says this, Rodrigo and Eiko both return their gaze to their own books. The teacher repeats the form with an exaggerated nod, and Nobu and Yoro belatedly raise their hands following this confirmation, while Sachiko puts her hand down. This is the peak of embodied participation here, with six students raising their hands. After the teacher's explicit positive assessment (EPA, Waring 2008) 'good' in line 8, Eiko and Michiko drop their hands. Nobu and Yoro, having just raised their hands a moment before, put their hands down following the teacher's 'okay', joined by Clara, who seems to have maintained eye gaze to the book throughout.

This fine-grained analysis of the sequentiality of actions shows how the students make their understanding visible to the teacher and each other. Some students demonstrate their understanding without delay and without first seeing embodied displays of understanding by others (i.e., Eiko, Sachiko, and Mizuki raise their hands first, followed by Michiko, who had her gaze toward her book the whole time). However, other students (Nobu and Yoro) wait until this "chorus" of hands builds and the grammatical form has been confirmed by the teacher. There are yet other students who decline to provide a response at all, whether embodied or not (e.g., Rodrigo and Hyon Joo), though in some cases, their embodied actions indicate continued engagement despite their unwillingness to participate (e.g., Rodrigo's gaze to the teacher, his neighbor's book, and his own book).

What then can we say about different students' (lack of) participation and engagement in this brief sequence? Nobu, who was seen to pursue a turn prior to the teacher's prompt for multimodal action, orients to the multimodal responses of his classmates, but does not raise his hand until the correct answer has been confirmed by the teacher. He is certainly engaged in the task, as evidenced by his precision timing (particularly his raised gaze at the beginning), but also by his careful monitoring of the multimodal actions of the teacher and his classmates; however, his actions index his uncertainty around this answer (or unwillingness to publicly display his understanding). Eiko raises her gaze precisely with the teacher's introduction of a new prompt and is the first to raise her hand and among the last to lower it. Nobu and Yoro's delayed lowering of their hands seems due to the belated nature of their initial response.

Nobu, Yoro, Mizuki, and Eiko all simultaneously drop their hands following the teacher's repetition of the correct response (delivered with an exaggerated head nod to reinforce its correctness). We can see that the retraction of Clara's multimodal response is somewhat delayed. Not only does she not lower her hand following the repetition of the correct response (as most of her classmates do), she also does not lower it following the explicit positive assessment (EPA, Waring 2008) as the rest do. It is only following the teacher's boundary-marking 'okay' that she drops her hand, and it is possible that while she is participating in this exercise, she is not sufficiently attentive to it (i.e., *engaged*) to time her actions more precisely.

Student embodied actions following requests for multimodal responses show their attention to, and engagement in, the participation framework of whole-class discussion. Note that the lack of student embodied responses where they are projected does not *necessarily* index non-participation and/or (dis)engagement, particularly for students who have no wish to "perform" participation and engagement to a level that might lead to their being called on to participate verbally or in a more public way. In particular, the temporality and sequentiality of their responses demonstrates their variable levels of engagement and willingness to display understanding or claim knowledge. Temporality is important because precision timing of student action shows their engagement through their careful monitoring of expectations for participation. The sequentiality of multimodal responses shows us the wave-like nature of such embodied "choral" responses. Some student responses, coming after an initial round of responses by their classmates, may be occasioned *by* the choral demonstration of participation. That is, in seeing their classmates raise their hands, some students may be "going along with" what is expected of them, regardless of whether they were initially engaged in the interaction, understand what is being discussed, or agree with the question.

Teacher requests for multimodal responses by their nature do not necessarily project responses from all students; when taking a poll, not everyone will agree. In these cases, lack of embodied response from any individual student does not necessarily indicate disengagement. A student might be unwilling to make their understanding public, may be disengaged, or may not self-identify within the group the teacher is targeting. As seen in sanctions like 'gotta raise your hands' (see Extract 7.2), teachers have some expectations about how many students should respond to a given prompt, and can make parameters for appropriate participation explicit (see also Looney and Kim 2019, where a teacher orients to the inadequacy of a student's embodied response). At other times, the teacher directs students to perform an embodied action, creating an interactional expectation that all will comply. Following directives that project multimodal responses from everyone, a lack of response (or delay in response) tells us about those students' participation and engagement in the interaction. These directives tend to occur at transition places between activities, or in what Walsh (2006, 2011) calls managerial mode, where the teacher is giving instructions for an upcoming activity or task. Extracts 5.10a and 5.10b (from the ESL Data) shows a typical example of this kind of directive. The teacher had just polled the students on whether they believed certain sentences written on the board to be grammatical, and following her announcement that they were all grammatical, she announced the focus of the upcoming grammar unit, the subjunctive form (line 1 below). A video of this extract is also available online (edinburghuniversitypress.com/multimodal).

Extract 5.10a Turn to page 85
```
1    TEA    okay this form is called
2           the subjunctive form.
3           that's what we're gonna study today.
4           so can everybody turn to
5           page *(.) eighty-five?
     ss        *upright posture
```

Lines 1–2 serve to end the previous discussion of the grammaticality of the sentences on the board; line 3 serves as a pre-sequence for the upcoming grammar lesson and also as a tie between the activity that just ended and the upcoming activity, acting as a signal of transition for students. The request comes in lines 4–5, with a micro-pause before the page number is named, potentially to secure the recipiency of the students (Goodwin 1980). It is in this brief pause that four of the visible students adjust their posture, leaning back slightly and sitting more upright than previously. While I have been arguing against oversimplification of transcripts, this collective movement has been included in the transcript in line 5 as "ss" because to include each student's action would add multiple identical lines to the transcript, impacting readability. This change in postural alignment marks these students as "publicly available . . . for engagement" (Hellermann 2008a: 49). Watching this moment very clearly shows a shift from embodied listening (i.e., leaning forward, gaze toward the teacher) toward some new activity as a group of students lean back and sit up. This truly simultaneous shift from several students is marked; much more common in the data are sequential waves of embodied action as seen in the prior extract in this chapter. However, even this "simultaneous" moment shows some features of the wave, and we turn now to examine the sequential detail of this postural shift.

Extract 5.10b Turn to page 85

```
1   TEA   okay *this *form is called       *
    nad        *.....*reaches for notebook*
    yas              *....................*gaze up*
2   TEA   *the *sub*junctive* form.
    mic   *....*up *
    yas   *gaze down and writing-->
    nad       *brings notebook to desk-->
3   TEA   that's what we're gonna *study   * today.
    mic                           *gaze up*gaze down and writing-->
4   TEA   *so *can *everybody turn to
    tea   *begins moving to desk, gaze to book-->
    nad   -->*opening notebook-->
    ame       *....*picks up pencil, clicks it closed
5   TEA   pa*ge *(.) *eighty-*five?*
    sac   *........*turns to grab bag
    eik   *head down-->
    ss        *upright posture
    yas              *gaze and body up
    rod                    *gaze to book-->
6   TEA   in the* textbook?
    mic         *stops writing, turns pages in text
```

Several student actions precede the postural change in line 5, and these show the beginning of the wave as students react to the activity shift. The teacher has indicated shift in several ways: (1) her transitional 'okay' and summative statement, (2) her transition marking 'so' (line 4), and (3) her physical movement in the classroom back toward her desk, with her gaze oriented toward her own book. Amelie's monitoring of these actions allows her to project activity transition, and she is able to participate in the postural shift in line 5, first closing her pencil in anticipation of moving to the next activity. Two other notable student actions prior to this simultaneous postural movement are from Eiko and Sachiko. Eiko orients to her book before the postural alignment from her classmates; she is engaged with the interaction, and slightly ahead of her peers in her reaction to the teacher's shift toward the book. Sachiko likewise began moving a moment before (during 'page' in line 5), turning to get her book out of her bag. Her "early" movement here shows her engagement in the interaction as she begins moving a moment before the rest of the class, potentially aware that it will take her longer to turn to the right page because her book is not yet on the table.

There are yet other students who are engaged, but who do not join the simultaneous postural alignment, because they are engaged in writing. Yasuko mirrors the movement her classmates just made, but briefly delayed. Rodrigo continues writing

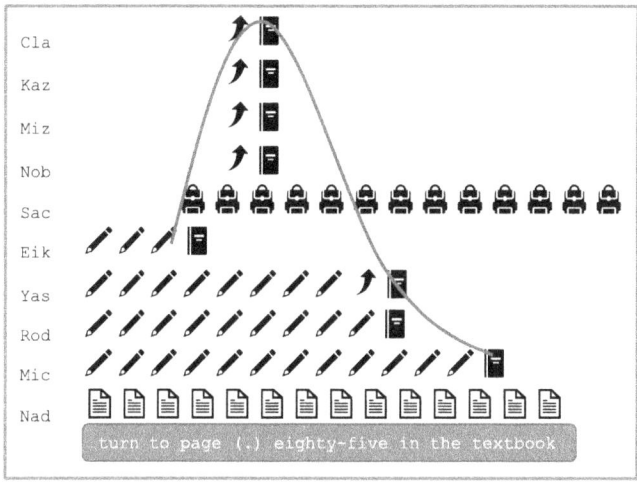

Figure 5.20   Waves of embodied response to teacher directive

until the end of the directive, when he then joins the embodied wave of students turning to the correct page in their books (without postural shift). Michiko, however, makes no visible movement at this point, continuing with her writing until midway through the teacher's increment in line 6. Figure 5.20 presents a new version of the wave image, this time showing students' enduring focus before the directive, and then how their actions fit within the ensuing wave of response. Eiko, Yasuko, Rodrigo, and Michiko are all writing, but their responses show their differential attention to the teacher directive, with Eiko reacting in anticipation of the request, and the others responding later. Of the students who are not writing, Sachiko likewise anticipates the request, reacting simultaneously with Eiko, but Clara, Kazumi, Mizuki, and Nobu all adjust their posture at the same moment. Nadia, as can be seen in the image, maintains her focus on her notebook throughout.

After the postural shift, the wave of embodied responses following the directive includes students putting away the prior papers and bringing out their textbooks. When teacher directives for multimodal action are given, students often have to cease a currently ongoing multimodal action in order to acquiesce. In this case, five students had their gaze fixed toward the teacher and the board, but four were writing (one of these four is only partially visible, so gaze direction is unknown). Of the students who were writing, they reacted differently to the directive for a multimodal response, with one anticipating the shift, and the other three students ceasing writing at the end of the request or during the increment. Even though they may be seen as having a delayed multimodal response, their persistence of the category-bound action of writing/taking notes marks them as participating as students, though not aligning with the pedagogical goal of the moment. These are examples of engaged studenting.

Interestingly, the student who seems least coordinated with the teacher's talk is, perhaps, not in alignment with the pedagogical task at all. Nadia begins reaching for her notebook during the teacher's explanation of the sentences on the board in line 1, and her activity of bringing the notebook to the center of her workspace and beginning to flip through it take up the entirety of the excerpt. Because Nadia begins this embodied action before the teacher's request, she seems to be engaged in her own goal-directed activity (a "parallel activity," per Koole 2007), potentially unrelated to the teacher's pedagogical focus. However, arranging her things and looking through her notebook are category-bound actions of the role student, and so the teacher may let such actions pass because they do not disrupt progressivity, despite the fact that the sequentiality of these actions marks them as non-participation in the current interaction (more on this in Chapter 7).

While in these first two cases, the teacher instigated the students' multimodal responses, in the next case, a student initiates a wave of motion that is then given the go-ahead by the teacher. Mondada argues that participants' "online analysis is embedded and embodied in their responsive actions" (2006: 126), and we have seen in the prior examples how students orient to teacher prompts for embodied action. In this next extract, we see the teacher's online analysis of students' multimodal actions. This final example of a wave of embodied action comes after the close of one part of an activity—a debate in small groups over whether a man who was taking coins from the Trevi Fountain should be considered to be stealing (ESL Data). After having each group report back on their discussion, the teacher directs students toward the other side of their handout, and just as she does this, Rodrigo looks around and begins to gather his things (line 3).

Extract 5.11 You can go back to your seats

```
1    TEA  ↑okay so now we're going to um (.)
2         look at the back (.)
3         *of *this * article.*
     rod  *gaze R     *
     rod       *gathers things-->
              *Eik/Nad flip paper and gaze down-->
4    TEA  *>okay< because this *actually um did go*# to*court.
     rod  *gets up............*walks-------------*   *walking-->
     nad                                              *writing-->
                                                      #fig. 5.21
```

```
5    TEA  *you can go *back to*your seats,*
     tea  *..........*hand wave
     ame               *gaze to T  *
     jin               *gaze to board-->
```

Extract 5.11 You can go back to your seats (continued)

```
6    TEA   if you- *if you want,        *
                   *Nob/Eik sit up-->
     eik             *gaze up-->
     fle             *gets up-->
     cla             *turns back to desk*
     mic             *gaze up-->
     ame             *.......paper to front table-->
     jin                           -->*gaze down-->
7          *(0.2)*(0.8)*(2.0)*(5.0)
     ame   .........-->*
     eik   *G up-*down-->
                   *Eik/Nob stand up-->
     jin           -->*moves to front-->
     nad                  -->*adjusts chair-->
8    TEA   *and this is     *how the court decided.
     jin   *puts things down*pulls chair to table
     ame   *puts pen down       *
9          (1.5)*
     nad      -->*
10   TEA   *let's read *it together.*
     jin   *..........*sits         *picks up pen, adjusts books-->
     jin                            *gaze to board-->
11         (4.2)*(0.8)*(1.2) *(0.8)*(0.8)
     jin      -->*writing-->
     ame   ((speaks to Fle at low volume))
     nad             *gaze L*to R *front-->
12   TEA   *the Italian court*rules in the <Trevi case.>
     nad   *papers upright    *
     eik   *................*sits
     ame   *moving papers-->
```

During the teacher's transitional talk in lines 1–3, several students shift their gaze between the teacher and their materials, and following her mention of the other side of their handout, most students flip their paper over and orient their gaze toward the paper. That is, their embodied actions are in alignment with the teacher's pedagogical and interactional goals at the moment. Rodrigo, however, looks to his right and then begins to pack up his papers, standing as the teacher begins to move on in line 4. He walks back toward his original seat, pausing midway through the teacher's turn, and then begins to walk again toward the projectable end of her utterance in line 4. While the teacher does not establish mutual gaze with him or endorse his continued movement in any way, he seems to take her lack of sanction as an indication that he may continue. The teacher orients to his initiation of movement, uttering the directive/permissive 'you can go back to your seats' while waving her hand. While the beginning of this turn may be understood as referring to Rodrigo

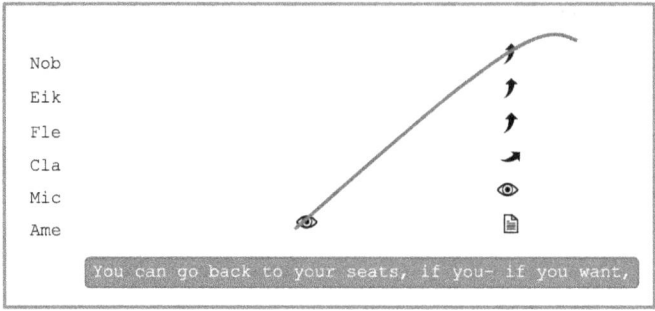

Figure 5.22 Student-initiated wave of embodied response

in particular, the plural "seats" makes it clear that "you" in this case refers to all the students. No other students get up at this stage; it is only when the teacher adds the restarted increment 'if you- if you want' that the students follow her prompt for embodied action. This increment and restart show her orientation to the lack of embodied action from the students; she is securing their embodied recipiency. Their reaction to this is clear in Figure 5.22 where we see several students adjust their posture or gaze toward the teacher in reaction to her permissive/directive. Amelie, we can see from the image, reacts first as the teacher's directive is being delivered.

Fleur, Eiko, and Nobu are some of the first to demonstrate their understanding of the teacher's directive with their bodies, orienting to the teacher (line 5) or shifting their postures forward in preparation for standing (line 6); Clara simultaneously turns back to the desk behind her. Eiko allows several students to pass her and so is one of the last to get to her original seat. Nadia, who was already sitting in her original seat, did not respond with the timeliness of her peers to the teacher's directive, understandably so because she did not need to physically move to meet it. However, even she orients to the need to reposition back into the whole-group participation framework, and after writing in her notebook, shifts her chair back and forth to adjust back to a seated position oriented toward the board. Jin-Ae was also writing prior to line 1 and continues writing until after the teacher's directive 'you can go back to your seats if you- if you want'. After picking up her things and moving her chair back to her original positioning, she sits down, rearranges her things, and returns to the activity she had been engaged in before the transition: writing information down from the board. The teacher's directive has thus acted as a temporary hold on Jin-Ae's activity-in-progress, which may be connected to the lesson, but is not in alignment with the teacher's managerial aims at the moment (i.e., it is a "parallel activity," per Koole 2007); she is studenting.

Students are still making final adjustments as the teacher moves on in line 12, reading the title of the article aloud, but all are in their original positions, and for the most part are oriented toward the material, gaze down. However, the teacher does not start the new task until the final student, Eiko, is visibly located at her seat and beginning to move to a seated position. That listener response can affect the design of turns-in-progress is well documented (cf. Goodwin 1979, 1980; Mondada

2016a). For example, Sahlström argues that teachers use multipart elicitation turns as they engage in "participation monitoring" (2002: 54), lengthening their questions to secure a critical mass of willing next speakers. Goodwin likewise notes that speakers may adjust the length of their turns to allow time for "the negotiation of an appropriate state of mutual orientation between speaker and hearer" (1979: 98). In this example, the teacher is seen to react to a student's embodied action (i.e., Rodrigo's move back to his seat), and also to maintain awareness of all the students' compliance with her directive, moving on only when their whole-group participation structure, including spatial orientation, has been re-established.

CA and second language researchers have shown interest in the social nature of teacher instructions, with regard to how they are interpreted by students, as well as how the design or delivery of instructions might affect ensuing task completion (Hellermann and Pekarek Doehler 2010: Markee 2015b; Seedhouse 2008). Both Markee (2015b) and Hellermann and Pekarek Doehler (2010) argue that a full understanding of instruction giving (and following) requires attention not only to verbal contributions but also to embodied actions, including participants' use of written materials and other objects. Mortensen notes that the design of instruction turns has consequences for "the interactional jobs the students are faced with" (2009: 491), as we saw in the examples here. While prior research has examined teacher instructions for small group or individual tasks, here we have instead focused on "small" requests or directives for action. Markee notes that "the most familiar courses of action are often the most interesting sites for developing novel insights into human behavior" (2015b: 118), and the analysis here of mundane and ubiquitous teacher actions in the classroom shows the complexity of equally mundane student responses.

5.5 SUMMARY

In all of the phenomena identified here, students' engagement in classroom interaction is visible primarily in their bodies. Building on the examination of students' participation and engagement in Chapter 4, this chapter highlights the crucial role of embodied resources in students' displays of participation and engagement, and particularly, how they work in concert with students' verbal contributions, or in some cases, their displays of unwillingness to participate verbally, to present a more nuanced view of student action in the classroom both individually and collectively as we saw waves of multimodal responses from students. I reproduce the matrix again here, highlighting how the examples from this chapter continue to illuminate the subtle differences between participation and engagement.

As in the last chapter, we have seen examples of *engaged participation* (Eiko and Sachiko in Extract 5.1, and student gestures in Extracts 5.5, 5.6, and 5.7). However, whereas in Chapter 4, a delay in verbal participation (as seen in Mahmoud's delayed contributions to choral responses) was glossed as *disengaged participation*, here by examining students' multimodal actions, we are able to see that delayed participation is sometimes also indicative of engagement, or *engaged non-participation* (Nobu's delayed hand-raise in Extract 5.2 and engaged displays of unwillingness to participate in Extracts 5.3 and 5.4). Finally, by returning to an example from Chapter 4 where

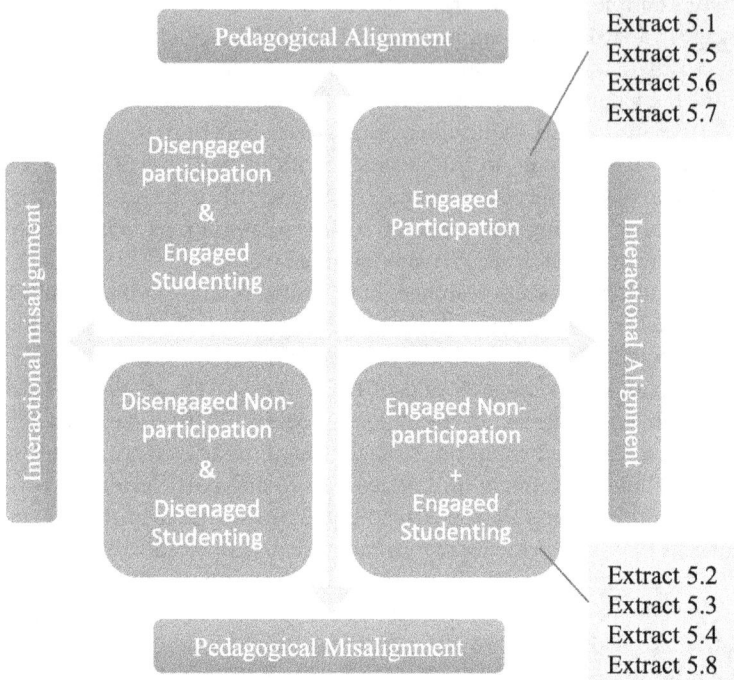

Figure 5.23 Embodied participation and engagement

several students were seen to "not" participate because they did not contribute verbal turns, we saw that students sometimes participate and demonstrate engagement through embodied means like writing, even when those actions do not fit within the current interactional constraints on student participation (Extract 5.8). Overall, through the detailed analysis here I hope to emphasize the complexity involved for students in displaying their participation and engagement, as well as the enormous job monitoring these displays entails for the teacher.

The difficulty for teachers in monitoring classroom interaction is also apparent in the complex waves of multimodal action seen in Section 5.5. Students' choral embodied responses, much like their verbal responses described in Chapter 4, show varying degrees of both participation and engagement. Some students decline to participate verbally at all, demonstrating through their multimodal actions an unwillingness to participate in this way (e.g., gaze aversion, writing). Others demonstrate their careful monitoring of interaction (i.e., their engagement) through the precision timing of their embodied responses to the ongoing interaction. We have also seen other students participating in such multimodal responses in a delayed fashion, showing their (at least minimal) attention to the ongoing interaction and their willingness to participate. While I have attempted to show how students' embodied actions can demonstrate their engagement, in the absence of action, we are limited in the conclusions we can draw. One of the difficulties of attempting to operationalize terms like "engagement," for both teachers and analysts, is that CA takes no interest in an individual's internal cognitive state, and so when a student is undertaking no action, we can't say with certainty whether they are or are not engaged. This will become particularly apparent when we turn to the next chapter where we will examine students' actions during extended turns when they are almost entirely silent and are engaged in what I am calling *multimodal listening*.

6
MULTIMODAL LISTENING

> One wants to make a distinction between 'having the floor' in the sense of being a speaker while others are hearers, and 'having the floor' in the sense of being a speaker while others are doing whatever they please. One wants not merely to occupy the floor but to have the floor while others listen.
>
> Harvey Sacks (1992: 683)

6.1 INTRODUCTION

How do teachers know if students are listening or if they are simply "occupy[ing] the floor while others are doing whatever they please"? While Goodwin (1981) discusses "hearership," as the Sacks quote above suggests, this does not necessarily entail "listenership" (McCarthy 2003). *Listening* (to the teacher or another student) takes up a large portion of whole-class time, and as students' actions during such extended teacher turns are visible to their co-participants, such actions can be a way to understand what "listening" looks like. As Edwards and Westgate dryly note, "appropriate participation requires of pupils that they listen *or appear to listen*, often and at length" (1994: 40; emphasis added). This chapter aims to uncover how students display (non-)participation and (dis)engagement when they are meant to be listening.

Goffman (1981), in talking about lectures, notes that the audience is also performing in a theatrical sense, but this performance has been relatively under-researched. Gardner (2001) notes that "listeners as a group have generally been neglected in language research" (2001: 1), a point echoed by others (cf. Kendon 1990; Mondada 2016a; Walsh 2011). Given that the vast majority of students' time (in traditional classrooms in particular) is spent listening, a more complete understanding of the nature of what I am calling *multimodal listening* is needed. As Mortensen says, listening is "something that current non-speakers *do* and display" (2009: 495; emphasis in original); Goodwin likewise notes that listeners engage in "participation displays" (1986: 283). While Gardner (2001) focuses particularly on listener *response*, Sahlström (2002) and others focus on listening *as recipiency*, and Sert (2019a) focuses on a *demonstration* of listening, my focus here is on the display, the performance of listening as action in and of itself, i.e., what does "doing-being-a-listener" look like in classroom interaction? Participation and engagement are context-sensitive, locally-contingent phenomena, and as such, I argue that they are constantly in flux.

This chapter aims to show different ways that students "do listening." In tracing how students' participation displays ebb and flow over the course of extended listening episodes, I demonstrate their orientation to the need to "do listening" in some visible way, even when interactional expectations are unclear. Finally, I focus on active listenership, proposing repair as one way students demonstrate active listenership, but I also show how students' embodied actions can make their engagement and participation in listening public.

6.2 DOING MULTIMODAL LISTENING

When the pedagogical focus in classrooms involves students reading silently or writing individually, there is an expected orientation toward materials, but when students are listening, where should they be looking? What should they be doing? Within multimodal conversation analysis, there is increasing attention to how objects in the environment become relevant to ongoing social actions (cf. Mondada 2011; Mondada and Svinhufvud 2016; Nevile et al. 2014a, 2014b), and in the course of normal classroom activities, a great many objects become relevant, such as notebooks, textbooks, handouts, writing implements, etc. The analysis to follow includes examination of how students engage with objects in the environment as they listen during a read aloud (Extract 6.1) and a freewriting prompt (Extract 6.2). In both cases, there is a joint attentional focus (the book or the task), but as we will see, students' displayed understanding of what listening looks like for each is varied.

6.2.1 MULTIMODAL LISTENING DURING A READ ALOUD

It is often the case in classrooms that one person reads aloud, sometimes a "new" passage that the class has not yet seen, though more often in these data from selections which students were already to have read individually, either at home or just previously in class. While one person reading aloud in a classroom may seem at first glance to be a solitary activity, such episodes are in fact collaboratively-constructed events, and ones that have been relatively understudied (Hall et al. 2019). Read alouds were particularly prevalent in the Reading Data; not surprising given the pedagogical focus of that class. In this first extract, the students had been in small groups discussing their summaries of the first twenty pages of *Fahrenheit 451* (Bradbury 1953). The teacher had also directed them to discuss questions they had about their reading. After the small group discussions, the teacher read the epigraph aloud ("If someone gives you ruled paper, write the other way."), and facilitated a whole-group discussion about its meaning. Following an extended teacher turn about the importance of asking yourself questions as you read, the teacher began to read aloud from the beginning of the book. As he finishes his reminder about vocabulary (line 41), students' foci of attention are varied. Isabelle and Chen both have their gazes up but not at the teacher, and several students are oriented toward their own materials, including Zeo, Alice, and Olivia. Figure 6.1 shows the teacher's posture as this extract begins: he is gazing toward the students and holding his book in his right hand but using both hands to gesticulate during his explanation. In line 41, we will see how he draws on first embodied, and then verbal, resources to index his shift into the read aloud.

Figure 6.1   Teacher's posture at beginning of extract

Extract 6.1 Ray Bradbury goes on
```
41   TEA   to build the vocabulary *as well.#
                                   *........Tea brings book up-->
                                        #fig. 6.2
```

```
42         (0.4)*(0.2)*
                *Gre gaze to book-->
                ............*Tea raises book-->
43   TEA   so then*# Ray *Bradbury goes on.
                  *Wen gaze to book-->
                        *Mah brings book up-->
                   #fig. 6.3
```

Extract 6.1 Ray Bradbury goes on (continued)

```
44   TEA   *he says *"it *#was a ↑special
           *........*Zeo brings book up, gaze to book-->
                   *Hea adjusting hair/posture-->
                       *Ali gaze to book-->
                   #fig. 6.4
```

```
45   TEA   *plea*sure *to see things *# (.)eaten.
           *..........*Kar opens book*
                *Ali gaze to binder and turning pages-->
                               *Oli holding papers-->
                               #fig. 6.5
```

```
46   TEA   to see *things *#blackened, and cha:nged."
                *Ali book to front-->
                    *Kar head on hand-->
                    #fig. 6.6
```

```
47         (0.4)
48   TEA   you *notice the word "changed"
                *Kar hair grooming-->
```

Extract 6.1 Ray Bradbury goes on (continued)

```
49        is in italics.*#
                    *Oli adjusting papers-->
                    #fig. 6.7
```

```
50        (0.8)(0.2)
51   TEA  empha*sizing *that.#
                *Kar head to chin, gaze to T-->
                    *Ali gaze to book-->
                        #fig. 6.8
```

```
52        *(0.2)*(0.2)
          *beat *Ali book to side/gaze to binder-->
53   TEA  "with the *#brass *nozzle in his
                *Kar gaze to book-->
                        *Oli pen to paper-->
                    #fig. 6.9
```

```
54        *fists,#       *with this great#    *python    *
          *Oli writing-->
          *Ali book down*both hands to binder*snaps open*
                    #fig. 6.10              #fig. 6.11
```

Extract 6.1 Ray Bradbury goes on (continued)

```
55        *spitting       *its venomous *kerosene,
          *.........................*Oli erasing-->
          *Ali holds book*............book moving to front-->
56        *upon the *world? *
          *Ali turning pages in binder with right hand-->
                    *Ali book to side*
                              *Oli stops erasing
57        the *blood# pounding in his head.
              *Oli gaze right-->
                    #fig. 6.12
```

```
58        and his *hands were the *#hands
                *Oli gathering papers-->
                                    *Ali gathering papers-->
                              #fig. 6.13
```

```
59        of some amazing *conductor playing
                              *Oli gaze to papers-->
60        all the *symphonies, (.) of *blazing
                *Isa gaze to Tea-->
                                    *Kar hair grooming-->
61        and burning,* to bring down the tatters*
                    *Isa gaze down-->
                                        *Kar done grooming
```

Extract 6.1 Ray Bradbury goes on (continued)

```
62        and charcoal *#ruins (.) of *history*#
                    *Ali book to side-->   *book move/gaze to
                                           book-->
                                        *Zeo closing book/gaze to T-->
                    #fig. 6.14             #fig. 6.15
```

```
63   TEA  so *#we have     *lots *#of-
                *Ali gaze to T*to book-->
                             *Isa/Oli gaze to Tea-->
             #fig. 6.16      #fig. 6.17 fig. 6.18
```

The teacher reveals his upcoming return to the book by slowly raising the book during the end of his utterance in line 41 and continuing to do so through the following silence. He delivers an announcement of his forthcoming reading as a pre-sequence (Schegloff 2007), saying in line 43, 'so then Ray Bradbury goes on'. While the students had been displaying their (non-)attention in a variety of ways during the extended teacher turn just prior (see Extract 8.1 for this teacher turn), the teacher's shift to the book occasions shifts from the students as well in their displays of multimodal listening (i.e., listening to a teacher lecture does not *look* the same as listening to the teacher reading aloud). Hall et al. note that participants "display their embodied alignment with the activity" (2019: 41) by orienting toward the materials that are being read aloud when they have a personal copy of the text in front of them, or alternatively, to the teacher who is reading aloud. This finding will become relevant as we examine students' gaze orientations and shifts throughout this extended teacher turn.

In response to the teacher's embodied move to his book, Greg orients his gaze toward his book before the pre-announcement (line 42), and several other students orient toward their books during the pre-announcement itself, including Wendy and Chen. Mahmoud begins to bring his book toward the front of his body, and Zeo demonstrably finishes writing, clicking her pen closed and orienting toward the teacher first and then toward her book just as the teacher begins to read in line 44. We can see that some students have been *engaged*, attending carefully to the teacher's talk, and thus able to anticipate his move back toward the book. Several other students turn their attention to the shared focus of attention, the book, just as the teacher begins reading, following the two pre-announcements (lines 43 'Ray Bradbury goes on' and 44, 'he says'). These students might be said to be slightly less engaged; they are a bit delayed, but their timing to join the collective read aloud demonstrates a certain level of engagement, or at least their *participation* in the multimodal listening event. Many of these students maintain their eye gaze toward their books throughout, with the exception of Jessica, who shifts her focus between the teacher and the book, both of which are appropriate foci of attention during multimodal listening during a read aloud.

In addition to the students whose engagement and participation are more inscrutable, there are others who may be said to be studenting, though in different ways. Alice, for example, suspends her ongoing activity of rearranging her papers in her binder to orient her gaze toward her book for the moment the teacher resumes reading in line 44. Notably, she does so in a side-task manner, with her book held to her side almost on the desk next to her, her actual desk taken up with her open binder. However, she also continually shifts her focus between the papers in her binder and the book. At times, she brings the book more prominently in her field of vision (lines 46, 51, 62, 63) but never in a sustained way. She seems to be quite literally touching back in with the activity at hand, demonstrably orienting her attention to the book at times during what appears to be her main activity, organizing her binder (which is, itself, a "parallel activity," per Koole 2007).

Olivia, on the other hand, spends the read aloud writing (including erasing) and organizing her papers, possibly finishing the summary of the first twenty pages of the novel that the teacher will be collecting following the read aloud. Olivia does not have a copy of the book out on her desk, and though writing is a category-bound action of the role "student," she does not attempt to *look like* she is doing the same thing as everyone else is, as Alice does at times. Olivia and Alice are both doing *disengaged studenting*, the first clear examples of student actions in the bottom left quadrant of the matrix. Interestingly, however, Alice is at times *participating* in an observable way, but her participation is *disengaged* at best. While Olivia could be placed in the bottom right quadrant for this extended teacher turn, Alice's constant shifting between disengaged participation and disengaged studenting makes her difficult to pin down. This state of flux is characteristic of most students' actions during any extended activity. As we have seen in earlier chapters, even within a brief moment, students' engagement and participation shifts. As an example of this, both Alice and Olivia gaze toward the teacher when he finishes reading and produces his commentary (line 63), showing their orientation to the teacher's read aloud as the primary activity (Koole 2007).

Two other students' multimodal actions during this read aloud are of note. The first is Isabelle, who, like Olivia, appears not to have a copy of the book. However, unlike Olivia, Isabelle does not engage in any visible "studenting," and maintains her gaze at mid-level, not toward a book or the teacher (see Figure 6.19). Her display of listenership gives more of a perception of non-participation to an observer (i.e., she could be daydreaming), but she *could* in fact be much more engaged than other students (even those with books), since she is not "doing" anything during this read aloud where students' only task is to listen. Karina likewise *looks* more disengaged than some of her peers, with slouched posture (seen seated on the far right in Figures 6.10, 6.12, 6.16) and continual hair grooming, but she is also orienting to the book and the teacher at appropriate times (line 51 to the teacher and 53 back to book); she is *engaged*.

Figure 6.19   Isabelle's mid-level gaze

It is impossible for us to know what any of the students are thinking as this read aloud progresses, and whether or to what extent they are "listening" is a matter of conjecture. The students' interpretations of *what the performance of multimodal listening looks like* differ, and the analysis above shows a range of actions, including active demonstrations of reading along (e.g., Chen, Jessica, Mahmoud, Zeo), less active participation (e.g., Karina), itinerant participation (e.g., Alice), non-participatory "studenting" (e.g., Olivia), and inscrutable actions which could be interpreted either as appropriate participation or complete disengagement (e.g., Isabelle), depending on one's predispositions toward a student. What all of the students *are* doing, however, is colluding with the teacher's pedagogical goal. While not everyone is aligning with the activity at hand, none of them is disrupting the progressivity of the interaction and the lesson.

6.2.2 TASK-BASED MULTIMODAL LISTENING

Students sometimes listen to the teacher as part of a task itself, as is the case in Extract 6.2 below. This type of listening differs from listening to "teaching" monologues in that the students are notionally engaged in a particular activity as part of task completion here. In this example from the ESL Data, the teacher introduces the students to visual writing, a journaling technique where the teacher leads students through sensory prompts about a memory they will write about. The students seemed unclear about the purpose of this activity and its parameters (e.g., whether they were to be writing during the prompt or not), as evidenced by their actions before, during, and after the teacher's reading of the prompt. Theoretically, students' gaze could be oriented in any direction for the purpose of reflecting on their own memories. However, of note here is students' almost constant shifting of gaze orientation, which indexes their uncertainty about what constitutes appropriate participation at this point: i.e., what does "doing-being-a-listener" look like for this over 3-minute task? As you read through the transcript, I invite you to imagine what you might do as a student listening to this prompt. Note: a full multimodal transcription of this episode, following Mondada's ([2001] 2019) conventions, is provided in Appendix 2, and two videos showing different camera angles are available on the companion website (edinburgh universitypress.com/multimodal)

Extract 6.2 Visual writing

```
28   TEA   "↑think back to yesterday, and find a memory.
29         can you find one (.) from ten years ago? (1.0)
30         when you were twenty? ten? (1.0) eight? (2.0)
31         six? (3.0) three? (3.0) does the month July?
32         send up a memory? (3.0) September? (3.0) a
33         particular time of day? (2.0) sunset, for
34         example.(2.0) midnight? (3.0) does the color
35         green trigger a memory? (2.0) aqua? (2.0) pink
36         or rose? (2.5) the smell of hyacinth? honeysuckle?
37         garbage? liver? (2.5) does the word dance give
38         you a picture? (2.0) do you see something in the
39         word under? (2.0) dream? (1.0) laugh? (2.0) kiss?
40         (2.0) tickle? (2.0) let your mind supply more
41         details.=until you can see the picture or event
42         clearly.(3.0) keep wandering until a memory you
43         would like to spend more time with (.) stands out.
44         (2.0) if several memories want your attention?
45         choose any one. (1.0) you can go back to another
46         one later. (3.0) look more carefully at this
47         memory. (2.0) where are you. (1.0) what kind of
48         light is there. what do you notice. (1.0) are
49         there any particular colors? (3.0) what do you
50         hear. clearly. in your mind. (.) in the distance?
51         (1.5) do you hear machines? animals? (1.0)
52         conversations? (2.0) do you notice a certain
53         smell? (1.0) is there an odor or fragrance
54         connected with this memory? (3.0) do you touch
55         specific surfaces? what tastes are associated
56         with this time. (2.5) what are you doing. (1.0)
57         how are you moving. (1.0) is there a particular
58         sensation in your body? (3.0) are there other
59         people around? (2.0) are they moving in
60         particular ways? do they have a relationship to
61         you? (2.0) do certain thoughts occur to you,
62         certain questions, is this memory ↑dark or light.
63         (1.0) fast or slow. hazy or distinct." (4.0)
64         okay, you may begin writing.
```

The constantly shifting nature of students' multimodal actions during this extract led to the decision to describe these actions in prose, following Koole (2007). Because this activity was designed to prompt students' internal exploration of a memory, any number of student actions which might normally be considered non-participation are potentially appropriate, including putting one's head down or closing one's eyes. Prior to the start of her read aloud of the prompt, the teacher explicitly told students they could close their eyes, and just before starting to read, she again reminded them 'eyes open or closed, but you um, you just have to listen'. However, no students elect to close their eyes, and only two students put their heads down at any point (Michiko and Clara); in both of those cases, they are also holding a pen with their head down, demonstrating that they are continuing to be ready to write, doing-being-a-student rather than resting, disengaged.

As the teacher began reading her prompt, most students were oriented toward the teacher (Yoro, Michiko, Rodrigo, Eiko, Clara, Nadia, Amelie, and Fleur), though several were gazing down at their desks (Nobu, Sachiko, and Jin-Ae). The students' general uncertainty about what constitutes participation for this task is evident in their continually shifting demonstrations of (dis)engagement in listening to the visual writing prompt. Many students look up toward the teacher (whose gaze remains fixed on the paper she is reading from throughout) for portions of the prompt, while others gaze toward their own notebooks, down to the table, or off into some undetermined space. Again, any of these gaze orientations is potentially appropriate for internal reflection on memory, but it is the students' continual shifting of gaze orientation that I argue demonstrates their uncertainty about where they should be looking and what they should be doing, i.e., what listening should look like for this task.

Changes in posture also index their disengagement from and re-engagement in "doing listening." As has been noted before, postural alignment can mark co-present persons as available for interaction (Hellermann 2008a; Kidwell and Zimmerman 2007), or conversely, as disengaging from it (Hellermann and Cole 2009). Most students at some point rest their heads or chins on their hands, a posture which looks like a disengagement from the whole-class interaction. They often come back to this posture after maintaining a more upright posture for some period of time (Michiko, Nadia, Rodrigo, Jin-Ae, Clara, Sachiko, and Nobu), i.e., after demonstrating more alert engagement for a period. Many of them also rub their eyes or part of their face (Rodrigo, Jin-Ae, Nobu, Clara, and Eiko), an embodied action which might indicate tiredness or an attempt to make oneself more alert. Again, the constantly shifting nature of students' posture and "self-care" actions seem indicative of their uncertainty about what might constitute appropriate participation. In addition, their movement between their "home position" (Sacks and Schegloff [1975] 2002) of "doing listening," seated upright or slightly leaning forward, and these other postures and actions shows their shifting (dis)engagement with the listening event.

Students' interaction with objects (particularly writing implements) in this extract is also illuminative of their (dis)engagement. Given that this is a writing prompt, it is perhaps not surprising that several students engage in writing as the teacher is reading aloud, including Yoro, Michiko, and Clara (each of these only briefly).

Interestingly, Sachiko does not write, but rather erases several times. Because this is the first time the students are hearing this prompt, it's unlikely that she would have written anything relevant prior to the task; thus, her erasing, while a category-bound action of *student*, appears rather to be an example of *disengaged studenting*, as she may be revising something unrelated to the task. Students' uncertainty about participation expectations is also seen in the fact that many students hold their pens throughout the reading of the prompt, but only three write anything. Instead, several students put their pens down on their desks at some point (Sachiko, Yoro, Nobu, Michiko, and Rodrigo), demonstrating their evolving understanding of the task, i.e., that it will involve writing at a later time.

When at last the teacher finishes reading the prompt and directs the students to begin writing, rather than taking up their pens and beginning to write, most students gaze at one another, some smiling, and some speaking at low volume with their peers. After several seconds of this, the teacher reminds the students that they should be 'writing what you imagined, what you saw' during the prompt. Some students talk with one another quietly after this reminder, and Rodrigo admits to the teacher that he 'didn't see anything'. The students' shared laughter following this extract indexes the interactional trouble occasioned by their lack of understanding of expectations for student action during the activity.

6.2.2 SUMMARY

The two examples included here show the varied displays of doing-listening by students in classrooms. While some students maintain a particular posture and focal gaze orientation, most students in these extracts were seen to shift in their displays of listening. Extract 6.1 showed that some of these gaze shifts demonstrate students' careful listening and engagement with the interaction, as when students move their focus to the book during the teacher's shift to a read aloud in Extract 6.1. In others, we see disengaged studenting, either in a display of attention (Alice's periodic touches back to the book during her main activity) or in a category-bound action that is not appropriate for the moment (Olivia's writing). In Extract 6.2, we see by students' constantly shifting posture, orientation, and interaction with objects their uncertainty about the "right" way to do listening. These examples have shown students listening in what might be glossed as a "passive" way, potentially engaged but not participating with the unfolding interaction in any way. We turn in the next section, however, to more active displays of multimodal listening.

6.3 ACTIVE MULTIMODAL LISTENING

In whole-class interaction, the students present in the room are designated from the outset as "entitled" to the talk in progress (Kidwell 1997: 85), though it is less clear what their responsibilities are *as listeners*. Recently, Sert (2019a) has argued for inclusion of demonstration of active listenership as a crucial component of second language classroom interactional competence (CIC), with, for example, collaborative turn completion serving as a clear demonstration of active listenership (cf. Waring 2002, "substantive recipiency"). In this section, I propose repair as another demonstration of active listenership, and as these examples will show, active listenership can also be demonstrated in entirely embodied ways. The first example shows students' embodied displays of active listening through gaze, as well as their demonstration of active listening through other-correction. The second example importantly shows that listening can *look like* non-participation; analysis of students' multimodal actions reveals a deeper truth, that students often engage in multiactivity while listening.

Repair is a "generic term" (Hutchby and Wooffitt 1998: 57), encompassing all sources of trouble in the talk to which participants orient. For example, trouble sources can include production trouble (e.g., stumbles or stuttering) or factual errors. In their seminal paper on repair, Schegloff et al. (1977) note an overwhelming preference for self-correction over other-correction in everyday interaction. Researchers of classroom discourse have noted that the same holds true in classrooms, though in many cases initiation comes from the teacher rather than the student themselves (cf. Kasper 1985; Kinginger 1995). McHoul (1990), for example, identifies other-initiated self-correction as the prevailing organization of repair in classrooms, with the teacher initiating repair but leaving it to the student to perform self-correction. When other trajectories of repair are found, they represent an interesting departure from these norms. Here we will look at two instances of students demonstrating active listenership by performing other-correction, generally after a failed self-correction attempt by the student who produced the original trouble source. These other-corrections show students' careful attention to the unfolding interaction, not simply in their ability to target an appropriate kind of repair correction, but in their ability to identify a failed attempt at self- or other-correction.

While repair can be a demonstration of active listening, participation and engagement in listening can also be demonstrated primarily through gaze (Mortensen 2013). While I focus on gaze, as the analysis below will demonstrate, students' embodied actions work as a complex multimodal Gestalt (Mondada 2014c) to demonstrate their (non-)participation and potentially their (dis)engagement as well. Notably, episodes of multimodal listening often take place within materials mode (or as side modes during materials mode activities), and so different foci of attention are available and potentially relevant, including texts, the board, notebooks, and other co-present participants. Students' shifting orientation can be seen as an indication of both their "immediate focus of attention" (Mortensen 2009: 498), as well as whether and to what extent any given student is available for what Goffman calls "focused interaction" (1961: 8).

The first example includes other-correction from two students, demonstrating active listenership in their ability to follow and resolve the interactional trouble. Importantly, this example also shows how rapid gaze shifts can demonstrate students' engagement in an interaction, showing that they are *listening*. In this skills and system mode (Walsh 2006, 2011) activity, students had been sharing phrases they composed using multiple adjectives and adverbs, and Amelie shares her sentence about how she admires another student's "incredibly big passion for life" in lines 1–2.

Extract 6.3 Big passion

```
1   AME   uh so Fleur? and her re- incredibly big
2         *#passion for life.
          *Nob/Rod/Yor gaze to Ame-->
          #fig. 6.20
```

```
3   TEA   her incredibly *#bi:g,
                         *Nob/Rod gaze to Tea-->
                         *Yor gaze to Ame-->
                         #fig. 6.21
```

```
4   AME   passion.*#
          *Nob/Rod/Yor gaze to Ame-->
          #fig. 6.22
```

```
5         (0.6)
6   TEA   *#patience? (0.6)      *#big patience,
          *Nob/Yor gaze to Amelie*Nob/Rod gaze to Amelie
          *Kaz/Rod gaze to Tea   *Yor gaze to Tea
          #fig. 6.23             #fig. 6.24
```

```
7         (2.2)
8   TEA   her incredibly *#big patience?
                         *Nob/Rod/Yor gaze to Tea
                         #fig. 6.25
```

Extract 6.3 Big passion (continued)

```
9            (0.8)
10    TEA    could we say *#that? her incredibly big- (0.6)*#patience?
                          *Kaz/Nob/Rod/Yor gaze to Tea    *N/R gaze to
                          Ame
                          #fig. 6.26                      #fig. 6.27
```

```
11           {(4.0) - ((Amelie and Fleur talk quietly))}
12    AME    P-A-S-S-I-O-N=not patience, passion. [I don' know]
13    NOB                                         [passion.  ]
14    AME    how you say that.
15    NOB    passion,=
16    ROD    =pa[ssion.]
17    TEA       [oh pa]ssion.
18    AME    passion.
```

Amelie pronounces the first vowel in "passion" as /e/, a notably non-native pronunciation that leads to the teacher mishearing her as saying "patience." This trouble leads to several attempts at repair. In line 3, the teacher repeats the first part of the phrase, ending just before the trouble source and using continuing intonation to mark it as a designedly-incomplete utterance (DIU, Koshik 2002). Amelie produces the word "passion," again with the same pronunciation, leading to further repair initiations from the teacher. Egbert (2004) notes that repair initiation is usually accomplished with one turn-constructional unit (TCU), and while two are possible (a "double," according to Schegloff, as cited in Egbert 2004: 1494), three TCU repair initiations are "exceptional." In this case, after the failed repair sequence in lines 3–4, we see a 5-TCU repair initiation from the teacher in line 6–10, even more marked by the extended pauses before and between the repair initiations.

Throughout this extended repair sequence, the other students look like spectators at a tennis match as they anticipate self-correction from Amelie or other-correction on the part of the teacher, shifting their gaze orientation back and forth. After speaking quietly with the student next to her, in line 12 Amelie spells the word she is trying to produce, rejects the teacher's candidate hearing ('not patience'), and repeats the word again, with stress on the first syllable to emphasize the contrasting vowel in that syllable. She then provides an account for the trouble, saying 'I don' know how you say that' (lines 12 and 14), a postmortem type that Egbert calls "post-trouble-resolution 'diagnosis'" (2004: 1472). This type of postmortem does the work of membership categorizing by making Amelie's status as a second language user of English salient to the repair sequence.

When no resolution is forthcoming, following Amelie's spelling and repetition of the word (i.e., her second attempt at self-correction), Nobu offers other-correction, pronouncing "passion" with the more target-like front/central low vowel /æ/, rather than the /e/ that Amelie has been producing. Nobu repeats his correction, orienting to the overlap with Amelie's 'I don' know how you say that', and then Rodrigo latches with Nobu to repeat the word. Finally, the teacher hears the correction and repeats it in line 17 following the change-of-state 'oh' (Heritage 1984a). Visually, we can see the other students in the classroom attending quite carefully to this extended repair sequence, shifting orientation between the repair initiator (i.e., the teacher) and the current speaker, Amelie. That they are closely following the continued interactional trouble and its consequences for progressivity is made clear when Nobu and then Rodrigo resolve the trouble through other-correction. They have understood their classmate, *and* importantly, they have targeted the source of the trouble for the teacher, and are able to resolve the interactional difficulties. I note that the teacher makes no move to open up the floor to other-corrections, keeping her gaze either on the board as she begins to write Amelie's contribution, or to Amelie as she initiates repair again. Nobu and Rodrigo self-select to perform the other-correction, demonstrating their active listenership of this interactional trouble. In this case, the shared focus is the interactional trouble itself, and the students' constant gaze shifts between the teacher and Amelie show their attention to the unfolding interaction. This next extract likewise shows a student's demonstration of active listening through repair, but importantly, highlights that engaged students can *look* like they are not listening.

While students in the Reading classroom often spend time listening to the teacher read materials, they also notably spend a significant amount of time listening to each other read aloud (this is also a prevalent activity in the ESL Data). Particularly in language classrooms, students engage in "performance reading" (Grabe 2009), where one student reads a passage aloud, often one which all students have just read silently to themselves. The pedagogical purpose of such activities can be to allow the teacher to monitor a particular student's reading fluency, though this purpose is not always clear to the students. In these cases, the attention of other students often wanders, as evidenced by their eye gaze or attention to other tasks (e.g., eating), while the focus of the teacher remains on the student who is reading aloud (as evidenced by proxemics and gaze). In describing students' attention as "wandering," I hope to suggest that at times it does rest on the pedagogical focus of the moment, i.e., the student reading aloud or the materials themselves. However, students shift their attention between the "official" business of the moment and other tasks. Some of these other tasks are examples of "studenting," while others appear to be non-participation (e.g., eating). Importantly, while some student actions appear to an observer to be non-participation, upon closer analysis, we can see that even these "off-task" actions do not detract from students' ability to simultaneously engage in the main activity. In addition, even when "studenting" means students are disengaged from the activity, if their actions do not disrupt progressivity, the teacher often lets such "studenting" pass.

As we will see when we look more closely, what initially appears to be a solitary activity for the student reading aloud, or a small "ecological huddle" (Goffman 1964) between the student and teacher, is actually a jointly-attended to activity involving many students. In some cases, students who appear to be disengaged from the interaction show that they are carefully attending to the read aloud and monitoring their classmate's performance, and are in fact, engaging in multiactivity (Haddington et al. 2014; Mondada 2014c). Koole (2007) proposes the term "parallel activities" to refer to the variety of "off-task" actions students take, and he goes on to argue that "students are capable of participation *in different activities at the same time*" (2007: 497). Mondada shows how participants can favor one parallel activity over another, but also how they can "embed[] different activities together" (2014c; 153), as we will see below.

This extract starts just as Alice, a struggling reader, begins to read aloud a passage which she and her classmates had just read silently. Elise, seated in the back row, had been writing since before the teacher solicited a volunteer to read, and continues writing as the extract begins. Heather had been eating her breakfast before this read aloud and continues to do so as it starts. Alice herself is already oriented toward her book, as is Chen, sitting between Alice and Heather. Robert, who has his book open to the correct page, is gazing "off into space" as it were, i.e., not at Alice, the teacher, or any identifiable object. Thus, students' performed attention to, and potential engagement with, this activity, is by no means uniform when Alice begins reading. Note: a full multimodal transcription of this episode, following Mondada's ([2001] 2019) conventions, is provided in Appendix 3.

Extract 6.4 I hope everybody's noticing

```
3    ALI   fifty years ago *American were sleeping an
                           *Hea gaze to food-->
4          average of e- eight hour to tw- twelve hour
5          a night. but by nineteen ninety# they were
                                          #fig. 6.28
```

```
6          down to only seven hour *a night.#
                                   *Eli gaze up-->
                                          #fig. 6.29
```

Extract 6.4 I hope everybody's noticing (continued)

```
7          *now many American# are getting only about six
           *Hea wiping hands and folding napkin-->
                         #fig. 6.30
```

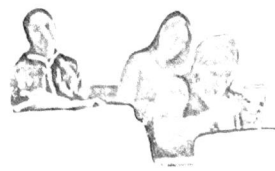

```
8          hours of sleep a night. sp- espensive research
9          show that    *lossing an hour or two *of sleep
                        *Eli gaze down-->       *Hea puts napkin under
                                                 book-->
10         every night, *week after week,    *# month after
                        *Eli gaze to side     *Hea gaze to book-->
                                       #fig. 6.31
```

```
11         month, makes* it more difficult for people to
                       *Eli gaze down-->
                       *Hea eating-->
                       #fig. 6.32
```

```
12         pay 'tention, *'specially *to (.) mono- (.)
                         *Eli gaze up*gaze down-->
13         [monoto- ]
14    TEA  [m- <mon]otonous.>
15    ALI  monotonous=°>tasks.<° *#and to remumber *thing.#
                                 *Eli leans forward, gaze to book-->
                                                 *Hea going into bag
                                 #fig. 6.33        #fig. 6.34
```

 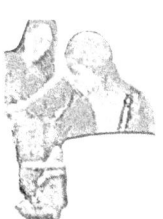

Extract 6.4 I hope everybody's noticing (continued)

```
16          (0.2)
17    ALI   reaction (.) time slow down. behavior
18          become inpractical. logic *re°action°
                                      *Eli gaze up-->
19          (.) reason is im- implay-=
20    TEA   =im↑paired?
21    ALI   empaired. and accident and urror in judge
22          *#increase. while productive and ability to
            *Hea gaze to book, eating
            #fig. 6.35
```

```
23          *#make a decision decleen- decleen. student
            *Eli writing-->
            #fig. 6.36
```

```
24          fel- fall 'sleep in class and fail learn
25          <all that they sh- (.) should>. marriage become
26          more stretsful as *sleep exhausted parent try to
                              *Hea gathers food trash-->
27          copy with their children and each other.
28          #truck and, and auto *driver fall asleep
                                 *Hea puts trash under book
            #fig. 6.37
```

Extract 6.4 I hope everybody's noticing (continued)

```
29         at the ( beach ) and *eps-  *and      *
                              *Hea wipes hands*
                                      *Ali traces words-->
                              #fig. 6.38
```

```
30         espet es- estimatt that
31         accident*# result        *in over one (.) f-
                   *Eli stops writing, gaze up-->
                   *Hea wipes mouth*traces words with finger-->
                   #fig. 6.39
```

```
32         one- f- one-
33  TEA    one $thousand?$=
34  ALI    =*one    * thh*ouhs   *and five *hundred death*
           *Hea nod*                       *Hea smile----*
                   * Eli gaze to book-->
                   *Mah nod*
35         in the country (.)* a year. worker perform
                             -->*Hea stops tracing words
36         less *ef- less effi-         *
                *Eli mouths "efficient"*
37  HEA    *efficient.
           *napkin under book-->
38  ALI    efficient.
39  TEA    mm-hmm?
40  ALI    and those in high (.) risk po- p- position can
41         endange us all.*# for example, sleeping (.) d-*
                          *Hea wiping desk--------------*
                          #fig. 6.40
```

Extract 6.4 I hope everybody's noticing (continued)

```
42          deprivation lead to the accident
43          *#at the nuclear power plant at#
            *Hea adjusting clothes and hair-->
            #fig. 6.41                    #fig. 6.42
```

```
44   ALI    three mile (      ) Pennsylvania.
45   TEA    excellent, really, your #reading has improved so much=
                                    #fig. 6.43
```

```
46   MAH    =mm [*#yeah. *]
47   TEA        [Alice,   ] I hope #everybody's noticing that.
                *Mah nod*
                *Hea gaze to Ali and smile-->
                                  #fig. 6.44
```

```
48   TEA    *rea    *lly, so much better than just *five* or six weeks
            *Mah nod*                              *nod *
49          ago.
```

There are a few students who begin this episode oriented toward their books, and who remain so oriented throughout, including Alice, Chen, and Nancy. Thus, we can see that one way of "doing listening," particularly during materials mode, involves continued gaze orientation toward the materials. However, several of the other students become more involved in listening than might at first be expected, revealing multimodal listening to involve more than just attention to the text. Mahmoud, for example, nods along with Alice when she is able to pronounce "thousand" in line 34, and echoes the teacher's praise in line 46, agreeing with the teacher's assessment that Alice's reading skills have improved. He nods along with his 'yeah' in line 46, and nods again twice during the teacher's continued praise in line 48. The four students discussed thus far are, however, the only ones for which an uncomplicated reading of their engagement with (or at least performed attention to) the task is possible.

Heather and Elise present interesting examples of the shifting attention that seems much more common during multimodal listening, though to differing degrees. Elise, who was writing before the excerpt began, and happened to be sitting next to the researcher, appeared to be doing a very convincing job of *disengaged studenting* through some parts of this episode. Her writing was personal in nature, unrelated to the task at hand or the topic of the day; but as has been argued before, writing in a notebook, being a category-bound action of student, marks her action as studenting, though in this example it would not be appropriate participation, let alone engagement. However, her engagement is in flux throughout the extract. After the teacher's other-correction in line 14, Elise leans forward with her gaze toward her book and then up for several lines. Her engagement fades in line 23 when she begins writing again, but again pronunciation difficulty seems to create a joint attentional focus as she gazes up in line 31. Following the teacher's other-correction in line 33, she also returns her gaze to the book in line 34. As Alice struggles with (i.e., initiates self-repair on) the word "efficient," Elise is seen to mouth the word to herself, gaze oriented toward the book (line 36). As Alice begins the last sentence of the passage in line 41, Elise again begins writing, withdrawing her engagement and becoming focused on her personal task rather than the joint pedagogical task. Elise is thus seen to weave in and out of engagement with the read aloud, withdrawing at times entirely as she writes for herself, and at other times attending carefully to the read aloud, and particularly, to the trouble sources and attendant repairs and corrections.

Heather, on the other hand, *looks* for much of the extract to be completely distracted with other tasks. She is eating her breakfast when the read aloud begins, and she continues to eat (lines 3–6, 11–15, 22–26), use napkins (lines 7–10, 15–21, 29, 37), deal with her breakfast trash (lines 26–28), clean her desk (lines 41), and adjust her clothes and hair (lines 43–47) throughout the entire read aloud, i.e., *she appears to be disengaged*. However, while she is engaging in these off-task actions, she is, in some cases simultaneously, attending to and demonstrating her engagement with the read aloud itself. She orients to her book noticeably in lines 22 and 29, tracing her finger along as Alice reads in line 31 (echoing the same action just undertaken by Alice herself in lines 29–31). She also engages affectively with the read aloud as a difficult task for Alice; she nods and smiles as Alice produces 'thousand' with smiley voice in line 34, and she orients directly to Alice and smiles during the teacher's praise in line 47.

Most noticeably, however, in line 37 it is Heather who provides the other-correction related to Alice's pronunciation difficulty. Prior to this instance, Alice has initiated repair herself 11 times, self-correcting in 9 of these instances. The other two represent cases where she initiated self-correction more than once, demonstrating continued trouble. In both these instances, the teacher provided other-correction. That the goal of this read aloud is not accuracy can be seen by the many instances of "incorrect" pronunciation that the teacher passes by because Alice herself does not orient to them as trouble. Rather, other-correction has only come when Alice herself indicates continued trouble that disrupts the progressivity of her read aloud. Notably, just two lines prior, Heather nodded and smiled as Alice repeated the teacher's corrected pronunciation, showing that she was carefully monitoring the unfolding of the repair episode and also affiliating with Alice's interactional trouble. Alice initiates self-repair with a cut-off (Laakso and Sorjonen 2010) as she begins the word "efficient," and she restarts the entire noun phrase again, proceeding one syllable more before cutting off again ('less effi-'). These multiple self-initiations of repair prompt Heather to provide correction in line 37, which Alice repeats in line 38, followed by confirmation from the teacher in line 39. Heather identified the pattern of self-initiated other-correction that had occurred twice before in this read aloud and provided the other-correction herself. Her ability to predict an appropriate use of other-correction shows her careful monitoring of the interaction thus far, i.e., it demonstrates her *engagement*. Van Compernolle (2015) includes other-correction as an element of learners' classroom interactional competence. However, he includes instances where a shift in teacher footing makes it clear that any student may participate in the repair sequence. Here as in Extract 6.3, the teacher makes no verbal or embodied action to indicate a shift in footing, and Heather's other-correction occurs quickly following Alice's failed self-correction, demonstrating her engagement with Alice's read aloud. In fact, Heather simultaneously utters the correct pronunciation and puts her napkin under her book, engaging in the interaction in a precise way while also orienting part of her body to "off-task" objects: she is multitasking. That students are engaging in both their own parallel activities and the teacher-led activity *at the same time* is made clear by students' responses to the teacher-led interaction at appropriate junctures. As Koole so perceptively puts it, for a student to have responded at some moments in the interaction, "she must have monitored more than just these" (2007: 496).

The only two other students visible throughout the excerpt are Brad and Robert, seated next to one another on the side of the classroom, and thus facing Alice, seated in the middle of the room facing the board. Because of his near constant movement, including Brad's multimodal actions in the transcript would result in readability issues (see Appendix 3 for the full multimodal transcript). Conversely, Robert makes very few visible changes in posture or gaze throughout the extract, and so he has almost no "actions" to include in the transcript. Rather, their actions will be described here following Koole (2007). Both Brad and Robert are studenting, though in different ways. Though he occasionally scratches his face, Robert returns to his slouched posture with one arm up on the ledge behind him, the other resting on his opened book, with his gaze up but not oriented toward any particular person or object (see Figure 6.45). He may or may not be listening to his classmate reading aloud (or to the various repairs ongoing), but he gives no observable evidence that he is doing so. His book is open to the required page and his eyes are open, and this is as far as his demonstration of studenting goes. He may, in fact, be listening closely, but he gives no observable evidence of this.

Figure 6.45   Robert's posture during the read aloud

Brad, on the other hand, is hardly still for a moment. Notably, Brad does not have the textbook, and the teacher had spoken with him in a prior class about this, learning that Brad could not afford to purchase one. While he is seated next to a classmate with the book (Robert), he does not look at Robert's book (perhaps because Robert is not looking at it), nor does he engage in a demonstration of doing-listening in any other way. Rather, Brad appears deeply engaged in copying down information from the board; he constantly shifts his gaze between his papers and the blackboard, and he writes throughout most of the read aloud. What is interesting about this action (particularly compared with Elise's personal writing and Robert's disengaged posture and inscrutable gaze orientation) is that Brad is very visibly doing *disengaged studenting*: writing down information from the board. This is not the appropriate time for this action, but given his limited options (i.e., lack of book and proximity to the teacher), Brad seems to have elected to be doing-being-a-student in this way. This draws no sanction from the teacher, but it is marked in that Brad demonstrates almost no observable "listening" during the read aloud (note: he does gaze to Alice briefly in line 34, but this action has been left out of the transcript for reasons discussed in Section 8.3).

Students' displays of multimodal listening are thus seen to be constantly in flux. Some students, by their actions, show appropriate participation, though not necessarily engagement, in the activity. Others appear to be disengaged (or participating in other tasks), but by their precisely timed multimodal actions, are shown to be carefully attending to the read aloud. Still other students are disengaged from the activity, though in differing ways. The nature of students' displayed non-participation and disengagement will be further explored in the next chapter.

6.4 SUMMARY

In their foundational treatise on turn-taking, Sacks et al. note that one consequence of the turn-taking system they describe is "an intrinsic motivation for listening" (1974: 727). They argue that a potential next speaker *must* "listen to and analyse" (1974: 727) each utterance, to determine whether they are being selected as next speaker or whether any other participant has been selected as next speaker. While not all students may desire to be the next speaker during classroom interaction, given the teacher's superior interactional rights, any given student *might* be selected as next speaker at potentially any time. Thus, while students may not display incipiency, they must be prepared to be next speaker, or else manage the resulting interactional trouble and problems of progressivity when they are unable to contribute in an expected way. Within CA, listeners can be considered incipient speakers (Mortensen 2009; Waring 2013b), and work in interactional linguistics in particular has demonstrated how hearer actions affect syntax-in-construction (cf. Goodwin 1980; Goodwin and Goodwin 2004) as well as how upcoming speakers secure displays of recipiency from others (e.g., Butler and Wilkinson 2013; Ford and Stickle 2012; Heath 1984). By analyzing what multimodal actions students take during extended turns in large multiparty classroom talk, this chapter has shown that listeners are not only incipient speakers but must also perform "doing listening." Engaged participation in listening includes a range of actions, including timely gaze shifts and changes in posture but also repair as a demonstration of active listenership.

Notably, we have also seen examples of disengaged studenting for the first time in this volume, as when Olivia and Alice engage in parallel activities during a teacher read aloud (Extract 6.1), or Brad copies down information from the board while Alice reads from the textbook (Extract 6.4). By investigating students' multimodal displays of "doing listening," I hope to highlight the complexity inherent in "listening," particularly when what is required of them may be unclear. Sahlström describes listening in whole-class participation structure as being silent and "display[ing] recipiency" (2002: 48), but what the *body* is doing while one is quiet is an area in need of further illumination. Sahlström also makes the key point that not all students must engage in a display of listening, saying instead that "a sufficient number of them [must be] doing so for the Student as a speaking partner to be recognizably doing listening" (2002: 48). The question of whether students are "recognizably" doing-being-students will be the consideration of our next chapter, as we turn to the ways in which students display their non-participation and disengagement in public and embodied ways.

7
NON-PARTICIPATION AND DISENGAGEMENT

> As long as ... control is not overtly threatened or blatantly rejected, much counter-activity will be possible. The individual acts to say 'I do not dispute the direction in which things are going and I will go along with them, but at the same time I want you to know that you haven't fully contained me in the state of affairs.'
>
> Erving Goffman (1961: 133)

7.1 INTRODUCTION

What kinds of "counter-activity" are possible in the classroom? Which actions are allowed to pass, and which are negatively sanctioned by the teacher? This chapter examines instances of non-participation and disengagement, focusing on their dynamic nature, as well as the ways in which they may be disambiguated from one another. Students' willingness to participate (WTP, Sert 2015) can be indicated in verbal and embodied ways, and likewise, students can communicate unwillingness to participate (UTP, Sert 2015) in a variety of ways. Sert notes that UTP is "dynamic and fluid" (2015: 141); just as students' participation and engagement have been shown to be reflexive phenomena, so too we must consider the context when examining UTP. An important distinction I make here is the use of the term *non-participation*. Rather than simply looking for ways that students communicate their unwillingness to be next speaker, I aim to show the many and varied ways that students fail to participate or resist particular forms of participation. Notably, some of these forms of non-participation are ignored by the teacher, while others are oriented to as accountable actions. In all the cases below, an important question is what doing-being-a-student looks like at that moment, in that classroom, and how students' embodied and verbal behaviors do or do not meet expectations. In addition, as we have seen in earlier chapters and as I argue below, non-participation does not always indicate disengagement.

In this chapter, we will examine how students use their bodies to demonstrate their non-participation and disengagement, while also problematizing a simple read of these embodied actions as always indexical of disengagement. I include examples of embodied unwillingness to participate, (dis)engagement at transition, and postural disengagement in Section 7.2. In Section 7.3, I turn my attention to how students orient to and interact with objects as they disengage from interaction, including clocks, bags, materials, and personal electronic devices.

7.2 EMBODIED (NON-)PARTICIPATION AND (DIS)ENGAGEMENT

There are many mundane misalignments that occur in the course of classroom interaction; for example, when students are unable to follow the interactional pattern of what Mortensen and Hazel (2011) call a "round robin" checking episode. While these incidents are relevant to my argument regarding participation and engagement, in the interest of space, I choose to focus instead here on more clearly *embodied* cases of (non-)participation and (dis)engagement, with particular interest in the presence of electronic devices in the classroom. Anyone with teaching experience in the last ten years has noted the drastic shift in the ubiquity of electronic devices in the classroom space, including "official" equipment like computers and projectors, as well as personal electronic devices like laptops, tablets, and smartphones. While the use of technology has been studied in what Mortensen (2013) calls "workplace studies," the focus has largely been on how participants interact with technologies during social interaction. Here, I am interested in how the presence of electronic devices affects participants' (non-)participation in and (dis)engagement with the ongoing classroom interaction. It is possible that students are engaging in multiactivity (Mondada 2014c), either by orienting primarily to their devices (to the detriment of their engagement with classroom interaction), or by engaging with them in parallel with their participation and engagement in the classroom interaction. This may be an instance of students engaging in "parallel activities" (Koole 2007) while attending in some way also to the primary, teacher-led activity. We turn here to instances where students display their non-participation and disengagement using their bodies, including embodied displays of unwillingness to participate, different kinds of hand-raises, delayed joint orientation, and postural disengagement.

7.2.1 EMBODIED UNWILLINGNESS TO PARTICIPATE

Students' unwillingness to participate (UTP) has been treated as a kind of interactional trouble (Sert 2013), particularly as it can often disrupt progressivity. Sert examines teachers' epistemic status checks, which are used following a delayed second pair part from a student. Long silences after a teacher's first pair part or a student's embodied (e.g., a head shake) or verbal (e.g., "I don't know") claim of insufficient knowledge (CIK) are both considered by Sert to be examples of interactional trouble in the classroom. He notes that students indicate their unwillingness to participate sometimes with a CIK, but often do so with other embodied resources, including long pauses, smiles, quiet responses, and gaze withdrawal. Sert (2015) also says that mutual gaze can communicate willingness to participate, and so a moment of mutual gaze orientation has the potential to lead to their being selected as next speaker. Mortensen (2008) shows how students withdraw their gaze as the teacher scans the classroom for a willing next speaker, and Sert (2015) likewise argues that withdrawal of gaze is an important part of students' display of unwillingness to participate. While Sert calls gaze withdrawal as part of UTP a kind of "disengagement" (2015: 78), I argue that students' unwillingness to be next speaker does not necessarily indicate their *disengagement* from the interaction. Rather, students' precisely timed gaze withdrawals, along with other embodied resources, demonstrate their *engaged*, careful monitoring of the unfolding solicitation from the teacher.

In this example from the ESL Data, students just completed their first freewriting exercise, where they were instructed by the teacher to write continuously for 5 minutes on the topic of influences. After explaining "the rules" of freewriting, the teacher noted 'we're freewriting right now to get our ideas going'. Notably, she did not prepare them ahead of time that they may be asked to share what they were about to write. After the allotted time had expired, the teacher brought the students back together and attempted to find a willing next speaker to share their freewriting with the class. Just as we have seen the wave-like pattern in students' embodied responses (Section 5.4), here we will see students' displays of unwillingness to participate unfold in a wave as the teacher seeks a willing next speaker.

Extract 7.1 Who would like to share

```
1    TEA   would #*anyone like to
                  *mutual gaze T w Miz and Sac
                  #fig. 7.1
```

```
2    TEA   *sha:re? what you *wrote?#
           *................*Miz/Sac gaze down
                            *T withdraws gaze
                            *Yas/Kaz/Mic/Eik/Jin/Nob/Sal gaze to T
                             #fig. 7.2 fig. 7.3
```

```
3    TEA   >because *influences is such a big topic.<*#
           *..............................*Miz/Sac gaze to T
                                           #fig. 7.4
```

```
4          it's a really big topic, so, (.)
5          you can literally write, >you know<
6          about >so many different things.<
```

Extract 7.1 Who would like to share (continued)

```
7         *um, who would like to #*sha:re
          *T scans class, walks from L to R across U-shape
          *Rod gaze down           *Kaz/Yas/Jin/Mic/Eik gaze down
                                   #fig. 7.5
```

```
8         <what they *#wrote.>
                    *Rod moves forward to desk, gaze down
                    #fig. 7.6
```

```
9         (4.4)*#(4.6)
               *Nob removes glasses, rubs eyes-->
               #fig. 7.7  fig. 7.8  fig. 7.9
```

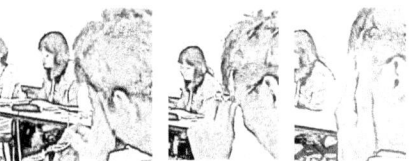

```
10  TEA   Amelie?
```

As the teacher begins to solicit a next speaker in line 1, she establishes mutual gaze with Mizuki and Sachiko, both seated to her left. Following a brief moment of mutual gaze orientation, both Mizuki and Sachiko begin to withdraw their gaze, with the teacher simultaneously shifting her gaze. Notably, after their mutual gaze is broken (line 2), Mizuki and Sachiko simultaneously shift their gaze back toward the teacher, demonstrating their continued engagement in the activity, despite their prior unwillingness to be selected as next speaker.

At the same moment that the mutual gaze is broken in line 2, most of the other visible students shift their gaze *to* the teacher. All of the students who engage in this gaze shift are seated farther from the teacher than Mizuki and Sachiko, and so they are not in imminent peril of inadvertently establishing mutual gaze with her (and potentially demonstrating their willingness to be next speaker). As the teacher rephrases her solicitation in lines 7–8, she simultaneously scans the classroom for a willing next speaker and moves in space from left to right across the U-shape. As the teacher shifts her gaze and moves in space, each of the students in her field of vision withdraws gaze. This gaze withdrawal does not happen one-by-one in a domino effect, but the effect is still wave-like, as first Rodrigo, then Kazumi, then Yasuko, then Jin-Ae, then Michiko and Eiko turn their eyes from the teacher. The ripple of students' gaze aversions, precisely timed to occur as the teacher scans the classroom for a willing next speaker and moves physically across the U-shape, shows their engagement with the interaction, if not their willingness to participate.

Likewise, when the "danger" of being selected as next speaker has passed, students demonstrate their continued engagement in the unfolding interaction. For example, after the teacher has physically moved passed them, Mizuki and Sachiko both return their gaze to the teacher (line 3). Following his gaze withdrawal from the teacher, Rodrigo moves forward in his chair, maintaining his gaze to his notebook (line 8). Prior to the excerpt, Nobu had maintained gaze orientation toward the teacher, nodding along with her comments and smiling. Now, as the teacher's scan reaches him at the far-right side, Nobu removes his glasses and rubs his eyes in a clear demonstration of his unwillingness to participate (line 9).

The unwillingness to participate seen by some students in Extract 7.1 occurs on the open floor when the teacher is seeking a next willing speaker, and so while it is likely that one student will speak next (either by self-selection or nomination by the teacher), there is no expectation that any given student will speak. The teacher is thus accepting of their displays of unwillingness to participate, though she does eventually nominate a student. Extract 7.2, from the Reading Data, is different in that the teacher is asking for self-identification of what he assumes to be a large group: those with several televisions in their homes. Like the excerpts examined in Section 5.5, this is a teacher prompt for multimodal action from the students, but here, the students' differential participation is sanctioned by the teacher, in what may be called a "reproach", where a teacher "explicitly refer[s] to the rules of 'correct' behaviour" (Margutti and Piirainen-Marsh 2011: 305), in this case, "correct" participation.

Like Extract 7.1, this next extract shows embodied waves, this time of both participation and disengagement. This excerpt comes from a discussion of the novel *Fahrenheit 451* (Bradbury 1953), which the class had just begun reading that week (note: this extract precedes Extracts 6.1 and 7.9). Students were to have read the first twenty pages, summarized them, and written down questions as they were reading. The students had just finished comparing their summaries in groups before the teacher brought them back together to a whole-class participation structure. Most students fully adjusted their chairs at this point, but one student, Heather, has her lower body facing the side and back of the room. The teacher makes connections between the first twenty pages and the epigraph, noting that in the main character's house, three walls of his living room are taken up with television screens. As the excerpt begins, 8 of the visible students have their gaze oriented toward the teacher, though Sara has her gaze to her notebook. A wave of embodied response unfolds here (as in Section 5.4), including a simultaneous movement from most students (as in Extracts 5.10a and 5.10b), though as we will see, a lack of clarity about expectations for participation leads to interactional trouble.

Extract 7.2 Gotta raise your hands

```
1    TEA   so how many of you have
2          more than *#two T-Vs in
                     *Sar gaze to T
                     #fig. 7.10
```

```
3    TEA   your (.) a↑partments.*#
                                 *Sar opens hand, Zeo raises hand
                                 #fig. 7.11 fig. 7.12
```

```
4          (.)
5    TEA   gotta *raise your *hands.*#
                 *Ali raises hands, Kar starts to raise, S1 opens hand
                               *Kar hand up/S1 raises hand
                                       *Hea raises hand
                                       *Ss hands up
                                       #fig. 7.13
```

```
6    GRE   the whole apartment,*#
                               *Sar closes hand
                               #fig. 7.14
```

Extract 7.2 Gotta raise your hands (continued)

```
7    TEA   in the *whole apartment.*#
                   *...............*Che gaze to Hea/Sar reopens hand
                                    #fig. 7.15
```

```
8          how many*# (.) have [more  ]
9    CHE                       [°two°?]
                   *Gre raises hand
                   #fig. 7.16
```

```
10   TEA   than *#two*     T-Vs. *#
                *Che 2 gesture/Sar closes hand/Zeo gaze to Gre/Gre hand
                down
                       *Sar reopens*Sar closes/Zeo hand down
                   #fig. 7.17,7.18 #fig. 7.19
```

```
11         (.)
12   TEA   *I- I'm not    *# including* handheld devices
           *Kar bends elbow*-----------*
                           #fig. 7.20
```

Extract 7.2 Gotta raise your hands (continued)

```
13      I mean an actual television.*#
                                *Ali elbow to desk
                                #fig. 7.21
```

```
14      *#mm.           *#
        *Ali closes hand*Kar lowers arm
        #fig. 7.22      #fig. 7.23 fig. 7.24
```

The teacher prompts the students for an embodied response with an informal poll: 'how many of you' in lines 1–2. This teacher action prompts gaze shifts from some of the few visible students who had not established mutual gaze with the teacher at the beginning of the excerpt, and indeed Sahlström (2002) notes that eye gaze to the teacher tends to precede hand-raising. Just after the teacher says, 'so how many' (line 1), Olivia orients her gaze toward the teacher, followed by Mahmoud and Sara (line 2), who had started the excerpt with her head down, writing. The first student to raise a hand in response to the prompt is Sara, though she does so with a small gesture, only opening her hand but not raising it. Zeo also raises her hand in the brief silence after the teacher delivers his full prompt. While most students have their gaze oriented toward the teacher at this point, the teacher orients to the embodied response of two students as inadequate, referring explicitly to appropriate participation for this context, saying 'gotta raise your hands' (line 5). As he delivers this sanction of their non-participation, three more students (Karina, Alice, and S1) raise their hands. Just at the end of the sanction, all students with a raised hand lift their hands slightly higher into the air (represented by "Ss hands up" in line 5). This wave of embodied response is shown in Figure 7.25. We see a wave of hand-raising, but also a simultaneous emphasis of those hand-raises, as all with their hands raised lift them higher.

Sahlström (2002) describes the basic "morphology" of hand-raising, noting that only one hand is raised, generally at 30–45 degrees; he goes on to argue that gaze orientation, face orientation, and orientation of the other (non-raised) hand are relevant to the interactional unfolding of hand-raising. Sahlström was looking par-

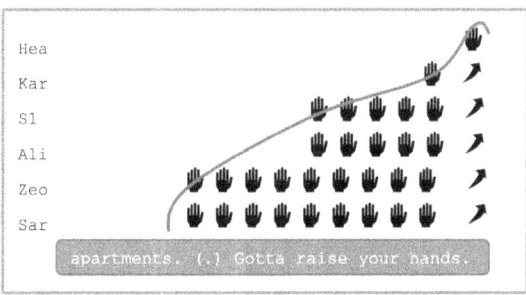

Figure 7.25   Embodied wave: hand-raises

ticularly at cases of hand-raising as bids for a turn; here, students are not bidding for a turn with their hand-raise, and so the interactional unfolding of hand-raising functions differently. I argue that in addition to gaze, head, and other hand orientations, other important considerations include (1) the *form* the hand-raising gesture takes, and (2) the duration of the hand-raise, as both may demonstrate differential (and changing) participation and engagement with the interaction. For example, following the collective lift in line 5, Sara, the first to raise her hand initially, closes her hand. Likewise, during the teacher's confirmation in line 7, Heather puts her hand down slowly, and Karina also adjusts her gesture, with her arm still up but her palm down rather than fingers pointed upward. These students seem to be orienting to the moment when most students lifted their hands higher (line 5, Figure 7.13) as sufficient for creating the critical mass of participation seemingly required by the teacher. This relates to Sahlström's (2002) finding that the teacher waits to nominate a student until "enough" students have identified themselves as willing next speakers.

After this peak of embodied participation in line 5, Greg initiates clarification of the teacher's prompt, asking whether the teacher is referring to 'the whole apartment' (line 6). The teacher's confirmation (line 7), along with his repetition of his original prompt (lines 8, 10), and his clarification (lines 12–13) all serve to extend the sequence, leading to several students lowering/closing their hands and then reraising/reopening them. However, following the peak of participation in line 5 when most of the visible students have raised their hands, students put their hands down in a gradual wave. This wave is seen as a gradual retraction of the gesture rather than withdrawal of it entirely, as several students move to a less emphatic gesture first before retracting the hand-raise. Compare Karina's bent elbow (line 12) and Alice's resting her elbow on the desk (line 13). Having moved her arm down to the desk, Alice retracts her hand-raise by simply closing her hand, similarly to Sara's hand closures (lines 6 and 10).

Of the other students who raise their hand after the initial prompt, we cannot say for certain whether the delay in their participation is due to a lack of engagement, uncertainty about expectations for participation, or uncertainty about the prompt itself. Notably, the teacher's prompt here is asking not for a display of understanding, but for what may be considered a display of wealth. Students may be unwilling to participate here because of their reluctance to mark themselves as either poor (or not) or nonconformist, given the design of the teacher's question to prefer an affirmative response ("how many" vs. something like "does anyone").

What of the other students who do not raise their hands at all? It is during the teacher's confirmation (line 7) that Chen establishes mutual gaze with Heather to initiate a side sequence confirming that the teacher is asking whether students have more than "two" televisions. Chen does this both by saying 'two' in overlap with the teacher's repeated prompt in line 8, and by making an iconic gesture for the number two, which coincides with the teacher's repetition of 'two' in line 10. Chen does not raise her hand at any point during the exchange, and given her confirmation with Heather, it is likely that it is because she does not have more than two televisions in her house, rather than an unwillingness to participate in general. Fanny reveals she has no televisions in her apartment at all in response to the teacher's question after this exchange, so her lack of participation in the embodied response is accounted for (note, however, that she maintains gaze toward the teacher throughout, an indication of her engagement). Olivia, who oriented her gaze toward the teacher during his initial prompt in lines 1–2, also does not raise her hand during the exchange, though she mostly maintains gaze toward the teacher throughout. Mahmoud starts with his gaze oriented toward the teacher, and then shifts his gaze toward the students to his left as they raise their hands, shifting back to the teacher following Greg's clarification in line 6. His continued gaze can be argued to represent a demonstration of his engagement with the exchange, even though he does not participate in the "choral" embodied response. Whether his lack of participation in the response is because he does not have that many televisions or because he does not understand what's being asked of him is unknown. This highlights yet another limit to observable behavior as an indication of engagement: when students do not answer, it is unclear without further probing *why* they do not answer.

Heather's body is oriented toward the side of the classroom and slightly toward the back, and thus at a glance, she seems particularly disengaged from the participation framework. She is one of the few students whose gaze is not oriented toward the teacher in the beginning of the excerpt, and she does not orient her gaze to him throughout. Rather, she establishes mutual gaze with Chen (line 7), who confirms with Heather that the teacher is asking about more than "two" televisions. Thus, while Heather does not establish mutual gaze with the teacher, she shows engagement with the discussion by establishing mutual gaze with and smiling at her fellow students, and she shows delayed participation by raising her hand following the teacher's explicit instructions about how to participate in line 5.

As mentioned above, in addition to the question of who is raising their hands and when, of note here is also the *form* students' hand-raises take and *how long* they maintain their gestures. Students raise their hands in different ways, making their participation in the embodied response more or less visible to both the teacher and their classmates. Sara, seated in the back row, raises her hand as a small movement, just opening her right hand, pen still held in her hand; her hand does not rise above chest level in a gesture seemingly designed primarily for the teacher. On the other hand, Karina, also seated in the back row, fully extends her arm initially in a clear display of participation (think of Hermione in Extract 1.1). Heather also extends her arm, but keeps her head resting on her other hand, with her entire body oriented toward the back of the room; her hand-raise is (delayed) embodied participation, and the rest of her body suggests she is less than fully engaged. The students with their hands raised the highest are in the second or third row of desks, and thus their more visible displays of participation may be occasioned by their physical distance from the teacher. In comparison, Zeo and Alice, sitting in the first row, only raise their hands from the elbow. These differential forms of hand-raising seem closely related to Sahlström's claim that the students exist as part of a collective "Student" interacting in dialogue with the teacher. The teacher's expectations for participation at this moment require that a critical mass of students join in the embodied display before he moves on. His sanction of their non-participation and his reformulations and repetitions show him in pursuit of a different kind of participation, in this case, *more* participation.

In the first two cases above, students are expected to self-select as next speaker (or in the case of Extract 7.2, to raise their hand to participate in the poll), and while the teachers pursue responses, they do not hold any one particular student responsible for doing so. In the next excerpt, however, we will see students who are nominated as next speaker decline the turn by nominating a different next speaker, a kind of active unwillingness to participate. These other-nominations can take verbal or embodied forms and are not necessarily related to the nominator's own unwillingness to participate. Rather, they show students carefully monitoring both the teacher's management of the unfolding interaction, as well as their peers' engagement and availability for participation.

In Extract 7.3, from the Reading Data, the teacher was leading the class through a checking episode with a "round robin" participation structure (Mortensen and Hazel 2011), and he had nominated Greg to answer number seventeen, but Greg had declined because he had not completed that question, and another student volunteered instead. The teacher then nominates Isabelle, seated beside Greg, to read the answer for the next item, number eighteen; he is following the row of students, nominating each one in turn to complete an answer.

Extract 7.3 You're dying to do number eighteen

```
1    TEA   nu:mber eighteen. Isabelle?
2          *#(0.4)
           *Gre gaze to T-->
           #fig. 7.26
```

```
3    ISA   I- *#(0.6)
              *point to Gre
              #fig. 7.27
```

Extract 7.3 You're dying to do number eighteen (continued)

```
4    TEA   you wanna do number eighteen?
5          you're dying to do number eighteen,
6    GRE   I mean [(I will,)]
7    TEA          [it's yours.]
```

A brief pause follows the teacher's nomination, during which Greg orients toward the teacher. Isabelle starts to speak in line 3, but almost immediately cuts herself off, and instead points to Greg. The teacher acquiesces to this change after confirming that Greg does want to answer that question. Because the teacher generally moves laterally through the classroom during checking episodes, Isabelle could predict that she would be next. However, she may have been monitoring the preceding interaction, i.e., Greg's inability to answer the previous number despite his desire to participate, and upon seeing Greg's gaze orientation toward the teacher here, interpreted it as a bid for a turn. She is able to nominate Greg with minimal action, barely speaking and instead pointing to him in response to the teacher's nomination of her in line 1. Isabelle's monitoring of the interaction, whether of Greg's ability to answer or his desire to do so, shows her engagement with the episode.

In another example from the ESL Data, the class had just watched a short video about disaster relief in Myanmar following Cyclone Nargis. The teacher had directed students to talk briefly to clarify what they saw and heard, and to ask questions of each other about anything they did not understand (Rodrigo and Yoro were partners for this activity). The teacher brings the class back together in line 1.

Extract 7.4 Something you heard

```
1    TEA   okay. (1.4) so, um, (2.0) what do you guys
2          remember from the video. >something
3          you heard or something you watched.<
4          (2.0)#       (1.2)#             (0.4)# (0.2)#
                  #fig. 7.28   #fig. 7.29        #fig. 7.30 #fig. 7.31
```

```
5          {(1.2)# - ((laughter from T and Ss))}
                  #fig. 7.32
```

Extract 7.4 Something you heard (continued)

```
6          (2.4)#
           #fig. 7.33
```

```
7          *(2.4)
           *Rod pushes his seat back, smiles, head down
8    ROD   that uh there is a- a man? who,
9          he used to be a chef? or a cook,
```

Following the teacher's prompt in line 1, Rodrigo turns his gaze toward Yoro after 2.0 seconds of silence (Figure 7.28). This could be seen as an implicit nomination or orientation to Yoro as next speaker, but instead, Yoro then points to Rodrigo, nominating him to take a turn (Figure 7.29). This deictic gesture is much more clearly a nomination; Yoro moves her hand toward Rodrigo, with her thumb pointing toward him. While this is a gesture made low in front of the body (and thus not particularly visible), she maintains gaze orientation toward the teacher, the participant with the most say about who the next speaker will be, and thus Yoro's point toward Rodrigo can most clearly be seen as communication *with the teacher* about her suggestion that Rodrigo speak. Immediately after Yoro's retraction of her point, Rodrigo and Yoro establish mutual gaze as Rodrigo points back to Yoro (Figure 7.30). Notably, his nomination might be read as more of an invitation to speak rather than a nomination exactly. He extends his right hand, palm up, toward Yoro, in a "go ahead" gesture, while establishing mutual gaze. Just as Rodrigo's gesture reaches its apex, Yoro begins to point back to Rodrigo, her gesture moving farther toward Rodrigo than before (Figure 7.31). These mutual other-nominations have sped up, with 1.2 seconds between Rodrigo's gaze movement and Yoro's point, then only 0.4 seconds between her point and his open-palm gesture, and then only 0.2 seconds before Yoro's final point. In fact, the preparation stage of Yoro's second point occurs simultaneously with the retraction of Rodrigo's gesture.

Both students, smiling, orient back to the teacher after this volley of nominations (Figure 7.32), and the teacher and several students audibly laugh at this interactional trouble affecting progressivity. 2.4 seconds later, with both still gazing at the teacher, Yoro reaches out and touches Rodrigo's arm briefly in another clear other-nomination (Figure 7.33), before leaning back and away from Rodrigo, effectively withdrawing from the floor. He pushes his seat back, smiling, and then answers the teacher's prompt from line 1. This negotiation of next speaker, accomplished entirely without verbal turns, shows both students carefully attending to the other, while still orienting to the teacher as the ultimate arbiter. The teacher declines to intervene, and the students resolve the interactional difficulty themselves, with Yoro's increasingly close gestures to Rodrigo pushing him finally to accept her other-nomination. Yoro may be unwilling to participate herself, though I argue that her returning gaze

144   MULTIMODAL PARTICIPATION AND ENGAGEMENT

orientation toward the teacher marks her attention to the interaction and availability for participation. Rodrigo, likewise, seems rather to be offering the floor to his partner rather than actively declining to take a turn himself (e.g., he also returns his gaze to the teacher throughout). Rather, this example shows the embodied negotiations for speakership that can obtain following open-floor prompts from the teacher, as students carefully attend to the availability of other potential incipient speakers.

7.2.2 ENGAGEMENT AT TRANSITIONS

In addition to an unwillingness to participate when the teacher is pursuing a response, we can also see students' (non-)participation and (dis)engagement as delayed or anticipatory at moments of transition. Two examples of delayed engagement are provided here for comparison, showing teachers bringing students together at the beginning of class (Extract 7.5) and after a break (Extract 7.6), followed by an example of anticipatory disengagement (Extract 7.7), as students pack up early before the teacher has officially ended class. The students' delayed engagement and anticipatory disengagement have interactional consequences for the teacher-led interaction which we will explore below.

In the first example from the College Data (Extract 7.5), the professor of an introductory communications course is opening class, and students gradually turn their attention to her as she does so. Their engagement with the interaction is not uniform or immediate, but rather shows a general orientation toward the teacher and the screen. The professor of the communications class is seated at the computer station in the corner of the room, and students are arranged in a U-shape facing the projector screen. Prior to class, students have engaged in a variety of "off-task" actions, including speaking at reduced volume with other students, eating, and engaging with their devices.

Extract 7.5 Alright. So.
```
1    TEA   *#°alright. (0.6) so.°*#
           *Only Eve gaze to Tea
                             *Mia gaze to Tea
           #fig. 7.34         #fig. 7.35
```

```
2          (13.0)*(0.4)*#(0.6)
                *.....*Jam gaze to screen/Tea
                      #fig. 7.36
```

Extract 7.5 Alright. So. (continued)

```
3    TEA    alright so we're *#talking about
                          *Wil/Mia gaze to Tea;Cha gaze to device
                          #fig. 7.37
```

```
4           *#organizational culture here.*#
            *Sop->Tea/Emm->bag/Ame->phone  *Ame gaze to Tea
            #fig. 7.38 fig. 7.39              #fig. 7.40
```

```
5           and, (.) he- uh (>°I don't want
6           to mess with that°<) so:, this?*# idea
                                  *Cha starts to put away device
                                  #fig. 7.41
```

```
7           of studying an organization?*#
                              *Cha gaze to Tea
                              #fig. 7.42
```

As the teacher begins speaking, only Evelyn has her gaze oriented toward the teacher, and by the end of line 1, only one additional student has oriented toward her. The teacher's delivery of the transitional markers 'alright.' and 'so.' in line 1 are delivered at lower volume, and with a large pause between them. Unfortunately, the teacher was not captured on video so her gaze orientation is unknown to the researcher, but given what we can see of the technology, it seems the teacher is very much engaged with setting up the PowerPoint lecture for the day, and with turning on the equipment. This first line might thus be seen as similar to the "self-talk" Hall and Smotrova (2013) discuss, where teachers effectively talk to themselves out loud during technical difficulties, though in this case, this is at the moment class begins, rather than in the middle, so it does not require a suspension of participation frameworks. Rather, the teacher has not yet established the participation framework, and so this is a transitional moment of self-talk. While the lower volume matches Hall and Smotrova's findings, each of the teacher's utterances here is also delivered with falling intonation, suggesting that they are not projecting further immediate talk, but are holding the floor for the teacher. The teacher's turn in line 1 acts as a preface, projecting the start of class without actually launching it; as such, it prepares the students for the opening.

When the projector turns on after 13 seconds of silence (line 2), James shifts his gaze toward the screen, and less than 1 second later, the teacher restarts again with 'alright so', this time with no pauses and continuing on to introduce the topic for the day (lines 3–6). As she does so, we see several shifts in participation and engagement around the classroom. Two students (Will and Mia) orient toward her as she continues, while Charlotte shifts her gaze to her device (line 3). Sophia shifts her gaze toward the teacher in line 4, while Emma focuses more intently on her popcorn bag and Amelia looks first toward her phone and then toward the teacher. By the end of line 7, six of the visible students have oriented toward the teacher in a gradual engagement with the interaction and away from their various other engagements prior to the start of class. Ten seconds from the teacher's relaunch (line 3), most of the visible students have shifted their orientation toward the teacher in a display of engagement with the interaction. The teacher's first opening 'alright.so.' is not designed as a true opening; it is followed by silence as the teacher continues with the technology setup. However, this preface, along with the switching on of the projector, prepares students for the reopening in line 3. Most students orient to the teacher by the end of her opening statement in line 4, and the last student joins them as the teacher moves on with the topic of the day in line 7.

In the second example (Extract 7.6), also from the College Data, the professor of an introductory philosophy course is restarting class after a break (this particular section meets only one day per week for several hours). In this second case, students' engagement with the whole-class interaction is markedly delayed, with several students engaged with their phones almost 6 minutes after the teacher has restarted class. In this case of marked delay in engagement at transition, the teacher is attempting to bring the students back to a whole-class participation structure following a break, during which students had engaged in similar "off-task" actions as those described in Extract 7.5. In this case, however, several students delay engaging with the whole-class interaction, instead engaging with their devices.

Extract 7.6 I think we should probably get started

```
1    TEA    *#alright guys.
            *Mel/Jac gaze to Mel phone
            *Kat/All/Joh gaze to personal devices
            #fig. 7.43
```

```
2           I ↑think we should probly get started.*#
                                        *Mel/Jac gaze to Tea
                                        *Kat/All/Joh gaze to
                                        phones
                                        #fig. 7.44 fig. 7.45
```

```
3           (3.6)
4    TEA    okay.*#
                    *Jac gaze to T
                    *Ale/Kat/All/Joh gaze to phone
                    #fig. 7.46
```

```
5           (8.0)
6    TEA    I think we should probly get
7           started=so:? this is the week
8           twelve schedule? and I have,
9           >if you look at C,< >that's the
10          name of the text.< okay?
11          (1.2)
12   TEA    and we- *#we'll look at that text
                    *Jac/All/Joh gaze to phone
                    *Ale/Kat gaze up
                    #fig. 7.47
```

Extract 7.6 I think we should probably get started (continued)

```
13        together. we'll look at it right
14        now together. okay? (.) >and
15        ↑hopefully have a discussion
16        about it.*# I think we'll have time
                  *Jac/Ale/Kat/All/Joh gaze to phones
                  #fig. 7.48
```

```
17        to do that.< we have an hour: and
18        ten minutes? I think? so we
19        should be able to (.) read it?
20        (0.6) an:d (0.8) um, discuss it.
21        okay? um, (2.0) ↑so:, (5.0) how bout we,
22        (2.0) I should introduce it in
23        some way. oh before I do that,
24        (1.8) I found the- >if you don't
25        have your book,< if you have your
26        textbook, it's on pa:ge,*# (.) what
                  *Jac gaze to T, holding phone
                  *Ale/Kat/Joh gaze to phone
                  *All gaze to T, putting down phone
                  #fig. 7.49
```

```
27        did I- what did it say there,
28   S    one-oh-seven to one-ten I think?
29   TEA  it's one-oh-seven to one-ten?*#
                  *Kat puts phone down, gaze to T
                  *All picks up phone, gaze to T
                  #fig. 7.50
```

Extract 7.6 I think we should probably get started (continued)

```
30        okay? thanks. if you don't, have
31        your book, apparently*# >you can
                        *Ale gaze to T
                        *Kat gaze to book
                        *Jac/Dan/All gaze to phones
                        #fig. 7.51
```

```
32        find a P-D-F of it online.< okay? (1.8) alright,
33        (5.2)
34   S?   ↑oh. 'is unwanted pregnancy a medical disorder'?
35   TEA  yes. (0.4) okay?
36        (6.8) ((S asks a question quietly))
37   TEA  mm-hmm? okay. good. um:, okay. so
38        why don't I introduce this a little
39        bit? (2.6) um, >but before I do
40        that, here are some words.< (1.0) *#that
                                   *Jac/Kat/All gaze to T
                                   *Joh gaze to phone
                                   #fig. 7.52
```

```
41        you might- that you might need
42        defined?* (1.2) menta- a medical
              *All gaze to phone
43        disorder is a physical or mental
44        condition that is not normal or
45        healthy. (0.4) okay?
```

As the teacher first brings the class back together after break in line 1, several students are oriented toward their devices, including Melanie, Jack, Kate, Allison, and John, and very few students are oriented toward the teacher. As the teacher continues with his second transition-oriented TCU in line 2, Melanie and Jack orient toward him, though Kate, Allison, and John continue with their gazes fixed on their phones. After several long gaps (lines 3, 5) and another transitional 'okay' (line 4), the teacher restarts with a repeat of his turn in line 2, this time continuing into managerial mode talk about the upcoming activity. The interactional features of managerial mode include extended teacher turns, use of transitional markers, and confirmation checks (Walsh 2006, 2011). This managerial talk continues through line 37 (a total of 1 minute and 45 seconds), and then the teacher transitions into materials mode talk for 1 minute and 50 seconds, preparing students for terms they will encounter in the text they are about to read. In contrast to Extract 7.5 above, which shows a gradual, but fairly quick, transition from disengagement to engagement for most students, here we see several students persisting in engaging with their devices, though in a variety of ways.

Notably, John, seated in the back row behind Allison, never engages with the interaction in an observable way, instead orienting to his phone throughout the excerpt, with the phone held at varying heights, making his disengagement more or less visible to the teacher and his fellow students. Allison likewise engages with her phone almost exclusively, with a notable exception in line 26 when she orients to the teacher and puts her phone down on the table. This attention to the teacher is short-lived, as she picks her phone back up again in line 29 and turns her gaze to the phone in line 31. She orients toward the teacher briefly again in lines 40–42 (just after he moves into materials mode talk), and again briefly in the part of the extract not shown here, but then remains focused on her phone for the remainder of the extract, scrolling and tapping with her fingers, i.e., she is not looking at the reading. Her engagement with the interaction is minimal, and she does not observably orient to *appearing to be engaged* either, holding her phone up at chest level at several points during the teacher's extended turn. Her persistent engagement with her phone affects the engagement of nearby students too, with her neighbor gazing at her phone as well several times.

Some students do engage with the whole-class interaction, but their engagement fades in and out as they re-engage with their devices. Jack, who had been oriented toward his neighbor's phone at the start of the excerpt, turns his gaze to the teacher at the end of line 2 through the next several moments of managerial mode talk. As the teacher transitions to materials mode in line 12, however, he brings out his own phone and orients toward it for most of the rest of the excerpt, looking up several times and even putting his phone down on top of his book, but never completely disengaging from it. While it is possible he is looking at the reading on his phone, he also has a physical copy of the book with him, suggesting that this is not the case. Kate likewise starts the excerpt engaged with her phone, and despite looking up briefly in line 12, doesn't engage with the interaction until line 29, when she puts her phone away and turns her gaze to the teacher. She subsequently brings out her book and shifts her gaze between the book and the teacher for the remainder of the excerpt. Alex, who has a laptop open in front of him, is holding his phone in front of the laptop until he looks up briefly in line 12, and then orients his gaze toward the teacher in a more sustained way in line 31.

This excerpt shows an extended delay in engagement on the part of a majority of students and highlights the impact electronic devices can have on student engagement. Allison and John seem *primarily* engaged with their devices, rather than with the ongoing interaction, while other students appear to shift their engagement between the teacher and their devices. This transition, coming after a break in the middle of a long class period, may be more difficult for students than transitioning into the start of class, when their attention and energy is potentially at its apex. As part of his managerial talk during the transition, the teacher advises students that the textbook may be freely available online if they do not have their text with them, but I note that there is no shift in orientation to phones following this news, suggesting that the students who have been engaging with their devices have been doing so for off-task purposes. This claim is also supported by the nature of the students' engagement with their devices, which is suggestive of texting and/or using social media, i.e., extended typing and scrolling. The on-record nature of students' use of their devices, with those devices often held up from the table, makes their non-participation in and disengagement from the classroom interaction publicly available. The teachers in Extracts 7.4 and 7.5 do not orient to students' engagement with their devices in any observable way throughout the recording, and without evidence that they do so on other occasions, these would not be instances of "letting it pass." Rather, the students' engagement with their devices does not seem to be an accountable action in this classroom, though their lack of engagement is oriented to by the teachers. The design of the teachers' turns, both with restarted openings, seems to show the teachers' orientation to the lack of engagement from the students as they pursue recipiency from the members of the class.

While these first two examples show the wave of students' delayed engagement at transition, a similar phenomenon is seen to happen in reverse, as students disengage from the interaction toward the end of class, packing up their things and beginning to engage with their electronic devices before class has been officially ended by the teacher. The extended delay in engagement in Extract 7.6 might be accounted for by the fact that after the opening (lines 1–7), the teacher continues for several turns with managerial mode talk, showing the students the course schedule, previewing their activity, and discussing other logistical talk like the availability of the reading. That is, because the teacher does not launch into the content of the class after the opening, some students do not orient to the need to attend closely to his talk. A similar issue seems to occur in this next extract from an undergraduate forensic linguistics class in the College Data, where teacher and students have been discussing the language-related difficulties faced by asylum seekers during government interviews. The teacher has just explained what "euphemism" means, and she transitions into telling the students a related joke which may not seem immediately relevant to their discussion. This occurs toward the end of the class period, and several students begin packing up before the teacher's joke is recognizably finished, a fact she orients to explicitly.

Extract 7.7 It's fast

```
1    TEA   it's like that whole ↑joke
2          about the person that died?
3          did you ever hear this joke?
4    S?    what?
5    TEA   right? so there's a- right
```

Extract 7.7 It's fast (continued)

```
6          so like you go and you-
7          >do we have time?< so you go
8          and you're watching your
9          friend's house. you're
10         watching your friend's house*
                                    *Ele closes notebook-->
11         and *#their cat while they're
              *Luc gaze to clock
              #fig. 7.53
```

```
12         away on vacation.*# right? and
                 *Luc gaze back to Tea
                 #fig. 7.54
```

```
13         uh, it's *#fast. Um and uh,
                 *Tea mutual gaze with Luc, points to clock
                 #fig. 7.55
```

```
14         and so,*# you're- you're- you're
                 *Jan closes handout
                 #fig. 7.56
```

```
15         watching their house, right?
16         and uh-*# they're gone like (.)
```

Extract 7.7 It's fast (continued)

              *Meg closes notebook
              #fig. 7.57

17   a couple days, right? um,*# and
              *Meg packs up, Jes/Jan close papers
              #fig. 7.58 fig. 7.59

18   uh, their, her- their parents
19   live in a like a house next
20   door, right?*# and the person
            *Meg gets bag from floor
            #fig. 7.60

21   calls and they say "hey, so
22   how's everything up at my
23   <u>house</u>,"*# say "well your house
            *Jan closes notebook, Meg packs up
            #fig. 7.61 fig. 7.62

24   looks great, everything's fine,
25   but you know, I'm sorry, but
26   your mom died."

Extract 7.7 It's fast (continued)

```
27   S     what?
28   TEA   and they're like "oh my-" yeah,
29         they're like "what?" like, you*#
                              *Meg packs up, Jes closes
                              papers
                              #fig. 7.63
```

```
30         can't just sa::y?
31   S     (    )
32   TEA   you can't just sa:y, you know,
33         uh:,*# that my mom died? you
              *Cha brings back up, begins to pack up
              #fig. 7.64
```

```
34         gotta like warm me up. you
35         gotta like, you know you gotta
36         say like "your mom's, you know,
37         not feelin so good." and then
38         the next time I call, you say
39         "you know, your mom's, you
40         know, uh: (.) you know,"
41   S     (    )
42   TEA   "yeah, she's not eating so much."
43         right? and then you finally say,
44         "you know your mom's on the roof."
45         *#right? and then all of a sudden
              *Ele closes notebook, Meg/Jes/Cha packed up, Cha using phone
              #fig. 7.65 fig. 7.66
```

Extract 7.7 It's fast (continued)

```
46        you say she passed away. right?
47        so then, you know, so there-
48        they really yell at ya,*# wait,
                    *Ele/Lau packing, Meg/Jes/Cha packed,
                    Cha on phone
                    #fig. 7.67 fig. 7.68
```

```
49        then, WAIT, I'm not done with
50        my joke. THEN,
51   Ss   ((laughter))
52   TEA  you call back like two weeks
53        later, and you're like "alright,
54        now how's the house?" *#and
                    *Ele/Cha on phones
                    #fig. 7.69
```

```
55        they're like "well, your cat's
56        on the roof."
```

The teacher herself orients to the time constraints of class in line 7, quickly asking 'do we have time?' as she checks the clock before launching into her joke. As the teacher goes through the joke, students begin visibly orienting to the fact that they are reaching the end of the class period. In line 10, Eleanor starts to close her notebook, and in line 11, Lucas turns his body 180 degrees to look at the clock mounted on the rear wall of the classroom. The teacher orients to this movement with an account for why she is continuing to hold class, establishing mutual gaze with Lucas as she points to the clock and notes that 'it's fast' in line 13 before shifting back to her joke. Despite this explicit reference to the time, several other students also start packing up their things, with Janice closing the handout in line 14, and Megan closing her notebook in line 16 and continuing to pack up in line 17. Charlie, seated near her, joins her in this, and Janice puts away her papers as well. Janice and Megan continue packing up over the next several lines, and Jessica joins in (line 29). In line 45, Eleanor closes her notebook, and Megan, Jessica, and Charlie are completely packed up. Charlie takes her phone out and holds it at chest level, her packed bag on her lap. Eleanor starts packing up in line 48 and begins using her phone in line 54 (Charlie has continued using her phone during this time).

Hellermann and Cole describe disengagement from face-to-face interactions as including resources such as "postural alignment ... and re-engaging with one's personal belongings" (2009: 190). We thus see a mirror image of Extracts 7.5 and 7.6 here as students slowly, and in a growing wave, disengage from the classroom interaction. Where before we saw students slowly orienting their bodies toward a whole-class participation framework, here their observable actions of packing up their things, and in some cases engaging directly with their devices in on-record ways, makes their disengagement publicly available to both the teacher and their fellow students. The teacher orients to this wave of embodied disengagement in lines 48–50, explicitly formulating the situation to make it clear that class is not yet over; however, the teacher is not ultimately able to make the connection between her joke and the pedagogical topic, and instead orients to the students' disengagement by closing class with managerial mode talk about upcoming deadlines. Goodwin and Goodwin note that "speakers must have systematic methods of determining whether or not someone is positioned as a hearer to their talk" (2004: 229), and point to the many embodied displays of attention employed by silent listeners for evidence of this. The examples in this section show how students' embodied waves of delayed engagement and disengagement may affect the unfolding of the teacher's turn.

7.2.3 POSTURAL DISENGAGEMENT

As seen above, students often disengage in embodied ways that make their disengagement from the interaction visible to other participants, including the teacher. As with all the kinds of (non-)participation and (dis)engagement discussed thus far in this book, these embodied actions are made meaningful in the particular context in which they occur, and some occur at more "appropriate" times for disengaging than others. In this first example from the ESL Data, one student puts her head down on her arm as the teacher is distributing materials and transitioning between activities. The transitional nature of this moment may allow students more latitude in stepping away from their performance of doing-being-a-student, as we see below.

Extract 7.8 Head down
```
1    TEA    *#like Spanish and French. you guys
            *Cla gaze to Tea, head resting on hand
            #fig. 7.70
```

Extract 7.8 Head down (continued)

```
2         usually do run-on. an' the Asian
3         like Korean Japanese you guys
4         do fragments. (1.0) $I don't' know
5         why.$ maybe it's just different
6         thinking.
7         (3.0)
8    TEA  *#native language. um okay so be on
          *Cla head on arm
          #fig. 7.71
```

```
9         the lookout for that, watch out for
10        that when you write tomorrow, (1.0)
11        okay the last thing we're going to
12        do today is a speaking exercise.
13        (1.5)
14   TEA  we're going to practice using gerunds
15        and infinitives? .HHH plus subjunctives.
16        (.5)
17   TEA  which I think most people forgot.
18        (1.0)
19   TEA  because HEHEHE $we didn't- we didn't
20        um get that subjunctive sentence
21        *#correct during um grammar auction.
          *Cla rests head on arm
          #fig. 7.72
```

```
22        I was very surprised.
23        (1.0)
24   TEA  okay so we'll practice that.*#
                              *Tea stops in front of Cla
                              #fig. 7.73
```

Extract 7.8 Head down (continued)

```
25         (1.8)*#(4.2)
              *Cla begins to sit up
              #fig. 7.74
```

```
26    TEA  *#okay?
              *Cla is upright
              #fig. 7.75
```

This sequence comes at a transition between activities, another example of Walsh's (2006, 2011) managerial mode. The teacher is summarizing her advice for the students about their upcoming exam the next day, and simultaneously distributing materials for the next activity they will do in class. As the extract starts, Clara has her gaze oriented toward the teacher, her head resting on her hand. As the teacher goes on, Clara moves to rest her head more completely on her arm, as seen in line 8 (Figure 7.71). The teacher begins distributing the materials, walking from one side of the classroom to the other, and Clara puts her head completely down on her arm (line 21, Figure 7.72). She maintains this posture until the teacher stops in front of her, and after 1.8 seconds of silence, she slowly returns to an upright posture.

Clara's postural moves here do not preclude her from listening to the teacher's instructions, but they do observably demonstrate a disengaged stance to the teacher and other students. In certain participation structures (e.g., individual writing, listening), this might be less accountable than in managerial mode, a whole-class participation structure with the teacher giving instructions and distributing materials. By the same token, this is a mode "at the seams" (Mehan 1979), and the expectations for students' participation may simply be that they will sit and wait as the teacher reveals what to do next. Clara's posture here does not demonstrate her engagement in the interaction, but it does not impede progressivity or her ability to monitor the interaction. There are many examples throughout all three corpora of students leaning back or resting their head on hands/arms/desks/walls, all of which can be perceived by teachers (or analysts) as disengaged postures. On the more extreme end of such postural choices projecting disengagement, there are examples of students appearing to sleep in both the Reading Data and the College Data. In the image in

Figure 7.76   Displayed disengagement

Figure 7.76 from a first-year undergraduate philosophy course (the same class seen in Extract 7.6), as the teacher prepared to show a video, Andy made a pillow out of a piece of clothing and put it under her head as she rested on the table behind her seat. Maintaining this posture with eyes closed for almost 5 minutes of the video, this student is projecting complete disengagement from the interaction. While she might be listening despite her posture and closed eyes, the fact remains that she is assuming a prototypical posture for sleeping. She is thus *displaying* disengagement, whatever may be going on cognitively.

The element of posture is an interesting one in that there are certainly postures that seem more clearly to project participation and engagement (e.g., sitting up straight, hands on the desk or materials, eye gaze to the current speaker and/or materials), though whether a student *is* engaged while maintaining such a posture is not immediately obvious. We saw in Extract 6.1 that two students, Isabelle and Karina, seem by their postures not to be observably "doing listening," but they could in fact be more engaged in the read aloud than other students who are projecting "doing listening," sitting upright, holding their books, and with eye gaze oriented toward the book or the teacher. Posture and gaze can be used to do "studenting," i.e., looking like one is doing an appropriate student-related action, or they can be used to project disengagement and unwillingness to participate. It is only by examining students' precisely-timed actions, including verbal contributions and shifts in gaze or posture, that we can begin to speculate about whether any given student is actually *engaged* and closely monitoring the interaction. However, in many cases, we are unable to speculate in this way, and students with "engaged" postures may not be involved in the interaction in any way, while those with "disengaged" postures may be attending to it quite carefully.

7.3 SELF-PRESENTATION AS (DIS)ENGAGEMENT

While some object orientation, like writing in a notebook or gaze toward the blackboard, might represent disengagement when occurring at inapt moments, in those cases, students might at least be said to be performing category-bound actions of "student," whether arranging papers in a binder (Alice in Extract 6.1), writing in a notebook (Olivia in Extract 6.1), or looking at the board and taking notes (Brad in Extract 6.4). In other cases, students' orientation toward objects and/or materials can seem to represent a marked disengagement, even when analysis of the students' multimodal actions reveals their engagement.

Teachers' and students' orientation to technology use as problematic (or not), will be seen in several examples below that show self-presentation with electronic devices (i.e., wearing earbuds) as examples of how what Goffman (1959) calls the "personal front," e.g., appearance (including clothing) and manner (multimodal resources), can communicate students' (dis)engagement. Instances where students are observably wearing headphones in class are interesting for several reasons. First, wearing headphones does not necessarily mean that one is listening to anything else. Second, even if one is listening to something else, in some cases, it is entirely possible that one is *also engaging* with the class in some meaningful way, as we will see particularly in Extracts 7.9 and 7.10. Teachers can choose to explicitly sanction such behavior, whether verbally or in embodied ways, or let it pass, but other teachers seem not to orient to such self-presentation as disengagement. One of the complex tasks for students when they enter a new classroom with a new teacher is deciphering the unspoken expectations for classroom interaction. What does doing-being-a-student look like for *that* class, with *that* teacher?

In Extract 7.9, from the Reading Data, the class was reviewing a vocabulary exercise, and they had been talking about what "innuendo" means when the teacher orients toward Robert, seeming to have just noticed that he is wearing earbuds. Robert participated appropriately at the beginning of this checking episode, reading the first item in the exercise aloud. Robert is not visible for parts of the recording, so it is not clear at what point he put the earbuds into his ears (he was visibly *not* wearing them earlier in the class), but by all accounts, the presence of his earbuds does not seem to have affected his ability to participate.

Extract 7.9 Take those things out of your ears
```
1     TEA   *that's a good thing perhaps.*
            *Tea is walking towards Rob--*
2     TEA   *#°take those (.) things out of your*
            *Tea stands in front of Rob--------*
            *Zeo/Mah/Ali/Oli/Sar/Che gaze to Tea and Rob
            #fig. 7.77
```

```
3           *ears please.°
            *Tea walks back towards center-->
4           (1.8)
5     TEA   Alright. Let's go on,
```

As the teacher finishes his turn directed toward another student in line 1, he moves toward Robert, and then while standing in front of him, says at low volume 'take those (.) things out of your ears please' (lines 2–3). He begins moving away from Robert before he finishes this turn, and following 1.8 seconds of silence, he transitions to the next item. While there is no sign that Robert's participation and engagement have suffered because of his headphones, the teacher orients to their visible presence as a problem worth disrupting the progressivity of the checking episode. While he delivers his reproach (Margutti and Piirainen-Marsh 2011) at low volume, his movement toward Robert in the classroom creates a spotlight of sorts, with the attention of most other students drawn toward this sanction (Figure. 7.77).

Fifteen minutes earlier in this class session, the teacher had small conferences with individual students to go over their homework from the prior day, and Robert had his conference with the teacher while holding his earbuds, so he likely put them in shortly after this when he went back to his desk to complete the vocabulary exercise. Interestingly, the presence of his earbuds does not seem to have impeded Robert's ability to participate in other, more acceptable ways in this classroom. Robert is also seen wearing his earbuds during Extracts 4.1 and 5.8 (Utopia), and in those instances he also demonstrates his engagement with the interaction through his precisely-timed writing activity. Likewise, here, as noted above, Robert answered the first item of the checking episode, demonstrating his participation and engagement with the interaction. However, wearing earbuds at this juncture of class seems to the teacher to be an unacceptable display of disengagement from the interaction. This reproach includes explicit reference to the offence, but as Margutti and Piirainen-Marsh note, such reproaches may also be done "through more implicit means" (2011: 305), as we will see in a similar instance below, this time with an embodied sanction.

In Extract 7.8, from the Reading Data, Robert comes to class wearing his earbuds, and keeps them in as students silently work on vocabulary exercises, as is normal routine for this class. In Figure 7.78, we see Robert first sitting down, his earbuds clearly visible in his ears. In Figure 7.79, he continues to participate in expected and appropriate ways despite his earbuds, turning to the chapter review in the workbook as instructed by the teacher (i.e., he is engaging multimodally).

Figure 7.78   Robert wearing earbuds as he arrives

Figure 7.79   Robert turning to the chapter review in his workbook, earbuds visible

As we turn to the extract, we can see that the teacher stops his ongoing action (taking attendance) to address the fact that Robert has his earbuds in during this silent activity.

162   MULTIMODAL PARTICIPATION AND ENGAGEMENT

Extract 7.10 Off, please

```
1          *(2.4)
           *Tea gaze to Rob
2    TEA   .hh HH. °Robert?°
3          (0.4)
4    TEA   >Robert.<
5          (0.6)*#
                *Tea slams pencil down & withdraws gaze
6          (0.6)*(3.8)
                *Tea walks towards Rob
7    TEA   *#Rob,
           *Tea stands in front of Rob
           #fig. 7.80
```

```
8          (0.4)*#(0.2) *#(0.2)
                *Tea claps twice in front of Rob's face
                        *Rob looks up at second clap
                #fig. 7.81 #fig. 7.82
```

```
9          *#(0.4)*(0.8)
           *#Tea mimes taking out earbuds 3X, holds gesture-->
                *Rob takes out earbuds
           #fig. 7.83
```

Extract 7.10 Off, please (continued)
```
10   TEA   off, (0.6) please.*
                        -->*
```

In line 1, the teacher turns his gaze away from his papers toward Robert, seated a few feet to his right. He inhales and exhales audibly and then calls Robert's name softly in line 2. After 0.4 seconds, he pursues a response, saying his name again, this time louder and more quickly. After 0.6 seconds, the teacher withdraws his gaze from Robert and simultaneously slams his pencil on to the desk (line 5). He then walks toward Robert, stopping right in front of him and again uttering his name, this time a shortened nickname 'Rob' (line 7). Margutti and Piirainen-Marsh (2011) note that gaze and address forms may be used in order to orient to some untoward behavior from a student; here, the teacher's gaze and use of different varieties of Robert's name can be seen to be doing reproach. After a continued lack of response from Robert, the teacher claps twice near his face, and Robert looks up at the second clap (line 8). The teacher then mimes removing earbuds three times (line 9), and Robert quickly begins to remove his earbuds. The teacher then follows his embodied request with a verbal one, saying 'off, (0.6) please' in line 10, holding his iconic gesture until the completion of the turn.

Again, as was the case in Extract 7.9, Robert is participating in ways that are expected and appropriate, completing the vocabulary exercise. The issue here seems to be the *appearance* of disengagement, rather than any evidence of disengagement per se. The teacher's orientation to Robert's wearing earbuds may also be related to Hall's (1998) observation that teachers' differential perceptions of students as "good" or "bad" students affects the kinds of interactional opportunities they create for those students. Robert is a student whom the teacher had kicked out for sleeping, and who often did not put on a convincing performance of doing-being-a-student. It is an empirical question whether a "good" student whose "personal front" (Goffman 1959) suggested disengagement would be sanctioned in this same way, and I return to this question in Chapter 8.

7.3.1 DIFFERENT INTERPRETATIONS OF PERSONAL FRONT

Teachers' orientation to the use of technology is highly idiosyncratic, and so students' use of personal devices is often not addressed in the interaction, showing that for these teachers, this self-presentation alone is unproblematic. Teachers' decisions to let such technology use pass may also be an example of what Goffman calls a "protective practice" (1959: 13), whereby one participant employs strategies to avoid orienting toward a problematic role or situation orientation by another participant. However, deciding a priori what is problematic ignores the fact that without evidence to the contrary, for these teachers, this kind of self-presentation is not indexical of disengagement. Figures 7.84–7.86, from the CRT 3 and COM classrooms in the College Data, show students who wear both earbuds for the duration of class time, a fact that is never addressed during class by their teachers.

Figure 7.84 shows a student wearing earbuds and also engaging with her phone.

Figure 7.84
CRT 3 student wearing earbuds and using phone

Figure 7.85
COM student wearing earbuds

Figure 7.86
COM student wearing earbuds and using phone

While this student holds her phone for the duration of the class and can often be seen doing "off-task" things (e.g., looking at Facebook, shopping on Amazon), she also quite often participates verbally in class. Likewise, Figure 7.85 shows a student with earbuds in, but gaze oriented to the current speaker, i.e., she is possibly engaged in "parallel activities" (Koole 2007) in addition to monitoring the primary activity of the teacher. Figure 7.86 shows the same student with earbuds, oriented toward her phone, while the teacher speaks in the background. This student also participates verbally in class despite her occasional orientation toward her device and the continued presence of her earbuds.

These students seem to be setting the terms of their availability to participate, engaging with and disengaging from the interaction in a constant flow. As Koole (2007) shows, students' engagement with parallel activities does not preclude their active participation in the classroom interaction in appropriate ways. The presence of electronic devices does not necessarily indicate disengagement from the interaction, though it can be interpreted that way by the teacher or other students. While some teachers often have strict regulations on when and how students may use devices (or not), others set no restrictions, allowing students to set the terms of their own engagement. Whether one of these approaches has more pedagogical merit is an empirical question open for investigation.

7.4 SUMMARY

This chapter shows a full range of possibilities, from the engaged participation of Sara and Zeo in Extract 7.2 (and potentially Robert in Extracts 7.9 and 7.10) to the disengaged non-participation of students on their phones in Extract 7.6 and those packing up their things in Extract 7.7. I reproduce the matrix here again to summarize the findings of this chapter, examining how students' actions are indexical of their participation and engagement.

This chapter brings together many of the phenomena we have seen in earlier chapters, from students' verbal contributions and studenting (Chapter 4), waves of embodied (non-)participation and (dis)engagement (Chapter 5), and multimodal listening (Chapter 6). This chapter has extended our consideration of participation

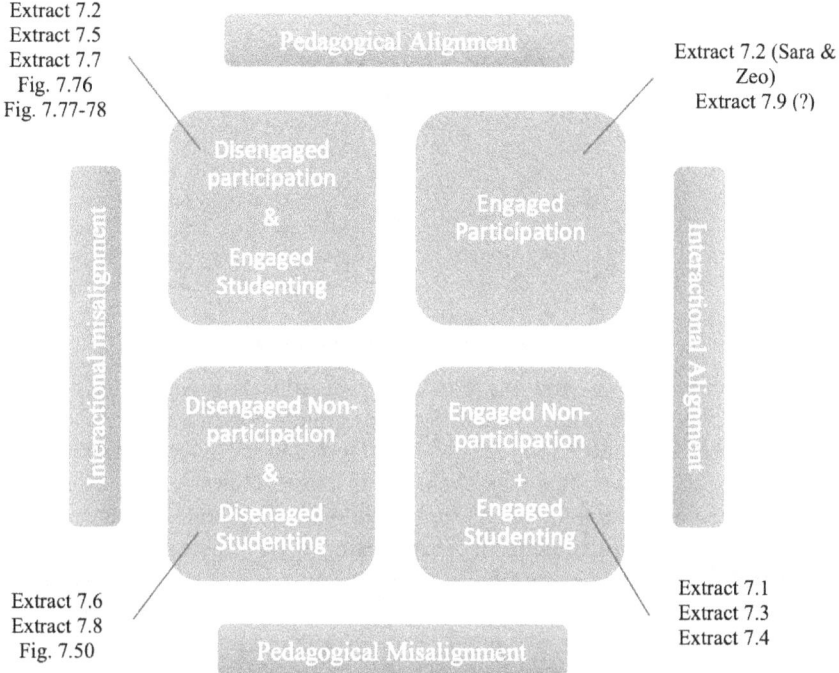

Figure 7.87   Reconceptualizing "participation" and "engagement"

and engagement to focus more particularly on instances where students display their non-participation and disengagement in public ways. It should be noted that I have selected cases where such non-participation and disengagement are visible, but again, I remind the reader that in most cases, observable behavior does not provide enough evidence for us to say one way or the other. The complexity of doing-being-a-student in a classroom should, by this stage in the book, be overwhelmingly apparent, and this chapter has placed a spotlight on non-participation and disengagement. While many students are invested in what I might call "the presentation of self as student," the energy required to produce that performance is not easily sustained over long periods of time, and so even students wishing to be "good" students have peaks and valleys in their engagement over the course of a class. In addition, there are some students who seem uninterested in this performance. In the final chapter, I offer some reflections for what this means for students and teachers in instructed-learning settings.

8

CONCLUSION

8.1 INTRODUCTION

Teachers, administrators, and the entire teacher–education industrial complex, including teacher preparation, certification, and evaluation (cf. Stanford Center for Assessment, Learning and Equity 2016), are interested in the question of how teachers can engage their students and get them to participate. However, the key concepts there, *participation* and *engagement*, are rarely defined. What is being measured when a teacher grades a student on "participation"? What does it look like when students are "engaged"? By specifying these concepts in interactional terms, this volume has expanded our conception of what participation means and how it differs from engagement. There are a number of theoretical and pedagogical implications of this way of looking at participation and engagement that I will touch upon here. The most general of these is that I hope through this analysis to have demonstrated the immeasurably complex work of doing-being-a-student in a classroom in all its varied forms, and have thus hinted at the monumental job teachers have in monitoring and trying to guide a roomful of people toward a common pedagogical goal. This final chapter reviews the contributions of this volume and presents several single-case analyses to springboard to a discussion of the challenges of multimodal analysis. Finally, I return to reflect on the concept of "participation," including the performance we require of students in the classroom, and the relationships between participation, engagement, and learning.

8.2 CONTRIBUTIONS

While participation is often equated with verbal contributions, this volume has presented a new way of looking at student participation in instructed-learning settings, and importantly, I have specified "participation" discursively by showing how it can be teased apart from engagement. Students' alignment with teacher-led activity, both interactionally and pedagogically, reveals their (non-)participation and (dis)engagement. Participation and engagement must be disambiguated; students can be engaged without participating, or participating without engagement, and all the variations in-between. Figure 8.1 shows the matrix one final time, as a reminder of the different shades of participation and engagement we have seen throughout the volume.

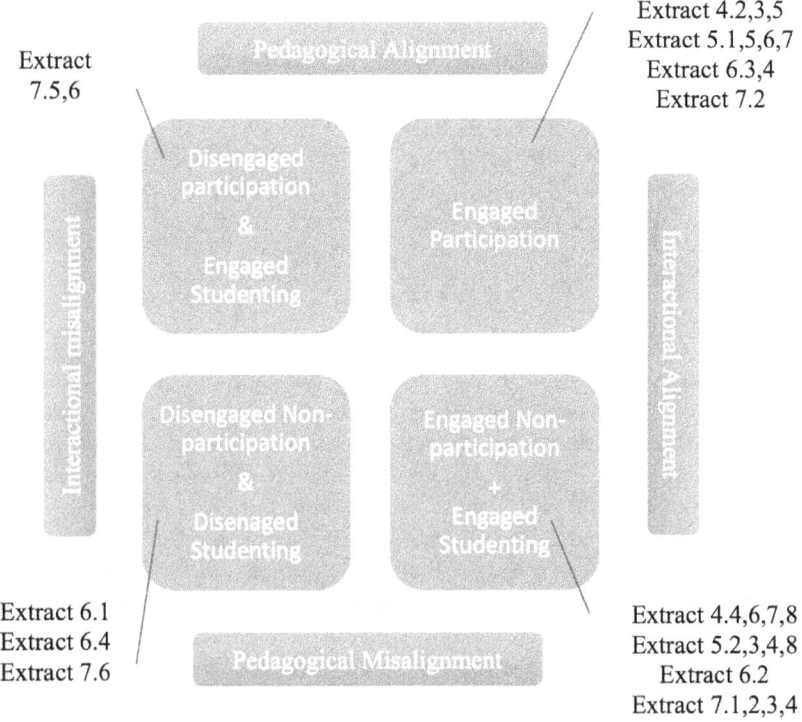

Figure 8.1   (Non-)participation and (dis)engagement

Each of the analysis chapters had as a goal a comparison between distinct quadrants in an effort to show the differences between superficially similar-looking student actions. Chapter 4 contrasted examples of participation and engagement, showing how the timing of students' verbal contributions can inform our characterization of their actions. Chapter 5 complicated the picture, introducing multimodal analysis to show how students can demonstrate engagement in the absence of expected participation, whether verbal or embodied. Chapter 6 showed what participation in listening looks like, demonstrating its dynamic nature. Finally, in Chapter 7, we turned to student actions that have been relatively under-researched, comparing engaged and disengaged participation and non-participation. In these chapters, I also introduced several new terms and concepts, including studenting, waves of embodied action, and multimodal listening, each of which is summarized below.

The complexity of the ways in which students participate and demonstrate engagement highlights the overwhelming job for teachers as they do "participation monitoring" (Sahlström 2002: 54). While teacher interactional awareness (Sert 2019b, forthcoming; Walsh 2003) is a crucial element of reflective practice (Walsh 2006, 2011), my analyses here show that there is a complex array of observable student action available for monitoring by teachers, and even with "constant multi-tasking"

(Sert 2019b), teachers are unlikely to be able to attend to it all in real time. I thus ask, when we grade participation, which actions are we attending to, and how representative are they of any individual student's participation and engagement in the interaction? I hope that my analyses will prompt teachers to reconsider their grading practices as regards participation, particularly when these grades are assigned holistically based on our general perceptions of students' involvement in class activities. The analyses here have shown that this involvement is complex, multimodal, and in constant flux.

8.2.1 STUDENTING

This volume introduced the term "studenting" to refer to the undertaking of a category-bound action of the role "student" at an inappropriate time, i.e., out of pedagogical or interactional alignment with the teacher-directed activity. The examples in the analysis chapters have shown that not all studenting is alike, however. For example, in Chapter 4, we saw a student attempting to self-select as next speaker at inapt sequential locations. This student was engaged, but unable to identify interactional spaces for his contribution during an extended teacher turn. He was doing-being-a-student in the wrong way for that moment. In the same chapter, we also saw students engaging in conversations with their peers during teacher-fronted interaction or resisting a shift in participation structure to teacher-led interaction. While these ways of doing-being-a-student were also "wrong" given their interactional environments, I argued that they show students as agents of their own learning, pursuing understanding, and so I termed these engaged studenting-cum-learning.

These examples of engaged studenting and engaged studenting-cum-learning contrast with the many examples of disengaged studenting we saw in Chapters 6 and 7. Students can be quite adept at finding ways of pursuing their "parallel activities" (Koole 2007) whether or not they are simultaneously monitoring the main interaction. As long as these studenting episodes do not disrupt the ongoing lesson, they are often ignored by the teacher, though most teachers will confess to being aware of them. I will return to the discussion of studenting in the final section of this chapter, discussing its relevance to the performance of doing-being-a-student in a classroom. Here, however, I reiterate the likelihood that given the limitations of the human senses, teachers are attending to only some portion of the class at any one time. Thus, while teachers may let some cases of studenting pass, it is just as likely that other students are participating in unobserved ways while not getting "credit" for doing so, as may also be the case when students participate in choral responses or waves of embodied action.

8.2.2 WAVES OF EMBODIED ACTION

In addition to expanding our understanding of the differences between participation and engagement, this volume also brings to light the wave-like nature of students' embodied action in the classroom. Waves are described as metachronal in biology when they involve sequential action (e.g., movement of cilia or segments of worms) rather than simultaneous action, and my analysis throughout the book likewise highlights the sequentiality of what are often glossed as simultaneous student actions. This wave metaphor is applicable to several different phenomena we have seen here, including students' choral verbal (Extract 4.1) and embodied responses (Chapter 5). The practice of transcribing such group actions in one line obscures the detail of each individual student's participation and engagement in the interaction, and the nature of these interactions potentially impacts the teacher's ability to monitor individual students.

It seems an impossible task for the teacher to monitor the unfolding of each student's actions during embodied waves of response, and given this reality, it is worth asking what such choral prompts accomplish pedagogically. Jacknick and Creider describe checking episodes as "highly ritualized institutional interactions, where teacher and students are more focused on a text and on answers than on each other" (2018: 85). Walsh (2011) notes that goals for materials mode include language practice and checking answers; as my analysis shows, choral responses are often produced by a small subset of students, so the question is, who exactly is getting language practice? Checking answers could be done more efficiently by the teacher reading the answers aloud, but as Creider (2016) notes, teacher questions and student responses offer the comforting appearance of engagement. However, if we are interested in actually engaging (most if not all) students, different participation structures or other teacher actions may have more pedagogical value.

The wave metaphor can also be seen in the temporal unfolding of (dis)engagement at transitional moments in the classroom (Chapter 7). While the slower building of these waves makes them difficult to represent linearly, they occur in strikingly similar ways to the waves seen in Chapter 5. There is often a student or two at the front, anticipating the wave, and then there is a moment of critical mass when other students join in, followed by delayed responses from others. These slow-building waves of engagement or disengagement may be a way of analyzing fuzzy concepts like "rapport," common in teacher evaluation and certification rubrics. How does the teacher bring the students together into a whole-class participation structure? How does she react when the students as a group begin to disengage before the lesson is over? These are areas ripe for further study that can help us to understand the specialized work of teaching, and thus to prepare teachers-in-training for the demands of managing classroom interaction.

8.2.3 MULTIMODAL LISTENING

In Chapter 6, we turned to a consideration of what I called multimodal listening, highlighting the nature of doing-listening as multiactivity. In this chapter, I also suggested repair and embodied engagement as demonstrations of active listening (cf. Sert 2019a). While an idealized version of a listener may include upright posture, constant gaze orientation toward the speaker, and perhaps even an eager face (e.g., Malfoy in Extract 1.1), the reality is much different. Co-present persons do not gaze unflinchingly at one another during interaction (Goodwin 1979, 1980), and particularly in the classroom, many other foci of attention are available, including materials, the board, clocks, one's breakfast, etc. Students' understanding of what doing-listening entails is made evident in the gaze orientations and postures they adopt during listening episodes; as we saw in Extract 6.2, students' uncertainty about expectations for participation led to constant multimodal action on the part of most students. When students are so observably engaged in "doing listening," are they *actually* listening? Or are they like the student Sartre (1956) describes, so intent on looking engaged that they are unable to maintain focus? Likewise, how can we characterize the students who do not display "doing listening" in any observable way?

Extract 6.4, in which Alice reads aloud, was the very first multimodal transcript I created as I started this research project. As a researcher sitting in the classroom the day that interaction was recorded, I remember being struck by the impressive disengaged studenting accomplished by Elise, seated next to me, as she wrote in her personal journal. However, transcribing this episode in full multimodal detail (see Appendix 1) allowed me to appreciate how she interwove her own parallel activity into the main, teacher-led activity, touching back in with the read aloud as the teacher's other-corrections recreated a joint attentional focus. Likewise, at the time, I remember thinking that Heather was completely disengaged, absorbed in eating her breakfast. However, the process of transcribing her multimodal actions demonstrated to me her skillful multitasking as she simultaneously monitored the interaction *and* ate her breakfast, cleaned the desk, removed trash, etc. Heather's other-correction demonstrates her active listenership, but I want to stress that active listenership may be demonstrated by embodied actions as well, and thus her tracing of the words, her nods and smiles, all precisely-timed with the unfolding read aloud, also demonstrate active listening. This excerpt, including the different kinds of studenting by Robert and Brad, shows the complexity of students' displayed participation and engagement, and how little we know about the experience of being a student in a classroom. Transcribing and analyzing multimodal action can be a daunting undertaking, but this excerpt more than any other underscores the value of such analysis for an understanding of social action.

8.3 THE CHALLENGES OF MULTIMODAL DATA

This project, particularly the transcription of multimodal detail, led to many challenging moments where the tensions between representation, readability, and analytic precision felt irresolvable. In creating icon-based transcriptions of the waves of verbal and embodied actions, I have tried to create new ways of visualizing action in large multiparty interaction. However, several issues with transcription were never resolved to my satisfaction. For instance, in Extract 6.4, I maintained several of Heather's most obvious orientation shifts during Alice's read aloud, but the resulting transcript does not fully convey how she shifts back and forth from parallel to main activity, and sometimes juggles both simultaneously. In addition, Brad's constant movement could not be included without introducing readability issues. Similarly, the visual writing prompt (Extract 6.2) produced a restless wave of multimodal action from the students that a transcript could not adequately represent.

While they were not perfect, the transcriptions I created using Mondada's ([2001] 2019) conventions allowed a precision of analysis that was crucial for the kinds of claims I wanted to make in this book. I include sample multimodal transcripts of Extracts 6.2 and 6.4 as Appendices 2 and 3, respectively, in order to show the reader not just the precision afforded by Mondada's ([2001] 2019) conventions, but also the readability issues produced when they are applied to such large multiparty interactions. I also include links to videos when permissions allow, and I urge readers to view for themselves the multimodal phenomena I am trying to capture "in flight." An open question remains whether linear transcripts of the type we have become accustomed to retain their utility for the analysis of multimodal action and the dissemination of findings, or whether a more multimodal approach, with annotated videos for example, is the future for our field.

The wave-like nature of students' disengagement and re-engagement in classroom interaction was found in all three corpora, in a variety of ways, and it is not surprising given the demands of doing-being-an-*engaged*-student in classroom interaction. For example, in Extract 6.4, we saw Elise shifting her orientation from the main activity (a student read aloud) to her writing and back. In the same excerpt, Heather's multitasking shows her monitoring of the interaction *while* she accomplishes other tasks such as eating and grooming. Her display of attention to the task at hand (i.e., listening) is not constant, but is rather intermittent as she shifts her gaze and hands toward other focal points (e.g., her hair, clothing, food, etc.). Particularly in the College Data, there are many instances of students orienting toward their phones but still touching in with the primary activity, engaging in embodied ways and participating verbally at times (e.g., the students seen wearing their earbuds and orienting toward phones in Figures 7.84–7.86; Allison in Extract 7.6). We will need to find new ways of disseminating data to adequately capture this dis- and re-engagement. As Jenks (2011) notes, transcripts as we know them were developed to represent audio-recorded data, and it is therefore unsurprising that transcripts built from words alone do not adequately represent the complexity of multimodal social action.

While each of the phenomena identified in earlier chapters represents a collection, I present several single-case analyses here to highlight some of the methodological challenges I foresee in future research on students' multimodal actions in the classroom, particularly as relates to students' orientation toward personal electronic devices. A wealth of research into students' use of phones and related devices has been undertaken in the last few decades, with most taking a quantitative approach to examining the impact of device usage on learning (e.g., Bradstreet Grinols and Rajesh 2014; McCoy 2013; Tindell and Bohlander 2012). At the same time, researchers within the conversation analytic framework have examined the use of devices *for* learning, whether "in the wild" (e.g., Hellermann et al. 2017) or in online environments (e.g., Balaman 2018; Thorne 2010). A fundamental question unanswered by either of these fields of inquiry is *how students engage with devices during classroom interaction*. While an answer to this question is beyond the scope of this book, I include several sample extracts to propose a few lines of inquiry that seem ripe for pursuit, including what I am calling *covert disengagement* and *domino (dis)engagement*. Caution: transcription challenges ahead.

8.3.1 COVERT DISENGAGEMENT

One issue familiar to most teachers and students is that of *covert disengagement*. By this I refer to instances where students engage in off-task behaviors but do so in an off-record way. We have seen several "low-tech" examples of this in Chapter 6; for example, in Extract 6.1, Olivia writes (possibly doing homework) and Alice organizes her binder as the teacher reads aloud. Seated in the back of the room, Olivia's writing does not disrupt progressivity of the teacher's read aloud. Alice, however, seated right in front, orients to the need to *appear* as though she is following the read aloud, keeping her book in her hand and occasionally bringing it to the center of her vision. However, the covert use of electronic devices is also common in classrooms, as seen below in this example from the Reading Data. The teacher is delivering an extended turn about how students should be reading the novel, and Greg is seen just before the excerpt with his book in one hand and his phone in the other, gaze shifting between the two.

Extract 8.1 Who, what, when, where, why

```
1    TEA   who, what, when, *#where, why.#
                   *Gre gaze to device-->
                   *Gre book down-->
                   #fig. 8.2 #fig. 8.3
```

```
2          (1.0)
3    TEA   you hafta keep going back and
4          asking those questions. even if
5          you don't have answers to the questions.
6          (1.0)
7    TEA   cause that's why we're doing this.
8          it's one of the reasons we're
9          doing this. is that when you come
10         and talk to each other, instead
11         of just some professor giving you
```

Extract 8.1 Who, what, when, where, why (continued)

```
12          all the *answers,*# you can get the
                    *........*Gre gaze to book-->
                         #fig. 8.4
```

```
13   TEA    answers among yourselves. °it's°
14          much better.
15   S?     *#mm-mm. *
            *Gre gaze to T*
            #fig. 8.5
```

```
16   TEA    *#you will learn much more
            *Gre gaze to device inside book-->
            #fig. 8.6
```

```
17          that way. cause I could just come up
18          here and tell you what the book is
```

Extract 8.1 Who, what, when, where, why (continued)

```
19          about. but will *#you have accomplished
                             *Gre gaze to T-->
                             #fig. 8.7
```

```
20          anything*# if we do it that way?
                     *Gre gaze to book-->
                     #fig. 8.8
```

```
21          (1.0)
22   ALI    °no ( )°
23   TEA    that's like reading Cliffs Notes.
24          that's cheating.
25          (1.4)
26   TEA    so even if it's a struggle
27          for you, and that's perfectly okay,
28          okay? just keep fighting your way
29          through. but write down the *#questions.
                                         *Gre gaze to device-->
                                         *Gre device above book-->
                                         #fig. 8.9
```

```
30          (1.4)
```

Extract 8.1 Who, what, when, where, why (continued)

```
31   TEA  I put *#about, what about twenty words
                 *Gre device inside book-->
                 #fig. 8.10
```

```
32        on the board, (.) the other day?
33        (2.2)
34   TEA  make sure you can *#define        *
                              *Gre device up*
                              #fig. 8.11
```

```
35        *#those words.       *
          *Gre device to side*
          *Gre gaze to book-->
          #fig. 8.12
```

```
36        (0.4)*#(1.0)
               *Gre gaze to side
               #fig. 8.13
```

176   MULTIMODAL PARTICIPATION AND ENGAGEMENT

Extract 8.1 Who, what, when, where, why (continued)

```
37        *#(0.4)
          *Gre gaze to book-->
          #fig. 8.14
```

```
38   TEA  same *#way we do the vocabulary
               *Gre gaze to T-->
               #fig. 8.15
```

```
39        exercises?*#
                    *Gre hand to chin, orients head to T-->
                    #fig. 8.16
```

For the first part of this extract, Greg uses his device with little attempt to disguise his actions. In line 1, he holds his book down below his desk, and his phone is held up on top of the desk. However, in line 15, Greg shifts his gaze (and his attention) toward the teacher and simultaneously moves his phone inside his book. While he shifts his attention between the book and the device after that, he also moves to put the device behind the book again in line 29, and then rests the phone inside the book in line 31. Greg's attention is primarily engaged with his phone throughout, though he is also clearly monitoring the teacher's gaze and movement through the classroom. By line 35, he moves the device to the side and re-engages in the class, or at the very least does a more convincing job of looking like an engaged student, looking at his book in line 37, the teacher in line 38, and reorienting his head toward the teacher in line 39. Notably, this is the teacher who sanctioned Robert for wearing earbuds (Extracts

7.9 and 7.10), and has an explicit policy forbidding phone use in class. Is he letting this disengagement from Greg pass? Greg's move to covert disengagement shows his orientation to the reproachable nature of such an action, but it is unclear why the teacher does not reproach him. In transcribing these actions, I have attempted to focus on moments of change in Greg's orientation—for example, toward or away from his phone—but it is far from clear to me whether these are the most analytically relevant moments to include in transcription. The current transcript shows his shifting displays of participation and (dis)engagement, but it is unclear if those shifts do in fact relate sequentially or temporally to the teacher's turn, as they are shown in the transcript above.

Similar instances were found throughout the College Data. In the examples in Figures 8.17–8.19 from the forensic linguistics class, Charlie is seen holding her phone behind a handout. By hiding her phone, she is attempting to display participation as she simultaneously disengages from the interaction, engaging instead with her device.

Figure 8.17 Charlie using phone while another student reads

Figure 8.18 Charlie using phone after the read aloud is over

Figure 8.19 Charlie holding phone in front of paper, gaze to teacher

In Figure 8.17, Charlie is seen holding her phone in front of the handout while another student reads aloud from the handout. In Figure 8.18, the read aloud has concluded, and other students have put their handouts down, but Charlie's static posture shows her engagement with the phone, and her continued attention to maintaining the appearance of attention to the interaction. These actions in fact betray her disengagement: by failing to orient to the shifting participation framework, she demonstrates that she is not monitoring the interaction. In Figure 8.19, Charlie orients her gaze toward the teacher, but maintains her posture of holding the phone in front of the handout. In these different snapshots of time, she does a more and less complete job of keeping up the façade, but the fact remains that she is engaged not only with her phone here, but also with maintaining the appearance of doing-being-a-student. She is touching in with the main interaction, but keeping one foot in her other engagement with her phone. Because her phone is on her desk during the entire class period, choosing which moments are worth transcribing becomes a difficult decision. The transcription in Extract 8.1 tracks shifts in orientation and posture, but without access to Greg's device, our analysis about what occasions those shifts is limited to the teacher's ongoing extended turn; it is akin to listening to half of a phone conversation. Conversation analysis is well suited to an examination of the sequentiality and temporality of students' orientations to devices, but the challenges of transcribing them in fruitful ways for analysis and dissemination of findings remains.

8.3.2 DOMINO (DIS)ENGAGEMENT

Another phenomenon worthy of future study is what I am calling *domino (dis) engagement*. In these instances, disengagement from the interaction by one student seems to lead to nearby students also disengaging. There is an example of this in Extract 7.6, where one student seems to be drawn in by a neighboring student's use of her phone, sometimes looking at her phone and other times pointing toward the phone itself. While he may have been attempting to get her to engage in the classroom interaction, his focused attention on his neighbor at these moments necessarily meant that he himself was disengaged from the interaction as well. We saw a similar example unrelated to phones in Extract 7.7, where Megan begins to pack up early, seemingly prompting Jessica and Charlie, seated nearby, to do the same. Further study of these moments is needed in order to determine whether the original student's action does, in fact, lead to the domino effect, or whether it is a simpler wave of disengagement.

There are many examples throughout the College Data of domino phone orientation. While most of these lead to disengagement from the interaction, in some cases, they can occur in on-task ways as well, though with interactional consequences. Extract 8.2, from the CRT 2 classroom in the College Data, shows an example from small group interaction. In this introductory philosophy course, students were placed into small groups to discuss how they might test the hypothesis that someone has seen the mythical creature Bigfoot. In this group, one student's orientation to her phone seems to prompt another student to bring out his phone as well, and the two students' orientation to their phones leads to an extended silence in their group. Note: in order to show how the focal student, Esme, engages both with her phone and her groupmates, I have transcribed her left hand (lh) and right hand (rh) separately for some lines.

Extract 8.2 On-task contagion

```
1    ESM   *(if you) *check# (*syl syl  *#syl).
     lh    *.........*hand to phone-----*phone to front-->
     rh                *drops pen*"hold"..*joins left hand-->
           *Esm gaze to Jef-------------*to phone-->
                        #fig. 8.20 #fig. 8.21
```

```
2    ESM   I know some people having a-
3          they have like an (apartment)
4          (and they *#don't)    *#
                      *LH wave--*back to phone-->
                        #fig. 8.22 #fig. 8.23
```

```
5    NAO   ((unintelligible*))
                         *Esm phone tilts to side
6    JEF   (not yet./ah yeah.)((unintellig[ible))
7    NAO                                [((laughter))
8    ESM                                [((laughter))
9    JEF   ((unin*tell[igible))] cost[ume.    ]
10   ESM              [mm-hmm. ]     [There's]
               *Esm gaze to phone-->
11         a whole *bigfoot# museum    *you guys.#
               *LH displays to Jef*to Nao
               *gaze to Jef-------*to Nao
                        #fig. 8.24          #fig. 8.25
```

Extract 8.2 On-task contagion (continued)

```
12   NAO    *really?=
            *displays phone to Jef
13   ESM    =yes. *Where they have these*# (museums).
                  *.....................*phone to self-->
                                        *hands to phone-->
                                        *gaze to phone-->
                                        #fig. 8.26
```

```
14          (where they have- in Georgia.)
15          *#(1.0)        *#(2.0)
            *Jef turns head*turns body, gathering phone-->
            #fig. 8.27   #fig. 8.28
```

```
16   TEA    they have a big foot museum?
17   ESM    *[yeah ] they have one in California,*
18   NAO    [mmhmm?]
19   JEF    [yeahh.]
            *Esm gaze to T-->
            *Jef turning-->
20   ESM    in Georgia,=*#
            ............*Jef turned
                        *Esm gaze to phone-->
                        *Esm scrolling-->
                        *Jef gaze to phone-->
                        *Nao smiling, gaze to Esm
                        #fig. 8.29
```

Extract 8.2 On-task contagion (continued)
```
21   TEA   cool.
22   NAO   °that's funny.°*#
                      *gaze down-->
                      #fig. 8.30
```

After several minutes of discussion, Esme picks up her phone from the adjacent desk with her left hand, simultaneously dropping her pen and then making a "hold on" gesture with her right hand, palm facing the others. Both hands join at the phone and she orients her gaze to it as well. As she engages with the phone, she also continues talking with her group members (lines 1–4, 8, 10–11). This continued talking may be akin to the self-talk identified by Hall and Smotrova (2013); the student is continuing to speak while using the technology as a way to manage the interactional trouble occasioned by her temporary gaze withdrawal and attention shift. The phone becomes a focal object for the interaction in lines 9–11 as she displays the phone to her groupmates. Thus far, the phone has been an on-task object mediating their discussion (Lantolf 2000).

In line 13, as Esme continues to confirm her finding that there are museums devoted to Bigfoot, she reorients the phone toward herself, bringing both hands to it and shifting her gaze down as well. Just after Esme finishes speaking in line 14, Jeff first turns his head and then his whole body, as he reaches for his own phone, located on the desk behind him (line 15). The teacher inserts himself into their small group interaction, confirming Esme's discovery in a loud voice from behind his desk. The students confirm in unison (lines 17–19), and again as Esme finishes speaking in line 20, Jeff and Esme orient to their phones. The teacher offers a postmortem 'cool' (a sequence-closing third, Schegloff 2007) in line 21, and Naomi produces one as well in line 22, saying 'that's funny.' at reduced volume. She also withdraws gaze from Esme, looking down and beginning to write. Following this, the three students sit in silence for 1 minute and 20 seconds, Jeff and Esme continuing to look at their phones and occasionally scrolling. Naomi looks down at her notebook, up toward the board, and down again to her bag as she gets her water bottle. The engagement with devices by Jeff and Esme seems to have completely shut down the group interaction for this period of time, whereas in the other group in the class, no students brought out phones at any point, and continued talking throughout this time, i.e., it was an "encounter" (Goffman 1959: 15). While the initial impulse to orient to the phone does seem to have been related to an on-task query, the interactional consequence of orientation toward phones, in this case at least, is disengagement from group interaction. Because my original focus was on whole-group interactions, cameras were unable to capture audio sufficiently during small group interactions, and so this transcription is partial. If we hope to examine students' orientation toward and engagement with personal devices as they simultaneously engage in small group work, more creative camera placement will be needed to capture the interactional unfolding of moments like these.

8.3.3 PARTICIPATION FRAMEWORKS FOR ENGAGEMENT

In noting that teachers often abruptly shift participation structure, Hellermann posits that students' skill at recognizing these shifts is likely due to "students' and teachers' mutual monitoring of each others' behavior" (2008a: 112). While monitoring of interaction and of co-present parties has been an important part of my analyses of participation and engagement, in focusing so emphatically on the multimodal actions of students, I was not able to include the multimodal affordances of classroom spaces themselves in the analyses here, though this is an area with important consequences for classroom interaction. Spatial organization in the classroom can create participation frameworks with more or less opportunity for participation and engagement, as we will see below.

Interactions that might be glossed as "classroom discussions" occur in all three data corpora, and while some students engage in mutual gaze orientation with each other during these episodes, most students' gaze follows the teacher's movements throughout the classroom. They engage with the teacher as one interlocutor, "the Student," as Sahlström (2002) describes this participation structure. Even when the students are taken as a group, the teacher dominates the discussion, uttering twice as many words in some cases, and often directing the talk toward particular answers. Figure 8.31 showing the configuration of the room in the Reading Data helps to explain why this participation structure prevails during "discussions." Most students are facing the teacher, and except for those seated at the sides of the classroom, it would take a complete twist of the body to face another student. Establishing mutual gaze with one another is thus more difficult than doing so with the teacher, and it is also clear that while students can display incipiency, the teacher is in charge of selecting next speakers in verbal and embodied ways. No individual student in particular is expected to participate verbally, and indeed, participation for this kind of discussion mostly involves a display of listening.

Figure 8.31   Reading classroom spatial configuration

In contrast, we turn now to an example from the College Data where, by virtue of their spatial orientation and the participation structure it entails, individual students are central participants in the discussion. The teacher for this class often uses this participation structure where students volunteer to be part of an "inner circle" to discuss a reading. These participants manage their own turn-taking, with the teacher intervening only when the discussion strays away from the topic of the reading. The students in the "outer circle" who are listening can also bid for turns, with the teacher pausing the inner circle discussion to allow the outer circle students to contribute (i.e., the teacher still maintains superior interactional rights and obligations, but turn-taking is mostly locally managed). This is the same introductory philosophy course seen in Extract 7.6, where students showed marked delays in their engagement with the whole-class interaction following a break. As is clear from Figure 8.32, the inner circle discussion students are configured in such a way that the boundaries of the participation structure are clear. They are seated in a circle around a table and can easily establish mutual gaze with one another in an excellent example of an "encounter" or "ecological huddle" as described by Goffman (1961); they can monitor one another for displays of incipiency, recipiency, and embodied participation. I also provide a key to students' seating arrangements in Figure 8.33 to aid with speaker identification.

Figure 8.32 CRT classroom inner circle spatial configuration

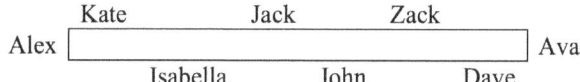

Figure 8.33 CRT inner circle seating arrangement

Prior to the establishment of the inner circle discussion, the class had gone through a reading about contraception. The discussion had been going for 13 minutes prior to this extract and continued for another 20 minutes after; this selection is representative of the nature of the interaction. As noted, this is the same class as seen in Extract 7.6, and several of the students who were engaging with their phones in that excerpt are notably engaged participants here, including Kate, John, Alex, and Dave. Whereas in most discussions throughout the corpora, the teacher facilitates a discussion with the Student, here we see an entirely student-led discussion.

Extract 8.3 Student-led discussion

```
1    AVA   okay I feel like if you make (.) sex
2          less taboo then you >really wouldn't
3          have to enforce< contraceptive as much.
4          like the only reason that, like, part
5          of the reason why the teens even would
```

Extract 8.3 Student-led discussion (continued)

```
6          go out and have unprotected sex and
7          everything is because of how negative
8          people make it seem? in- in a way it
9          kind of makes them want to do it even more.=
10   ALE   *=mmm.=
           *nodding-->
11   AVA   =and *as far as the- the whole
                -->*Ale stops nodding
12         injection? stuff?
((lines omitted))
21   AVA   you have to let medicine grow. before
22         you start trying tuh- (.)
23   JOH   make it mandatory.=
24   AVA   *=yeah. make it mandatory.
           *Ale nodding-->
25   ALE   mmm.*
              -->*
26   AVA   it should just be something you teach, stop
27         making it so:, make it seem like such
28         a bad thing and let people know that
29         it's natural and stuff like that.
30   S?    yeah.
31   AVA   and then, then they will start to, be
32         like, okay fine, I'll use a condom.
33         =Like it's everybody's choice and
34         everybody's decision.
35   KAT   [>can I ask a question,<]
36   DAV   [I-        I-          (.) ]
37   ZAC   [>there']s a  ]huge< difference [between vaccines]
38   KAT   [you      ]said,]               [oh- (let him.) ]
39   DAV   [I-       ]
40   ZAC   and like (actually) that stuff.=
41   DAV   =no, because,=
42   KAT   =>↑no no no no.< it's nothin bad (like,)
43   DAV   >no no no no.< hold on, I'm tryin to explain,
44         [like,]
45   KAT   [you  ]said when, um, when people talk about
46         sex negative, it make kids want to have mo-
47         sex more than they: (.)
48         [pssh]
49   ALE   [when] they say <unprotected sex:,> ]
50   AVA   [yeah] if somebody's tellin you like,]
51   KAT   that it's some, [if you told me,]
52   JAC                   [I ra- I ra-    ]
```

Extract 8.3 Student-led discussion (continued)

```
53   JOH                    [nah I agree. ]
54   KAT   somebody [told me if you could]
55   ALE            [make them (ballsy.) ]
56   KAT   *#catch#* S-T- a S-T-D from unprotected sex,
     zac   *kind of*
           #fig. 8.34    fig. 8.35
```

```
57         I'm not gonna [ < have sex >        ]
58   ALE                 [>that's not< what she] meant=
59   KAT   =li:ke,=
60   DAV   =that's not- that's not what she's talking
61         about. I,
62   JAC   I just feel like, um, someone could tell
63         me something as much, but if (.)
64   DAV   mmm.
65   JAC   genetically? I am (.) feeling it?
66   DAV   *yeah *#exact*[ly.]*
67   JAC                 [I  ]am,=
     dav   *.....*point-*,,,,,*
                        #fig. 8.36
```

```
68   AVA   =you're still gonna do it.
69   JAC   right.
```

In this discussion, we see students managing the turn-taking themselves, and showing much more engaged participation than we saw from them in Extract 7.6. Alex, seated directly across from Ava at the head of the table, maintains the most sustained eye gaze toward Ava throughout her extended turn (lines 1–34), nodding often and producing the response token 'mmm' (Gardner 2001) in lines 10 and 25. Other students also participate in Ava's extended turn, with John providing a collaborative turn-completion in line 23, confirmed by Ava in line 24, and another student agreeing with 'yeah' in line 30.

Following the conclusion of Ava's turn, Dave, Kate, and Zack all self-select as next speaker in overlap (lines 35–36). When both Dave and Kate restart in lines 38–39, they are also overlapped by Zack (line 37), who persists in his turn while Dave and Kate abandon theirs. After Zack's turn, both Dave and Kate jump back in again, latching on to one another until they again overlap (lines 44–45) and Dave abandons the turn again. When Kate finishes her turn, Alex and Ava both self-select as next speaker, with Alex continuing his turn to completion, overlapping Ava, and also being overlapped by Jack, John, and Kate. As Kate continues her turn, Zack contributes an embodied assessment, joining the discussion without disrupting its progressivity. Alex overlaps Kate's talk in line 57 in recognitional onset, clarifying on behalf of Ava with '>that's not< what she meant', with Dave joining in as well saying 'that's not- that's not what she's talking about' (lines 60–61). Jack comes in with a related point in line 62, with Dave providing response tokens ('mmm' in line 64) and agreement ('yeah exactly' in line 66). Ava provides collaborative completion in line 68 which is confirmed by Jack in line 69 with 'right'.

Seven of the eight "inner-circle" students contribute verbally in this short extract, and all demonstrate their embodied participation and engagement through the establishment of mutual gaze with speakers. The teacher is physically located several feet away from the group, and while his superior interactional rights and obligations mean that he can interrupt the group (as no students in the outer circle can), he does so only three times during this over 35-minute discussion. This minimal participation by the teacher allows space for the students to participate and engage in the discussion (Jacknick 2011b); we see this through their skillful management of turn-taking as well as their embodied participation and engagement while their peers are speaking. Goodwin argues that participants' postural orientations help to establish participation structures, "mak[ing] possible the production, reception, and joint constitution of a variety of *different kinds of action* built through gesture and talk" (2000: 1519; emphasis added). Here, we see that students' postural orientation does just this: it allows for different participation frameworks entailing different rights and obligations for them as both speakers and listeners. Not only this, but the overall participation structure leads to a shift in the participation and engagement of the outer circle students as well. Several of those students who were the most demonstrably disengaged in Extract 7.6 are engaged in this discussion, including not only Jack, Alex, Kate, and John in the inner circle, but also Allison, demonstrably *doing listening* in the outer circle. Considering the interactional consequences of different spatial configurations in the classroom, and particularly the affordances they offer for mutual monitoring, will shed important light on the kinds of participation structures that might facilitate opportunities for learning.

8.4 REFLECTIONS ON "PARTICIPATION"

Every time they start a new class with a new teacher, students are learning how to do-being-a-student in *that* classroom, with *that* teacher. What will be expected of them interactionally? What kinds of sideplay or byplay will be allowed? While classroom interactional competence (CIC) is defined by Walsh as "teachers' and learners' ability to use interaction as a tool for mediating and assisting learning" (2006: 132), this definition excludes student actions which may not be *for learning*. However, I argue that the term classroom interactional competence should apply just as well to students' ability to covertly use their phone as to their ability to find interactional space on the open floor to air a problem in understanding. There is competence in participating and engaging, but also in managing one's own participation and engagement over the course of a class session, and both of these are learned through processes of socialization. I note again that no one lives in the upper right quadrant of the matrix; even those of us who are adept at the performance of student (and I count myself among them) find ourselves in all the quadrants throughout the course of any given class. Rather than conceiving of classroom interactional competence as related only to learning, I suggest that we see it as an umbrella term. While some social actions in the classroom might be more conducive to learning than others, the way that classrooms are currently structured requires collusion more than engagement. If only some students must be observably participating (as in a choral checking episode), then what is required of the others is simply that they do not disrupt the progressivity of the interaction.

Returning to the impetus for this book, and my enduring interest in the interactional work undertaken by students, I suggest that we as teachers radically reconceive of the classroom space by asking what kinds of participation structures might benefit the students seated in front of us. Researchers of classroom discourse can aid in this effort by examining how different participation structures and spatial orientations affect the kinds of participation available to students. Likewise, teachers can be attentive to the "small" displays of engagement I have highlighted throughout the book, while maintaining awareness of how much student action is beyond their monitoring capabilities. The complexity of student action goes beyond our ability to analyze it in situ, and micro-analysis based on video recordings has the capacity to broaden our sense of what doing-being-a-student looks like; and in fact, video recordings are necessary for such analysis (Mondada 2019).

Finally, I suggest teachers abandon the practice of grading participation. What does it mean to grade a student on their participation? This is a question that has come to occupy my mind more and more throughout my career as a teacher and a researcher. As a novice ESL teacher, I knew that I wanted my students to speak, though I did not really understand why. As a researcher of language and social interaction in classrooms, I became interested in moments where students self-selected, hoping to discover how teachers and students work together to create interactional space. As a teacher and researcher, I took for granted that students wanted to be in the classroom, and that they would do-being-a-student in the same way I had. As a white graduate of an Ivy League school of education entering a teaching position at an urban community college, I was confronted with the realization that I was not standing in front of a room full of twenty-five copies of myself, sitting up straight, looking at me, prepared to show their engagement in ways I expected. It is crucial that we as teachers examine where our norms for participation come from, understanding that if they are based on ourselves, we are creating a model that sets many students up to fail. Examining the under-researched classrooms in the Reading and College Data corpora from a multimodal analytic lens shows the many and varied ways students participate and engage in classroom interaction, including those that do not align with mainstream ways of doing-being-a-student. When I began teaching, I saw these students' divergence from my own ways of doing-being-a-student as indications of their lack of engagement, but I argue that the reality is much more complex. Walsh highlights the danger of looking for "easy" classroom interactions:

> By following learnt behaviours, which are the product of many years of being socialised into classroom rituals and practices, we may be facilitating the kind of 'smooth' discourse profile, which prevails at the moment. But are we helping to create interactions that result in learning? (Walsh 2011: 189)

Some students are better than others at doing-being-a-(certain type of)-student for longer periods of time, and it is also possible that some students are not even aware of what is involved in such an endeavor. Through the many examples of studenting throughout the data analysis chapters, we have seen students' demonstrations of which actions they associate with the category "student," things like writing, or gazing at a book or the board. However, we have also seen several examples where students' engagement is more inscrutable, but from a lay perspective, we might say that these students "look" disengaged. In his book arguing for a reconceptualization of pedagogy in urban schools, Christopher Emdin (2016) recounts an exercise he uses with teachers-in-training in which he shows screenshots of students of color[1] in classrooms around the United States and asks the teachers-in-training to speculate about what is going through the students' minds at the moment the photo was taken. Emdin himself describes the students as in "varying poses" of disengagement, including heads on hands and "blank, emotionless stares" (2016: 28), and the teachers-in-training invariably describe the students as bored and/or angry. Reading Emdin's description of the still images and the teachers' gloss of the students' mindsets at the moment, I immediately thought of several students from the Reading Data, particularly Isabelle and Robert, whom we saw earlier in Extract 6.1 (Figure 6.19) and Extract 6.4 (Figure 6.45). These figures are reproduced here as Figures 8.37 and 8.38.

Figure 8.37 Isabelle's posture from Extract 6.1

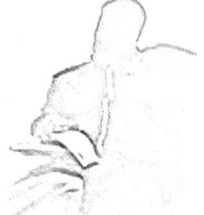

Figure 8.38 Robert's posture from Extract 6.4

---

[1] I use Emdin's own terminology here in describing the exercise. Note, however, that in the literature, there has been a move away from the phrase "people of color," with researchers/theorists instead using terms like "racialized groups/populations," "racially minoritized populations," and similar variations (cf. Flores and Rosa 2015; Rosa 2016). Thank you to Jen Delfino for bringing this to my attention.

In the training exercise, Emdin then shows the videos from before and after these moments, which often show students attempting to participate in the "right" way but being unable to find a way in. He also shares interviews with the students themselves so teachers can hear from the students' perspective about their frustration with prevailing participation structures in classrooms. Goffman notes that role distance can have "defensive functions" (1961: 112), allowing participants to account for their less than competent performance by suggesting that they "have no serious claim" to the role, and thus their shortcomings are not to be taken seriously. Having spent a lifetime within schooling systems that have treated them as "bad" students, they may opt instead to engage in role distance and display non-participation and disengagement. Re-examining participation and engagement through the lens of my analysis intersects with research on culturally-relevant/sustaining pedagogy (Ladson-Billings 1995, 2014; Paris and Alim 2017), with my analyses suggesting that the ways we grade participation in both K-12 and higher education may be not only flawed, but culturally insensitive as well.

While role distance is one explanation for the students' displays of (non-)participation in Figures 8.37 and 8.38, I include these particular still photos here because I argued earlier that we cannot say that these students are disengaged, only that they do not engage in any demonstrable display of engagement. Even though they may be engaged, the impression their postures and facial expressions[2] give of disengagement is a powerful one, deeply rooted in historical "ideas about what school should look like" (Emdin 2016: viii). To my fellow teachers and researchers, I propose we ask ourselves, who is the performance for? A decade into my tenure at an urban community college, I have begun to question what forms of participation are necessary to make things easier for me as the teacher as the facilitator of a large multiparty interaction, and what forms of participation relate to learning. This volume has shown how analysis of students' multimodal actions in the classroom can start to answer this question.

---

[2] Discerning Robert's facial expression in the videos is difficult. While he is seated near a window with the light behind him, across the corpora, students with darker skin tone are consistently less clearly captured by the video recording. The racial bias built into video recording and facial recognition technology is well documented by both research and anecdotal accounts (Harwell 2019a, 2019b; Noah 2016), and we must acknowledge the impact this has on the data we collect and the analyses we are able to produce.

APPENDIX 1
TRANSCRIPTION CONVENTIONS[1]

(1.8) Numbers enclosed in parentheses indicate a pause. The number represents the number of seconds of duration of the pause, to one decimal place. A pause of less than 0.2 seconds is marked by (.).

[ ] Brackets around portions of utterances show that those portions overlap with a portion of another speaker's utterance.

= An equals sign is used to show that a second speaker begins their utterance just at the moment when the first speaker finishes.

:: A colon after a vowel or a word is used to show that the sound is extended. The number of colons shows the length of the extension.

? A question mark indicates that there is slightly rising intonation.

. A period indicates that there is slightly falling intonation.

, A comma indicates a continuation of tone.

- A dash indicates an abrupt cut off, where the speaker stopped speaking suddenly.

↑↓ Up or down arrows are used to indicate that there is sharply rising or falling intonation. The arrow is placed just before the syllable in which the change in intonation occurs.

° This indicates an utterance which is much softer than the normal speech of the speaker. This symbol will appear at the beginning and at the end of the utterance in question.

>< 'Greater than' and 'less than' signs indicate that the talk they surround was noticeably faster than the surrounding talk.

<> 'Less than' and 'greater than' signs indicate that the talk they surround was noticeably slower than the surrounding talk.

'the' Quotation marks are used to designate meta-talk, specifically talk about focal language from materials of some kind (textbook, workbook, handouts, or the blackboard).

tea Participant doing embodied action is identified in lower case when (s)he is not the speaker.

---

[1] Adapted from Mondada [2001] (2019), available at: <https://lorenzamondada.net/multimodal-transcription> (last accessed July 18, 2020).

APPENDIX 1

* *	Gestures and descriptions of embodied actions are delimited between two asterisks. In the full multimodal transcripts, different symbols are used for each participant, with separate symbols used for gaze and embodied actions to allow for simultaneous transcription of several modalities. These symbols are synchronized with corresponding stretches of talk.
*--->	The action described continues across subsequent lines ---->* until the same symbol is reached.
>>	The action described begins before the excerpt's beginning.
--->>	The action described continues after the excerpt's end.
....	Action's preparation.
----	Action's apex is reached and maintained.
,,,,,	Action's retraction.
fig	The exact moment at which a screen shot has been taken is indicated with a specific symbol (#) showing its position within the turn at talk.
gaze	Embodied actions are italicized.
bold	Focal lines are bolded, whether they represent text or embodied action.

APPENDIX 2
MULTIMODAL TRANSCRIPT OF EXTRACT 6.2 VISUAL WRITING

MULTIMODAL SYMBOL KEY FOR EXTRACT 6.2

∅	Teacher gaze	%	Clara gaze
&	Teacher embodied action	\	Clara embodied action
*	Eiko gaze	√	Jin-Ae gaze
@	Eiko embodied action	♣	Jin-Ae embodied action
∂	Michiko gaze	⊗	Nadia gaze
∞	Michiko embodied action	#	Nadia embodied action
≅	Nobu gaze	⊗	Rodrigo gaze
+	Nobu embodied action	∇	Rodrigo embodied action
¬	Sachiko gaze	≥	Yoro gaze
∧	Sachiko embodied action	≈	Yoro embodied action

Extract 6.2 Visual writing

```
28   TEA   "think back to yesterday, and ¬find a memory.
     saG                                 ¬to T-->
29   TEA   can you ¬find one ¬∞ (.) from ten years ago?
     saG        -->¬down-----¬up-->
     mic                 ∞head down, puts down pen
30         ♣(1.0)
     jin   ♣puts bag on chair
31   TEA   when you were √♣∞∂twenty?
     jiG                 √down-->
     jin                 ♣chin on L hand-->
     miG                 ∂to T-->
     mic                 ∞chin on L hand-->
32   TEA   #ten? (1.0) eight?
     nad   #chin on both hands-->
33         ∇(2.0)
     rod   ∇rubbing eyes-->when does this end?
34   TEA   six?
35         (3.0)
36   TEA   three?
```

APPENDIX 2   193

```
37          √(3.0)  √♣
     jiG    √up to TV down-->
     jin           ♣head in hands-->
38   TEA    does the month July? send up a ∇memory?
     rod                                 ∇head in hands down-->
39          ∂∞(3.0)
     miG    ∂down-->
     mic    ∞starts to play with pen-->
40   TEA    ∧September?
     sac    ∧gets eraser, erases-->
41          (3.0)∧
     sac       -->∧
42   TEA    ♣a particular time of day?
     jin    ♣takes off glasses, rubs eyes-->
43          ≥(2.0)
     yoG    ≥down-->
44   TEA    ∞≅≈sunset,  ≈≥≥for example. ≅
     mic    ∞starts writing-->
     noG    ≅around-------------------≅
     yor    ≈flips paper≈back to previous-->
     yoG            -->≥≥to T-->
45          ≅(2.0)
     noG    ≅down-->
46   TEA    ⊗midnight?
     naG    ⊗-->down
47          ⊗#(3.0)
     naG    ⊗up-->
     nad    #playing with fingers-->
48   TEA    ♣does the color green ♣trigger a ∂∞memory?♣
     jin    ♣....................♣putting glasses on ♣
     miG                             ∂to T-->
     mic                                ∞chin to R hand-->
49          (2.0)
50   TEA    ∧≥aqua? ∧
     sac    ∧erasing∧
     yoG    ≥down-->
51          ♣ (2.0)
     jin    ♣head back in L hand, R hand holding pen to paper-->
52   TEA    pink or ∂rose?
     miG            ∂down-->
53          ≈(2.5)
     yor    ≈writing-->
54   TEA    the smell of ≥≈hyacinth, honeysuckle,
     yoG                 ≥to T-->
     yor                    ≈pen in hand-->
```

```
55  TEA   garbage, ♣liver?
    jin           ♣head up
56        ♣(1.0)%(1.5)
    jin   ♣takes glasses off to clean-->
    clG         %down-->
57  TEA   #⊗does the word dance ♣give you a ∂%picture?
    nad   #hands down, holding pen-->
    naG   ⊗up-->
    jin                           ♣puts glasses down, gaze up-->
    miG                                     ∂to T-->
    clG                                     %to T-->
58        ♣(1.4)\(0.6)
    jin   ♣rubbing R eye with R hand-->
    cla         \chin on R hand, L hand on cheek-->
59  TEA   ∧do you see something in the      ∧
    sac   ∧R hand w pen to head, back down ∧
60  TEA   word under? (2.0)
61  TEA   ⊗dream?
    naG   ⊗down, up, down-->
62        (1.0)
63  TEA   laugh?
64        (2.0)
65  TEA   kiss?
66        (2.0)
67  TEA   tickle?
68        (2.0)
69  TEA   let your ∂mind √♣supply more details.
    miG            ∂to left (board?)-->
    jiG                  √down-->
    jin                   ♣head resting on R hand-->
70  TEA   until you can see the ∂picture or event clearly.
    miG                         ∂to T-->
71        (3.0)
72  TEA   ∧keep wandering∧ until a memory you would like to spend more
    sac   ∧erasing-------∧pen to paper, erasing, then pen to paper-->
73  TEA   time with (.) stands out.
74        (2.0)
75  TEA   if ≈several memories want your attention, ≥≈choose
    yor      ≈pen down, hands together--------------≈head on hand
    yoG                                             ≥up-->
76  TEA   any one.
77        (1.0)
78  TEA   +≅you can go back to another one later.
    nob   +pen down, leans back, arms crossed-->
```

APPENDIX 2   195

```
      noG  ≅down-->
79         (3.0)
80    TEA  ¬∧look more carefully at this memory.
      saG  ¬to T-->
      sac  ∧pen to paper, head in L hand-->
81         ∂⊗∇(2.0)
      miG  ∂down-->
      roG  ⊗to left, then down-->
      rod  ∇chin on left hand-->
82    TEA  where are you.
83         (1.0)
84         what kind of light is there. what do you notice.
85         (1.0)
86    TEA  +≅are there any ∞≈≥particular colors?
      nob  +leans forward, head on L hand-->
      noG  ≅down-->
      mic              ∞sits back-->
      yor              ≈head in palms,
      yoG              ≥down-->
87         +(3.0)     ++∞
      nob  +rubs nose++hand covers face-->
      mic          -->∞∞puts down pen
88    TEA  ∂∞what do you hear ⊗clearly.
      miG  ∂gaze to T,
      mic  ∞hands under table-->
      naG                  ⊗up, chin on R hand-->
89    TEA  in your mind. (.) in the distance?
90         (1.5)
91    TEA  do you +≅hear machines? Animals?
      nob        +rubbing forehead-->
      noG        ≅down-->
92         (1.0)
93    TEA  conversations?++
      nob              -->++hand covers forehead, head down-->
94         #+≅(2.0)
      nad  #turns back to bag and back again
      nob  +forehead resting on L hand-->
      noG  ≅gaze down-->
95    TEA  do you notice a certain smell?
96         (1.0)
97    TEA  is there an ∂¬odor or fragrance connected with this memory?
      mic              ∂down-->
      saG          -->¬down-->
98         (3.0)
99    TEA  @do you ∂touch specific \surfaces?      \
```

```
        eik   @rubbing eye-->
        miG          ∂up-->
        cla                         \rubs forehead\
100 TEA   &*≅what @\tastes are associated with this time.
        eik   &arms crossed-->
        eiG   *down-->
        noG   ≅up, chin on L hand-->
        eik         -->@
        cla         \head rests on arm, pen in hand-->
101       \⊗♣(2.5)
        cla   \writing, head still down-->
        naG   ⊗down-->
        jin   ♣head up, chin on R hand-->
102 TEA   what are you doing. (1.0) how are you ⊗moving.
        naG                                        ⊗up-->
103       (1.0)
104 TEA   is there a ≅+particular sensation in your body?
        noG             ≅down-->
        nob               +head on L hand-->
105       (3.0)
106 TEA   are there other people around?
107       ∇⊗(2.0)
        rod   ∇puts pen down, head back in hands-->
        roG   ⊗down-->
108 TEA   are they moving in ⊗particular ways?
        naG                   ⊗down-->
109 TEA   #+do they have a relationship to you?
        nad   #turns to bag and back again
        nob   +leans back, head/gaze up-->
110       +⊗ (2.0)
        nad   #head in hands-->
        naG   ⊗down-->
        nob   +slow rocking forward and back, arms crossed, head/gaze
              up-->
111 TEA   do certain thoughts occur to you, certain questions,
112       is this ⊗memory dark or light.
        naG           ⊗up-->
113       ∇(1.0)                          +
        rod   ∇head up, face on hands-->
        nob             stops rocking-->+
114 TEA   fast or slow. hazy or distinct.
115       ∂∞(4.0)
        miG   ∂down-->
```

```
        mic  ∞leans forward, pen to paper-->
116 TEA      #Øokay?
        nad  #chin on R hand -->
        teG  Øup-->
117 TEA      you may *begin Øwriting.
        eiG            *to T-->
        teG                     Ødown-->
```

APPENDIX 3
MULTIMODAL TRANSCRIPT OF EXTRACT 6.4
I HOPE EVERYBODY'S NOTICING

MULTIMODAL SYMBOL KEY FOR EXTRACT 6.4

*	Teacher gaze	∈	Brad gaze
\	Teacher embodied action	%	Brad embodied action
⊗	Alice gaze	∝	Elise gaze
√	Alice embodied action	§	Elise embodied action
∂	Heather gaze	≅	Mahmoud gaze
√	Heather embodied action	+	Mahmoud embodied action
®	Nancy gaze		
∇	Nancy embodied action		

Extract 6.4 I hope everybody's noticing

```
3   ALI   ∈fifty ®years ago ≅∂American were sleeping ∈∈an
    brG   ∈down----------------------------------∈∈to board-->
    naG        ®to book-->
    maG                    ≅to book-->
    heG                    ∂to food-->
4   ALI   aver∈age of e- eight hour to tw- ∈∈twelve hour
    brG     ∈down---------------------∈∈to board-->
5   ALI   a night. but by nineteen ninety they were
6         down to only seven hour ∈∈∝§a night.
    brG                     -->∈∈to papers-->
    elG                     ∝up-->
    eli                     -->§ (stops writing)
7   ALI   √now ∈∈many American are getting only about six
    brG   -->∈∈to board-->
    hea   √folding napkin-->
8   ALI   hours of sleep a night.∈∈%sp- espensive research
    brG                  -->∈∈to papers-->
    bra                       %writing-->
9   ALI   show that ∝lossing an hour or two√√∈∈of sleep
    elG          ∝down-->
    hea                            -->√√eating-->
    brG                               -->∈∈to board-->
```

APPENDIX 3   199

```
10  ALI  every night, week after ∈∈week,∈∈month after
    brG                        -->∈∈down-∈∈to board-->
11  ALI  month,∈∈ make it more difficult for people to
    brG     -->∈∈down-->
12       pay 'tention, ∝∝'specially∝∝to (.)√√mono- (.)
    elG             -->∝∝up--------∝∝down-->
    hea                                    -->√√using napkin-->
13  ALI  [monoto- ]
14  TEA  [m- <mon]∈∈otonous.>
    brG         -->∈∈to board-->
15  ALI  monotonous=°>tasks.<° ∝∝§and to remumber thing. §
    elG                     -->∝∝to book-->
    eli                           §leans forward----------§
16       (0.2) reaction (.) time slow down. behavior
18       become inpractical.∈∈ logic ∝∝§re√√°action°§
    brG                  -->∈∈to board-->
    elG                            -->∝∝up-->
    eli                              §.....leans back§
    hea                                     √√eating-->
19  ALI  (.)%reason is im- implay=
    bra  -->%stops writing, holding pen-->
20  TEA  =im↑paired?
21  ALI  empaired. and accident and urror in judge
22       increase.∂∂√while §productive and ∈∈ability to
    heG      -->∂∂to book-->
    hea       √left hand to book-->
    eli              §writing-->
    brG                              -->∈∈up-->
23  ALI  ∈∈make a decision decleen- decleen.∈∈%student∈∈
    brG  ∈∈down--------------------------->∈∈to Rob--∈∈to board-->
    bra                                %left hand palm up-->
24  ALI  fel- fall 'sleep in class and %%fail     %%learn   %
    bra                            -->%%twists l. hand%%head shake%
25  ALI  ∈%<all that they sh- ∈∈ (.) should>.∈∈marriage become
    brG  ∈down---------------∈∈to board----∈∈down-->
    bra  %writing-->
26  ALI  more∈∈ stretsful √as sleep ex∈∈hausted parent try to
    brG   -->∈∈to board--------------∈∈down-->
    hea                  √gathering trash-->
27  ALI  copy with ∈∈their∈∈children and∈∈each other.
    brG          -->∈∈up---∈∈down--------∈∈to board-->
28  ALI  truck∈∈ and, and ∈∈auto    ∈∈driver fall asleep
    brG  -->∈∈down------∈∈to board∈∈down-->
    hea                        >>putting trash under book
```

```
29  ALI  at ∈∈the √( beach )∈∈ and √∂eps-\ ∈∈ and √
    brG  -->∈∈to board------∈∈down---------∈∈to board-->
    hea        -->√              √wipes hands √
    heG                          ∂head/gaze down to book-->
    ali                               \traces words with finger-->
30  ALI  espet∈∈ es- estimatt∈∈
    brG  -->∈∈to board------∈∈down-->
31  ALI  acc\ident§∝∝∈∈√result in  √ ∈∈over one (.) f-
    ali  -->\
    eli         -->§
    elG         -->∝∝up-->
    hea              √wipes mouth√traces words with finger-->
    brG         -->∈∈to board---∈∈down-->
32  ALI  one- f- \on \e-
    ali         \nod\
33  TEA  one $thousand?$=
34  ALI  =√one√ ∝∝thh+ouhs+and five √∈∈%hundred death√ in the country
    hea  √nod√                      √smile-----------√
    elG       -->∝∝to book-->
    mah            +nods+
    brG                      -->∈∈to Ali-->
    bra                          %stops writing...capping pen-->
35  ALI  (.) √a year.% ∈∈∂worker perform less§   §ef- \∂∂less effi- §
    bra  ....caps pen%
    brG         -->∈∈up (to Tea?)-->
    hea  -->√ (stops tracing)
    heG         -->∂gaze/head up------------------>∂∂to book-->
    eli                              §leans§mouths "efficient" §
    ali                                         \traces words-->
36  HEA  √efficient.                √
    hea  √leans back, napkin under book√
37  ALI  \efficient.
    ali  \hand to lap-->
38  TEA  mm-hmm?
39  ALI  and those in high (.) risk ∈∈po- p- position can∈∈
    brG                      -->∈∈to right----------∈∈up-->
40       ∝∝§endange §us all. §∝∝√for example, sleeping (.)
    eli       §leans back§        §writing-->
    elG  -->∝∝up--------------∝∝down-->
    hea                      √wiping desk-->
41       d- √deprivation lead to the accident
    hea  -->√
42       √at the nuclear power plant at
    hea  √adjusting clothes and hair-->
43  ALI  three mile ( ) Pennsylvania.
```

```
44   TEA   excell≅ent, really, your reading has improved so much√=
     maG   ----->≅to Tea-->
     hea                                                       -->√
45   MAH   =mm [+yeah.+ ]
46   TEA       [\∂∂Alice,]* I hope ®everybody's noticing that.
     mah       +nod->+
     teG       *to Ali-->
     tea       \moves back towards Mah-->
     heG   -->∂∂to Ali--->
     naG                           ®to Tea-->
47   TEA   +rea+lly, so much better than just +five+ or six weeks ago.
     mah   +nod+                              +nod +
```

REFERENCES

Allwright, R. L. (1980), "Turns, topics, and tasks: patterns of participation in language learning and teaching," in D. Larsen-Freeman (ed.), *Discourse Analysis in Second Language Research*, Rowley, MA: Newbury House, pp. 165–87.

Antaki, C. (ed.) (2011), *Applied Conversation Analysis: Intervention and Change in Institutional Talk*, Basingstoke: Palgrave Macmillan.

Appel, J. (2010), "Participation and instructed language learning," in P. Seedhouse, S. Walsh, and C. Jenks (eds.), *Conceptualising 'Learning' in Applied Linguistics*, Basingstoke: Palgrave Macmillan, pp. 206–24.

Arnold, L. (2012), "Dialogic embodied action: using gesture to organize sequence and participation in instructional interaction," *Research on Language and Social Interaction*, 45, 269–96. Available at: <https://doi.org/10.1080/08351813.2012.699256> (last accessed July 7, 2020).

Balaman, U. (2018), "Task-induced development of hinting behaviors in online task-oriented L2 interaction," *Language Learning & Technology*, 22(2), 95–115.

Bannick, A. (2002), "Negotiating the paradoxes of spontaneous talk in advanced L2 classes," in C. Kramsch (ed.), *Language Acquisition and Language Socialization: Ecological Perspectives*, London: Continuum, pp. 266–88.

Beun, R. J. (2000), "Context and form: declarative or interrogative: that is the question," in W. Black and H. C. Bunt (eds.), *Computational Pragmatics: Abduction, Belief and Context*, Amsterdam: John Benjamins, pp. 311–26.

Bezemer, J. (2008), "Displaying orientation in the classroom: students' multimodal responses to teacher instructions," *Linguistics and Education*, 19, 166–78.

Bolden, G. B. (2009), "Implementing incipient actions: the discourse marker 'so' in English conversation," *Journal of Pragmatics*, 41, 974–98.

Box, C. D. (2011), "Embodied (non)participation in a tutoring session." Special Issue of *Language and Information Society*, 16, 79–108.

Bradbury, R. (1953), *Fahrenheit 451*, New York: Simon & Schuster.

Bradstreet Grinols, A. and R. Rajesh (2014), "Multitasking with smartphones in the college classroom," *Business and Professional Communication Quarterly*, 77(1), 89–95.

Butler, C. and R. Wilkinson (2013), "Mobilising recipiency: child participation and 'rights to speak' in multi-party family interaction," *Journal of Pragmatics*, 50(1), 37–51.

Candela, A. (1999), "Students' power in classroom discourse," *Linguistics and Education*, 10(2), 139–63.

Clayman, S. E. (2013), "Turn-constructional units and the transition-relevance place," in J. Sidnell and T. Stivers (eds.), *The Handbook of Conversation Analysis*, Malden, MA: Blackwell, pp. 150–66.

Cole, M. and Y. Engeström (1993), "A cultural-historical approach to distributed cognition," in G. Salomon (ed.), *Distributed Cognitions: Psychological and Educational Considerations*, New York: Cambridge University Press, pp. 1–46.

Columbia, C. (Director), (2001), *Harry Potter and the Sorcercer's Stone* (Film), Warner Bros.

Couper-Kuhlen, E. and M. Selting (2018), *Interactional Linguistics: An Introduction to Language in Social Interaction*, Cambridge: Cambridge University Press.

Creider, S. (2016), "Encouraging student participation in a French-immersion kindergarten class: a multimodal, conversation analytic study," Unpublished doctoral dissertation, Teachers College, Columbia University, New York.

Cullen, R. (2002), "Supportive teacher talk: the importance of the F-move," *ELT Journal*, 56(2), 117–27.

De Fornel, M. (1992), "The return gesture: some remarks on context, inference, and iconic gesture," in P. Auer and A. Di Luzio (eds.), *The Contextualization of Language*, Amsterdam and Philadelphia: John Benjamins, pp. 159–93.

Diamondstone, J. (2002), "Keeping resistance in view in an activity theory analysis," *Mind, Culture, and Activity*, 9(1), 2–21.

Dobs, A. M. (2019), "Collective translations: translating together in a Chinese foreign language class," in J. K. Hall and S. D. Looney (eds.), *The Embodied Work of Teaching*, Bristol: Multilingual Matters, pp. 198–217.

Dorr-Bremme, D. W. (1990), "Contextualization cues in the classroom: discourse regulation and social control functions," *Language in Society*, 19, 379–402.

Drew, P. (1997), "'Open' class repair initiators in response to sequential sources of troubles in conversation," *Journal of Pragmatics*, 28(1), 69–101.

Drew, P. and J. Heritage (eds.) (1992a), *Talk at Work: Interaction in Institutional Settings*, Cambridge: Cambridge University Press.

Drew, P. and J. Heritage (1992b), "Analyzing talk at work: an introduction," in P. Drew and J. Heritage (eds.), *Talk at Work: Interaction in Institutional Settings*, Cambridge: Cambridge University Press, pp. 3–65.

Edwards, A. D. and D. P. G. Westgate (1994), *Investigating Classroom Talk*, 2nd edn., Washington, DC: Falmer Press.

Egbert, M. (1997), "Some interactional achievements of other-initiated repair in multiperson conversation," *Journal of Pragmatics*, 27, 611–34.

Egbert, M. (2004), "Other-initiated repair and membership categorization – some conversational events that trigger linguistic and regional membership categorization," *Journal of Pragmatics*, 36, 1467–98.

Emanuelsson, J. and F. Sahlström (2008), "The price of participation: teacher control versus student participation in classroom interaction," *Scandinavian Journal of Educational Research*, 52(2), 205–23.

Emdin, C. (2016), *For White Folks Who Teach in the Hood . . . and the Rest of Y'all Too*, Boston: Beacon Press.

Evnitskaya, N. and E. Berger (2017), "Learners' multimodal displays of willingness to participate in classroom interaction in the L2 and CLIL contexts," *Classroom Discourse*, 8(1), 71–94.

Evnitskaya, N. and T. Morton (2011), "Knowledge construction, meaning-making and interaction in CLIL science classroom communities of practice," *Language and Education*, 25(2), 109–27.

Evnitskaya, N. and E. Pochon-Berger (2012), "Embodied participation and interactional competence in the L2 classroom," in N. Evnitskaya, H. Martínez Ciprés, E. Moore, and C. Vallejo Rubinstein (eds.), *TRICLIL 2012 Proceedings: Better CLIL: More Opportunities in*

Primary, Secondary and Higher Education, Bellaterra: Universitat Autònoma de Barcelona, pp. 37–41.

Fanselow, J. F. (1977), "The treatment of error in oral work," *Foreign Language Annals*, 10(5), 583–93.

Fasel Lauzon, V. and E. Berger (2015), "The multimodal organization of speaker selection in classroom interaction," *Linguistics and Education*, 31, 14–29.

Flores, N. and J. Rosa (2015), "Undoing appropriateness: raciolinguistic ideologies and language diversity in education," *Harvard Educational Review*, 85(2), 149–71.

Ford, C. E. and T. Stickle (2012), "Securing recipiency in workplace meetings: multimodal practices," *Discourse Studies*, 14(1): 11–30. DOI:10.1177/1461445611427213.

Gardner, R. (2001), *When Listeners Talk: Response Tokens and Listener Stance*, Amsterdam: John Benjamins.

Gardner, R. (2015), "Summons turns: the business of securing a turn in busy classrooms," in C. J. Jenks and P. Seedhouse (eds.), *International Perspectives on ELT Classroom Interaction*, London: Palgrave Macmillan, pp. 28–48.

Gay, G. (2018), *Culturally Responsive Teaching: Theory, Research, and Practice*, 3rd edn., New York: Teachers College Press.

Gee, J. P. (2004), "Learning language as a matter of learning social languages within discourses," in M. Hawkings (ed.), *Language Learning and Teacher Education: A Sociocultural Approach*, New York: Multilingual Matters, pp. 1–31.

Goffman, E. (1959), *The Presentation of Self in Everyday Life*, New York: Doubleday.

Goffman, E. (1961), *Encounters: Two Studies in the Sociology of Interaction*, Indianapolis: Bobbs-Merrill.

Goffman, E. (1963), *Behavior in Public Places: Notes on the Social Organization of Gatherings*, New York: The Free Press.

Goffman, E. (1964), "The neglected situation," *American Anthropologist*, 66, 133–6. Available at: <https://doi.org/10.1525/aa.1964.66.suppl_3.02a00090> (last accessed July 7, 2020).

Goffman, E. (1981), *Forms of Talk*, Philadelphia: University of Pennsylvania Press.

Goffman, E. (1983), "The interaction order: American Sociological Association, 1982 Presidential Address," *American Sociological Review*, 48(1), 1–17.

Goldin-Meadow, S. (2010), "When gesture does and does not promote learning," *Language and Cognition*, 2(1), 1–19.

Goodwin, C. (1979), "The interactive construction of a sentence in natural conversation," in G. Psathas (ed.), *Everyday Language: Studies in Ethnomethodology*, New York: Irvington, pp. 87–121.

Goodwin, C. (1980), "Restarts, pauses, and the achievement of a state of mutual gaze at turn-beginning," *Sociological Inquiry*, 50(3–4), 272–302.

Goodwin, C. (1981), *Conversational Organization: Interaction Between Speakers and Hearers*, New York: Academic Press.

Goodwin, C. (1986), "Audience diversity, participation and interpretation," *Text*, 6(3), 283–316.

Goodwin, C. (2000), "Action and embodiment within situated human interaction," *Journal of Pragmatics*, 32, 1489–522.

Goodwin, C. (2006), "Human sociality as mutual orientation in a rich interactive environment: multimodal utterances and pointing in aphasia," in N. J. Enfield and S. C. Levinson (eds.), *Roots of Human Sociality: Culture, Cognition and Interaction*, New York: Berg, pp. 97–125.

Goodwin, C. (2007), "Participation, stance and affect in the organization of activities," *Discourse & Society*, 18(1), 53–73.

Goodwin, C. (2018), "Why multimodality? Why co-operative action?," *Social Interaction: Video-Based Studies of Human Sociality*, 1(2). DOI: 10.7146/si.v1i2.110039.

Goodwin, C. and M. H. Goodwin (2004), "Participation," in A. Duranti (ed.), *A Companion to Linguistic Anthropology*, Malden, MA: Blackwell, pp. 222–44.

Goodwin, M. H. (1999), "Participation," *Journal of Linguistic Anthropology*, 9(1–2), 177–80.

Goodwin, M. H. (2007), "Occasioned knowledge exploration in family interaction," *Discourse & Society*, 18(1), 93–110.

Gourlay, L. (2005), "OK, who's got number one? Permeable triadic dialogue, covert participation and the co-construction of checking episodes," *Language Teaching Research*, 9(4), 403–22.

Grabe, W. (2009), *Reading in a Second Language: Moving from Theory to Practice*, Cambridge: Cambridge University Press.

Green, J. L., R. Weade, and K. Graham (1988), "Lesson construction and student participation: a sociolinguistic analysis," in J. L. Green and J. O. Harker (eds.), *Multiple Perspective Analyses of Classroom Discourse*, Norwood, NJ: Ablex, pp. 11–47.

Groeber, S. and E. Pochon-Berger (2014), "Turns and turn-taking in sign language interaction: a study of turn-final holds," *Journal of Pragmatics*, 65, 121–36. Available at: <https://doi.org/10.1016/j.pragma.2013.08.012> (last accessed July 7, 2020).

Haddington, P., T. Keisanen, L. Mondada, and M. Nevile (eds.) (2014), *Multiactivity in Social Interaction: Beyond Multitasking*, Amsterdam: John Benjamins.

Hall, J. K. (1998), "A consideration of SLA as a theory of practice: a response to Firth and Wagner," *The Modern Language Journal*, 81(2), 301–6.

Hall, J. K. (2002), *Teaching and Researching Language and Culture*, New York: Routledge.

Hall, J. K. and S. D. Looney (2019), *The Embodied Work of Teaching*, Bristol: Multilingual Matters.

Hall, J. K., T. Malabarba, and D. Kimura (2019), "What's symmetrical? A teacher's cooperative management of learner turns in a read-aloud activity," in J. K. Hall and S. D. Looney (eds.), *The Embodied Work of Teaching*, Bristol: Multilingual Matters, pp. 37–56.

Hall, J. K. and T. Smotrova (2013), "Teacher self-talk: interactional resource for managing instruction and eliciting empathy," *Journal of Pragmatics*, 47, 75–92.

Hall, J. K. and M. Walsh (2002), "Teacher–student interaction and language learning," *Annual Review of Applied Linguistics*, 22, 186–203.

Harwell, D. (2019a), "Amazon racial-identification software used by police falls short on tests for accuracy and bias, new research finds," *The Washington Post*, January 25. Available at: <https://www.washingtonpost.com/technology/2019/01/25/amazon-facial-identification-software-used-by-police-falls-short-tests-accuracy-bias-new-research-finds/> (last accessed January 3, 2020).

Harwell, D. (2019b), "Federal study confirms racial bias of many facial-recognition systems, casts doubt on their expanding use," *The Washington Post*, December 19. Available at: <https://www.washingtonpost.com/technology/2019/12/19/federal-study-confirms-racial-bias-many-facial-recognition-systems-casts-doubt-their-expanding-use/> (last accessed January 3, 2020).

Hazel, S. and K. Mortensen (2014), "Embodying the institution – object manipulation in developing interaction in study counselling meetings," *Journal of Pragmatics*, 65, 10–29.

Hazel, S., K. Mortensen, and G. Rasmussen (2014), "Introduction: a body of resources – CA studies of social conduct," *Journal of Pragmatics*, 65, 1–9.

Heath, C. (1984), "Talk and recipiency: sequential organization in speech and body movement," in J. M. Atkinson and J. Heritage (eds.), *Structures of Social Action: Studies in Conversation Analysis*, Cambridge: Cambridge University Press, pp. 247–65.

Heath, C. (1986), *Body Movement and Speech in Medical Interaction*, Cambridge: Cambridge University Press.

Hellermann, J. (2003), "The interaction work of prosody in the IRF exchange: teacher repetition in feedback moves," *Language in Society*, 32, 79–104.

Hellermann, J. (2005), "Syntactic and prosodic practices for cohesion in series of three-part sequences in classroom talk," *Research on Language and Social Interaction*, 38(1), 105–30.

Hellermann, J. (2008a), *Social Actions for Classroom Language Learning*, Clevedon: Multilingual Matters.

Hellermann, J. (2008b), "The contextualization of participation in the asthma project: response sequences in classroom talk," in K.-M. Cole and J. Zuengler (eds.), *The Research Process in Classroom Discourse Analysis: Current Perspectives*, New York: Lawrence Erlbaum Associates, pp. 49–72.

Hellermann, J. (2009), "Practices for dispreferred responses using *no* by a learner of English," *IRAL*, 47, 95–126.

Hellermann, J, and E. Cole (2009), "Practices for social interaction in the language learning classroom: disengagements," *Applied Linguistics*, 30(2), 186–215.

Hellermann, J. and S. Pekarek Doehler (2010), "On the contingent nature of language-learning tasks," *Classroom Discourse*, 1(1), 25–45. DOI: 10.1080/19463011003750657.

Hellermann, J., S. L. Thorne, and P. Fodor (2017), "Mobile reading as social and embodied practice," *Classroom Discourse*, 8(2), 99–121.

Hepburn, A. and G. B. Bolden (2017), *Transcribing for Social Research*, London: Sage.

Heritage, J. (1984a), "A change-of-state token and aspects of its sequential placement," in J. M. Atkinson and J. Heritage (eds.), *Structures of Social Action: Studies in Conversation Analysis*, Cambridge: Cambridge University Press, pp. 299–339.

Heritage, J. (1984b), *Garfinkel and Ethnomethodology*, Cambridge: Polity Press.

Heritage, J. (1997), "Conversation analysis and institutional talk: analysing data," in D. Silverman (ed.), *Qualitative Research: Theory, Method and Practice*, London: Sage, pp. 161–82.

Heritage, J. (2005), "Conversation analysis and institutional talk," in K. L. Fitch and R. E. Sanders (eds.), *Handbook of Language and Social Interaction*, Mahwah, NJ: Lawrence Erlbaum Associates, pp. 103–47.

Heritage, J. and J. D. Robinson (2011), "'Some' versus 'any' medical issues: encouraging patients to reveal their unmet concerns," in C. Antaki (ed.), *Applied Conversation Analysis: Intervention and Change in Institutional Talk*, Basingstoke: Palgrave Macmillan, pp. 15–31.

Hester, S. and D. Francis (2000), "Ethnomethodology, conversation analysis, and 'institutional talk,'" *Text*, 20(3), 391–413.

Hudson, N. (2011), "Teacher gesture in a post-secondary English as a second language classroom: a sociocultural approach," Unpublished doctoral dissertation, University of Nevada, Las Vegas.

Hutchby, I. and R. Wooffitt (1998), *Conversation Analysis: Principles, Practices and Applications*, Malden, MA: Blackwell.

Jacknick, C. M. (2009), "A conversation analytic account of student-initiated participation in an ESL classroom," Unpublished doctoral dissertation, Teachers College, Columbia University, New York.

Jacknick, C. M. (2011a), "'But this is writing': post-expansions in student-initiated sequences," *Novitas-ROYAL*, 5(1), 39–54.

Jacknick, C. M. (2011b), "Breaking in is hard to do: negotiating classroom activity shifts," *Classroom Discourse*, 2(1), 20–38.

Jacknick, C. M. (2013), "'Cause the textbook says . . .': laughter and student challenges in the ESL classroom," in P. Glenn and E. Holt (eds.), *Studies of Laughter in Interaction*, London: Bloomsbury, pp. 185–200.

Jacknick, C. M. (2018), "Collaborative use of multimodal resources in discussions of L2 grammatical meaning: a microgenetic analysis," *Language and Sociocultural Theory*, 5(2), 130–74.

Jacknick, C. M. and S. C. Creider (2018), "A chorus line: engaging (or not) with the open floor," *Hacettepe University Journal of Education*, 33, 72–92.

Jacknick, C. M. and D. Duran (under review), "Transforming student contributions into subject-specific expression," Submitted to *System*.

Jacknick, C. M. and S. Thornbury (2013), "The task at hand: noticing as a mind–body–world phenomenon," in J. M. Bergsleithner, S. N. Frota, and J. K. Yoshioka (eds.), *Noticing and Second Language Acquisition: Studies in Honor of Richard Schmidt*, Honolulu: University of Hawai'i, National Foreign Language Resource Center, pp. 327–47.

Jenks, C. J. (2011), *Transcribing Talk and Interaction: Issues in the Representation of Communication Data*, Amsterdam: John Benjamins.

Kääntä, L. (2015), "The multimodal organisation of teacher-led classroom interaction," in C. J. Jenks and P. Seedhouse (eds.), *International Perspectives on ELT Classroom Interaction*, London: Palgrave Macmillan, pp. 64–83.

Kasper, G. (1985), "Repair in foreign language teaching," *Studies in Second Language Acquisition*, 7, 200–15.

Kasper, G. (2008), "Discourse and socially shared cognition," in J. Cenoz and N. H. Hornberger (eds.), *Encyclopedia of Language and Education*, 2nd edn., New York: Springer Science+Business Media, pp. 59–77.

Kendon, A. (1990), *Conducting Interaction: Patterns of Behavior in Focused Encounters*, Cambridge: Cambridge University Press.

Kendon, A. (2004), *Gesture: Visible Action as Utterance*, Cambridge: Cambridge University Press. Available at: <https://doi.org/10.1017/CBO9780511807572> (last accessed July 7, 2020).

Kidwell, M. (1997), "Demonstrating recipiency: knowledge displays as a resource for the unaddressed participant," *Issues in Applied Linguistics*, 8(2), 85–96.

Kidwell, M. and D. Zimmerman (2007), "'Observability' in the interactions of very young children," *Communication Monographs*, 73(1), 1–28. Available at: <https://doi.org/10.1080/03637750600559673> (last accessed July 7, 2020).

Kinginger, C. (1994), "Learner initiative in conversation management: an application of van Lier's pilot coding scheme," *The Modern Language Journal*, 78(1), 29–40.

Kinginger, C. (1995), "Task variation and repair in the foreign language classroom," in M. A. Haggstrom, L. Z. Morgan, and J. A. Wieczorek (eds.), *The Foreign Language Classroom: Bridging Theory and Practice*, New York: Garland, pp. 55–69.

Koole, T. (2007), "Central and parallel activities in classroom interaction," *Language and Education*, 21(6), 487–501.

Koshik, I. (2002), "Designedly incomplete utterances: a pedagogical practice for eliciting knowledge displays in error correction sequences," *Research on Language and Social Interaction*, 35, 277–309. Available at: <https://doi.org/10.1207/S15327973RLSI3503_2> (last accessed July 7, 2020).

Kunitz, S. (2018), "Collaborative attention work on gender agreement in Italian as a foreign language," *The Modern Language Journal*, 102, 64–81.

Laakso, M. and M.-L. Sorjonen (2010), "Cut-off or particle – devices for initiating self-repair in conversation," *Journal of Pragmatics*, 42, 1151–72.

Ladson-Billings, G. (1995), "Toward a theory of culturally relevant pedagogy," *American Educational Research Journal*, 32(3), 465–91.

Ladson-Billings, G. (2014), "Culturally relevant pedagogy 2.0: a.k.a. the Remix," *Harvard Educational Review*, 84(1), 74–84.

Lantolf, J. P. (2000), *Sociocultural Theory and Second Language Learning*, Oxford: Oxford University Press.
Lantolf, J. P. (2010), "Minding your hands: the function of gesture in L2 learning," in R. Batstone (ed.), *Sociocognitive Perspectives on Language Use and Language Learning*, New York: Oxford University Press, pp. 131–47.
Lantolf, J. P. and S. L. Thorne (2006), *Sociocultural Theory and the Genesis of Second Language Development*, Oxford: Oxford University Press.
Lave, J. and E. Wenger (1991), *Situated Learning: Legitimate Peripheral Participation*, Cambridge: Cambridge University Press.
Lemke, J. L. (1990), *Talking Science: Language, Learning, and Values*, Norwood, NJ: Ablex.
Lerner, G. H. (1987), "Collaborative turn sequences: sentence construction and social action," Unpublished doctoral dissertation, University of California, Irvine.
Lerner, G. H. (1995), "Turn design and the organization of participation in instructional activities," *Discourse Processes*, 19, 111–31.
Lerner, G. H. (1996), "On the 'semi-permeable' character of grammatical units in conversation: conditional entry into the turn space of another speaker," in E. Ochs, E. A. Schegloff, and S. A. Thompson (eds.), *Interaction and Grammar*, Cambridge: Cambridge University Press, pp. 238–76.
Leung, C. (2010), "English as an additional language: learning and participating in mainstream classrooms," in P. Seedhouse, S. Walsh, and C. J. Jenks (eds.), *Conceptualising 'Learning' in Applied Linguistics*, Basingstoke: Palgrave Macmillan, pp. 182–205.
Levin, J. S., S. Kater, and R. L. Wagoner (2006), *Community College Faculty: At Work in the New Economy*, New York: Springer.
Levinson, S. C. (2013), "Action formation and ascription," in J. Sidnell and T. Stivers (eds.), *The Handbook of Conversation Analysis*, Malden, MA: Blackwell, pp. 103–30.
Lindström, A. and M.-L. Sorjonen (2013), "Affiliation in conversation," in J. Sidnell and T. Stivers (eds.), *The Handbook of Conversation Analysis*, Malden, MA: Blackwell, pp. 350–69.
Liu, Y. (2008), "Teacher–student talk in Singapore Chinese language classrooms: a case study of initiation/response/follow-up (IRF)," *Asia Pacific Journal of Education*, 28(1), 87–102.
Looney, S. D. and J. Kim (2019), "Managing disaligning responses: sequence and embodiment in third-turn teases," in J. K. Hall and S. D. Looney (eds.), *The Embodied Work of Teaching*, Bristol: Multilingual Matters, pp. 57–80.
Love, K. (1991), "Towards a further analysis of teacher talk," *Australian Review of Applied Linguistics*, 14(2), 30–72.
McCafferty, S. G. (2002), "Gesture and creating zones of proximal development for second language learning," *The Modern Language Journal*, 86, 192–203. Available at: <https://doi.org/10.1111/1540-4781.00144> (last accessed July 7, 2020).
McCafferty, S. G. (2004), "Space for cognition: gesture and second language learning," *International Journal of Applied Linguistics*, 14, 148–65. Available at: <https://doi.org/10.1111/j.1473-4192.2004.0057m.x> (last accessed July 7, 2020).
McCafferty, S. G. and G. Stam (eds.) (2008), *Gesture: Second Language Acquisition and Classroom Research*, Philadelphia: Routledge.
McCarthy, M. (2003), "Talking back: 'small' interactional response tokens in everyday conversation," *Research on Language and Social Interaction*, 36(1), 33–63.
McCoy, B. (2013), "Digital distractions in the classroom: student classroom use of digital devices for non-class related purposes," *Faculty Publications, College of Journalism & Mass Communications*, 71. Available at: <https://digitalcommons.unl.edu/journalismfacpub/71> (last accessed July 7, 2020).

McDermott, R. P. and H. Tylbor (1986), "On the necessity of collusion in conversation," in S. Fisher and A. Todd (eds.), *Discourse and Institutional Authority*, Norwood, NJ: Ablex, pp. 123–39.

Macedonia, M., K. Bergmann, and F. Roithmayr (2014), "Imitation of a pedagogical agent's gestures enhances memory for words in second language," *Science Journal of Education*, 2, 162–9. Available at: <https://doi.org/10.11648/j.sjedu.20140205.15> (last accessed July 7, 2020).

Macedonia, M. and T. R. Knösche (2011), "Body in mind: how gestures empower foreign language learning," *Mind, Brain, and Education*, 5, 196–211. Available at: <https://doi.org/10.1111/j.1751-228X.2011.01129.x> (last accessed July 7, 2020).

Macedonia, M., K. Müller, and A. D. Friederici (2011), "The impact of iconic gestures on foreign language word learning and its neural substrate," *Human Brain Mapping*, 32, 982–98. Available at: <https://doi.org/10.1002/hbm.21084> (last accessed July 7, 2020).

McHoul, A. W. (1978), "The organization of turns at talk in the classroom," *Language in Society*, 7, 183–213.

McHoul, A. W. (1985), "Two aspects of classroom interaction: turn-taking and correction," *Australian Journal of Human Communication Disorders*, 13(1), 53–64.

McHoul, A. W. (1990), "The organization of repair in classroom talk," *Language in Society*, 19(3), 349–77.

McHoul, A. W. and M. Rapley (2001), *How to Analyse Talk in Institutional Settings: A Casebook of Methods*, London: Continuum.

McNeill, D. (1992), *Hand and Mind: What Gestures Reveal About Thought*, Chicago: University of Chicago Press.

McNeill, D. (2005), *Gesture and Thought*, Chicago: University of Chicago Press.

McNeill, D. (2016), *Why We Gesture: The Surprising Role of Hand Movements in Communication*, Cambridge: Cambridge University Press.

Majlesi, A. R. (2015), "Matching gestures – teachers' repetitions of students' gestures in second language learning classrooms," *Journal of Pragmatics*, 76, 30–45.

Majlesi, A. R. and N. Markee (2018), "Multimodality in second language talk: the impact of video analysis on SLA research," in D. Favareau (ed.), *Co-operative Engagements in Intertwined Semiosis: Essays in Honour of Charles Goodwin*, Tartu: University of Tartu Press, pp. 247–60.

Margutti, P. (2011), "Teachers' reproaches and managing discipline in the classroom: when teachers tell students what they do 'wrong,'" *Linguistics and Education*, 22, 310–29.

Margutti, P. and A. Piirainen-Marsh (2011), "The interactional management of discipline and morality in the classroom: an introduction," *Linguistics and Education*, 22, 305–9.

Markaki, V., S. Merlino, L. Mondada, F. Oloff, and V. Traverso (2014), "Language choice and participation management in international work meetings," in J. W. Unger, M. Krzyzanowski, and R. Wodak (eds.), *Multilingual Encounters in Europe's Institutional Spaces*, New York: Bloomsbury, pp. 43–74.

Markee, N. (1995), "Teachers' answers to students' questions: problematizing the issue of making meaning," *Issues in Applied Linguistics*, 6(2), 63–92.

Markee, N. (2005), "Conversation analysis for second language acquisition," in E. Hinkel (ed.), *Handbook of Research in Second Language Teaching and Learning*, Mahwah, NJ: Lawrence Erlbaum Associates, pp. 355–74.

Markee, N. (2008), "Toward a learning behavior tracking methodology for CA-for-SLA," *Applied Linguistics*, 29(3), 1–24. DOI:10.1093/applin/amm052.

Markee, N. (2013), "Contexts of change," in K. Hyland and L. C. Wong (eds.), *Innovation and Change in English Language Education*, New York: Routledge, pp. 28–43.

Markee, N. (ed.) (2015a), *The Handbook of Classroom Discourse and Interaction*, Hoboken, NJ: John Wiley & Sons.

Markee, N. (2015b), "Giving and following pedagogical instructions in task-based instruction: an ethnomethodological perspective," in N. Markee (ed.), *The Handbook of Classroom Discourse and Interaction*, Hoboken, NJ: John Wiley & Sons, pp. 110–28.

Markee, N. and S. Kunitz (2015), "CA-for-SLA studies of classroom interaction: Quo Vadis?," in N. Markee (ed.), *The Handbook of Classroom Discourse and Interaction*, Hoboken, NJ: John Wiley & Sons, pp. 425–40.

Matarese, M. (in preparation), *Policy Talk: The Discourse of Front-Line Policy Implementation*.

Matarese, M. and D. Caswell (2017a), "Neoliberal talk: the routinized structures of document-focused social worker–client discourse," in S. F. Schram and M. Pavlovskaya (eds.), *Rethinking Neoliberalism: Resisting the Disciplinary Regime*, New York: Routledge, pp. 2–20.

Matarese, M. and D. Caswell (2017b), "'I'm gonna ask you about yourself, so I can put it on paper': analysing street-level bureaucracy through form-related talk in social work," *The British Journal of Social Work*, 48(3), 714–33. Available at: <https://doi.org/10.1093/bjsw/bcx041> (last accessed July 7, 2020).

Matoesian, G.M. (2010), "Multimodality and forensic linguistics: multimodal aspects of victim's narrative in direct examination," in M. Coulthard and A. Johnson (eds.), *The Routledge Handbook of Forensic Linguistics*, London: Routledge, pp. 541–57.

Matsumoto, Y. and A. M. Dobs (2016), "Pedagogical gestures as interactional resources for teaching and learning tense and aspect in the ESL grammar classroom," *Language Learning*, 67(1), 7–42.

Maynard, D. W. (2013), "Everyone and no one to turn to: intellectual roots and contexts for Conversation Analysis," in J. Sidnell and T. Stivers (eds.), *The Handbook of Conversation Analysis*, Oxford: Blackwell, pp. 11–31.

Mehan, H. (1979), *Learning Lessons: Social Organization in the Classroom*, Cambridge, MA: Harvard University Press.

Mikkola, P. and E. Lehtinen (2014), "Initiating activity shifts through use of appraisal forms as material objects during performance appraisal interviews," in M. Nevile, P. Haddington, T. Heinemann, and M. Rauniomaa (eds.), *Interaction with Objects: Language, Materiality, and Social Activity*, Amsterdam and Philadelphia: John Benjamins, pp. 57–78.

Mondada, L. [2001] (2019), "Conventions for multimodal transcription." Available at: <https://lorenzamondada.net/multimodal-transcription> (last accessed September 28, 2020).

Mondada, L. (2006), "Participants' online analysis and multimodal practices: projecting the end of the turn and the closing of the sequence," *Discourse Studies*, 8, 117–29.

Mondada, L. (2009), "Emergent focused interactions in public places: a systematic analysis of the multimodal achievement of a common interactional space," *Journal of Pragmatics*, 41, 1977–97.

Mondada, L. (2011), "Understanding as an embodied, situated and sequential achievement in interaction," *Journal of Pragmatics*, 43, 542–52. Available at: <https://doi.org/10.1016/j.pragma.2010.08.019> (last accessed July 7, 2020).

Mondada, L. (2012), "The dynamics of embodied participation and language choice in multilingual meetings," *Language in Society*, 41(2), 213–35.

Mondada, L. (2013), "The conversation analytic approach to data collection," in J. Sidnell and T. Stivers (eds.), *The Handbook of Conversation Analysis*, Malden, MA: Blackwell, pp. 32–56.

Mondada, L. (2014a), "Bodies in action," *Language and Dialogue*, 4(3), 357–403.

Mondada, L. (2014b), "Pointing, talk and the bodies: reference and joint attention as embodied interactional achievements," in M. Seyfeddinipur and M. Gullberg (eds.), *From Gesture in Conversation to Visible Action as Utterance*, Amsterdam: John Benjamins, pp. 95–124.

Mondada, L. (2014c), "The local constitution of multimodal resources for social interaction," *Journal of Pragmatics*, 65, 137–56.

Mondada, L. (2016a), "Challenges of multimodality: language and the body in social interaction," *Journal of Sociolinguistics*, 20(3), 336–66.

Mondada, L. (2016b), "Multimodal resources and the organization of social interaction," *Verbal Communication*, 3, 329–49.

Mondada, L. (2018), "Multiple temporalities of language and body in interaction: challenges for transcribing multimodality," *Research on Language and Social Interaction*, 51(1), 85–106.

Mondada, L. (2019), "Goodwin, Charles, and Marjorie Harness Goodwin," in P. Atkinson, S. Delamont, A. Cernat, J. W. Sakshaug, and R. A. Williams (eds.), *SAGE Research Methods Foundations*. DOI: 10.4135/9781526421036809349.

Mondada, L. and S. Pekarek Doehler (2004), "Second language acquisition as situated practice: task accomplishment in the French second language classroom," *The Modern Language Journal*, 88, 501–18.

Mondada, L. and K. Svinhufvud (2016), "Writing-in-interaction," *Language and Dialogue*, 6(1), 1–53.

Mori, J. and A. Hasegawa (2009), "Doing being a foreign language learner in a classroom: embodiment of cognitive states as social events," *IRAL*, 47, 65–94.

Mori, J. and N. Markee (2009), "Language learning, cognition, and interactional practices: an introduction," *IRAL*, 47, 1–9.

Mortensen, K. (2008), "Selecting next speaker in the second language classroom: how to find a willing next speaker in planned activities," *Journal of Applied Linguistics and Professional Practice*, 5(1), 55–79.

Mortensen, K. (2009), "Establishing recipiency in pre-beginning position in the second language classroom," *Discourse Processes*, 46(5), 491–515.

Mortensen, K. (2012), "Visual initiations of repair – some preliminary observations," in K. Ikeda and A. Brandt (eds.), *Challenges and New Directions in the Micro-analysis of Social Interaction*, Osaka: Division of International Affairs, Kansai University.

Mortensen, K. (2013), "Conversation analysis and multimodality," in C. A. Chapelle (ed.), *The Encyclopedia of Applied Linguistics*, Malden, MA: Blackwell, pp. 1–8. DOI: 10.1002/9781405198431.wbeal0212.

Mortensen, K. (2016), "The body as a resource for other-initiation of repair: cupping the hand behind the ear," *Research on Language and Social Interaction*, 49(1), 34–57.

Mortensen, K. and S. Hazel (2011), "Initiating round robins in the L2 classroom – preliminary observations," *Novitas-ROYAL*, 5(1), 55–70.

Mortensen, K. and S. Hazel (2014), "Moving into interaction – social practices for initiating encounters at a help desk," *Journal of Pragmatics*, 62, 46–67.

Nevile, M. (2015), "The embodied turn in research on language and social interaction," *Research on Language and Social Interaction*, 48(2), 121–51.

Nevile, M., P. Haddington, T. Heinemann, and M. Rauniomaa (2014a), "On the interactional ecology of objects," in M. Nevile, P. Haddington, T. Heinemann, and M. Rauniomaa (eds.), *Interaction with Objects: Language, Materiality, and Social Activity*, Amsterdam and Philadelphia: John Benjamins, pp. 3–30.

Nevile, M., P. Haddington, T. Heinemann, and M. Rauniomaa (eds.) (2014b), *Interaction with Objects: Language, Materiality, and Social Activity*, Amsterdam and Philadelphia: John Benjamins.

Noah, T. (2016), *Born a Crime: Stories from a South African Childhood*, New York: Hachette.

Nuthall, G. (1997), "Understanding student thinking and learning in the classroom," in B. J. Biddle, T. L. Good, and I. F. Goodson (eds.), *International Handbook of Teachers and Teaching*, Dordrecht: Kluwer Academic, pp. 681–768.

Nystrand, M. (1997), "Dialogic instruction: when recitation becomes conversation," in M. Nystrand, A. Gamoran, R. Kachur, and C. Prendergast (eds.), *Opening Dialogue: Understanding the Dynamics of Language and Learning in the English Classroom*, New York: Teachers College Press, pp. 1–29.

Olsher, D. (2004), "Talk and gesture: the embodied completion of sequential actions in spoken interaction," in R. Gardner and J. Wagner (eds.), *Second Language Conversations*, New York: A&C Black, pp. 221–46.

Paris, D. and H. S. Alim (eds.) (2017), *Culturally Sustaining Pedagogies: Teaching and Learning for Justice in a Changing World*, New York: Teachers College Press.

Peräkylä, A. and J. Ruusuvuori (2006), "Facial expression in an assessment," in H. Knoblauch, B. Schnettler, J. Raab, and H.-G. Soeffner (eds.), *Video-Analysis Methodology and Methods: Qualitative Audiovisual Data Analysis in Sociology*, Frankfurt: Peter Lang, pp. 127–42.

Piirainen-Marsh, A. (2011), "Irony and the moral order of secondary school classrooms," *Linguistics and Education*, 22, 364–82.

Rampton, B. (1996), *Language in Late Modernity: Interaction in an Urban School*, Cambridge: Cambridge University Press.

Rosa, J. D. (2016), "Standardization, racialization, languagelessness: raciolinguistic ideologies across communicative contexts," *Journal of Linguistic Anthropology*, 26(2), 162–83.

Rosborough, A. A. (2010), "Gesture as an act of meaning-making: an eco-social perspective of a sheltered-English second grade classroom," Unpublished doctoral dissertation, University of Nevada, Las Vegas.

Rosborough, A. A. (2014), "Gesture, meaning making, and embodiment: second language learning in an elementary classroom," *Journal of Pedagogy*, 2, 227–50. Available at: <https://doi.org/10.2478/jped-2014-0011> (last accessed July 7, 2020).

Ruusuvuori, J. and A. Peräkylä (2009), "Facial and verbal expressions in assessing stories and topics," *Research on Language and Social Interaction*, 42(4), 377–94.

Sacks, H. (1984), "Notes on methodology," in J. M. Atkinson and J. Heritage (eds.), *Structures of Social Action: Studies in Conversation Analysis*, Cambridge: Cambridge University Press, pp. 21–7.

Sacks, H. (1992), *Lectures on Conversation*, ed. G. Jefferson, Malden, MA: Oxford University Press.

Sacks, H. and E. A. Schegloff [1975] (2002), "Home position," *Gesture*, 2(2), 133–46.

Sacks, H., E. A. Schegloff, and G. Jefferson (1974), "A simplest systematics for the organization of turn-taking for conversation," *Language*, 50, 696–735.

Sahlström, J. F. (2002), "The interactional organization of hand raising in classroom interaction," *Journal of Classroom Interaction*, 37(2), 47–57.

Sarangi, S. (2018), "Modes of En'gaze'ment and Analytic Accountability in Discourse and Interaction Studies," H. Z. Waring (Chair), Language and Social Interaction Working Group. Conference conducted in New York, October.

Sarangi, S. and C. Roberts (1999), "The dynamics of interactional and institutional orders in work-related settings," in S. Sarangi and C. Roberts (eds.), *Talk, Work, and Institutional Order*, Berlin: Mouton de Gruyter, pp. 1–47.

Sartre, J.-P. (1956), *Being and Nothingness*, trans. H. E. Barnes, New York: Philosophical Library.

Schegloff, E. A. (1984), "On some gestures' relation to talk," in J. M. Atkinson and J. Heritage (eds.), *Structures of Social Action: Studies in Conversation Analysis*, Cambridge: Cambridge University Press, pp. 266–96.

Schegloff, E. A. (1991), "Conversation analysis and socially shared cognition," in L. B. Resnick, J. M. Levine, and S. D. Teasley (eds.), *Perspectives on Socially Shared Cognition*, Washington, DC: American Psychological Association, pp. 150–71.

Schegloff, E. A. (1992), "On talk and its institutional occasions," in P. Drew and J. Heritage (eds.), *Talk at Work: Interaction in Institutional Settings*, Cambridge: Cambridge University Press, pp. 101–34.

Schegloff, E. A. (2007), *Sequence Organization in Interaction: A Primer in Conversation Analysis*, Cambridge: Cambridge University Press.

Schegloff, E. A., G. Jefferson, and H. Sacks (1977), "The preference for self-correction in the organization of repair in conversation," *Language*, 53(2), 361–82.

Schiffrin, D. (1987), *Discourse Markers*, New York: Cambridge University Press.

Schwab, G. (2011), "From dialogue to multilogue: a different view on participation in the English foreign-language classroom," *Classroom Discourse*, 2(1), 3–19.

Seedhouse, P. (1994), "Linking pedagogical purposes to linguistic patterns of interaction: the analysis of communication in the language classroom," *International Review of Applied Linguistics*, 32(4), 303–20.

Seedhouse, P. (2004), *The Interactional Architecture of the Language Classroom: A Conversation Analysis Perspective*, Malden, MA: Blackwell.

Seedhouse, P. (2008), "Learning to talk the talk: Conversation Analysis as a tool for the induction of trainee teachers," in S. Garton and K. Richards (eds.), *Professional Encounters in TESOL: Discourses of Teachers in Teaching*, London: Palgrave Macmillan, pp. 42–57.

Seedhouse, P. (2010), "A framework for conceptualizing learning in applied linguistics," in P. Seedhouse, S. Walsh, and C. J. Jenks (eds.), *Conceptualising 'Learning' in Applied Linguistics*, Basingstoke: Palgrave Macmillan, pp. 240–56.

Seedhouse, P. and S. Walsh (2010), "Learning a second language through classroom interaction," in P. Seedhouse, S. Walsh, and C. J. Jenks (eds.), *Conceptualising 'Learning' in Applied Linguistics*, Basingstoke: Palgrave Macmillan, pp. 127–46.

Seedhouse, P., S. Walsh, and C. J. Jenks (eds.) (2010), *Conceptualising 'Learning' in Applied Linguistics*, Basingstoke: Palgrave Macmillan.

Seo, M.-S. and I. Koshik (2010), "A conversation analytic study of gestures that engender repair in conversational tutoring," *Journal of Pragmatics*, 42, 2219–39.

Sert, O. (2011), "A micro-analytic investigation of claims of insufficient knowledge in EAL classrooms," Unpublished doctoral dissertation, Newcastle University, Newcastle upon Tyne.

Sert, O. (2013), "'Epistemic status check' as an interactional phenomenon in instructed learning settings," *Journal of Pragmatics*, 45(1), 13–28.

Sert, O. (2015), *Social Interaction and L2 Classroom Discourse*, Edinburgh: Edinburgh University Press.

Sert, O. (2019a), "The interplay between collaborative turn sequences and active listenership: implications for the development of L2 interactional competence," in M. R. Salaberry and S. Kunitz (eds.), *Teaching and Testing L2 Interactional Competence: Bridging Theory and Practice*, New York: Routledge, pp. 142–66.

Sert, O. (2019b), "Classroom interaction and language teacher education," in S. Walsh and S. Mann (eds.), *The Routledge Handbook of English Language Teacher Education*, New York: Routledge, pp. 216–38.

Sert, O. (forthcoming), "Transforming CA findings into future L2 teaching practices: challenges and prospects for teacher education," in S. Kunitz, O. Sert, and N. Markee (eds.), *Classroom-Based Conversation Analytic Research: Theoretical and Applied Perspectives on Pedagogy*, Heidelberg: Springer.

Sert, O. and S. Walsh (2012), "The interactional management of claims of insufficient knowledge in English language classrooms," *Language and Education*, 27(6), 542-56. DOI: 10.1080/09500782.2012.739174.

Sfard, A. (1998), "On two metaphors for learning and the dangers of choosing just one," *Educational Researcher*, 27(2), 4-13.

Sidnell, J. (2013), "Basic Conversation Analytic methods," in J. Sidnell and T. Stivers (eds.), *The Handbook of Conversation Analysis*, Malden, MA: Blackwell, pp. 77-99.

Sikveland, R. and R. Ogden (2012), "Holding gestures across turns: moments to generate shared understanding," *Gesture*, 12(2), 166-99.

Sinclair, J. M. and R. M. Coulthard (1975), *Towards an Analysis of Discourse: The English Used by Teachers and Pupils*, London: Oxford University Press.

Smotrova, T. (2014), "Instructional functions of speech and gesture in the L2 classroom," Unpublished doctoral dissertation, The Pennsylvania State University.

Smotrova, T. and J. P. Lantolf (2013), "The function of gesture in lexically focused L2 instructional conversations," *The Modern Language Journal*, 97(2), 397-416.

Stanford Center for Assessment, Learning and Equity (2016), *edTPA English as an Additional Language Assessment Handbook*, Stanford, CA: Board of Trustees of the Leland Stanford Junior University.

Stivers, T. (2008), "Stance, alignment, and affiliation during storytelling: when nodding is a token of affiliation," *Research on Language and Social Interaction*, 41(1), 31-57.

Stivers, T. and J. Sidnell (2013), "Introduction," in J. Sidnell and T. Stivers (eds.), *The Handbook of Conversation Analysis*, Malden, MA: Blackwell, pp. 1-8.

Sullivan, P. (2017), *Economic Inequality, Neoliberalism, and the American Community College*, New York: Springer.

Tadic, N. (2018), "'My brain hurts:' incorporating learner interests into the classroom," *Language and Education*, 33(1). Available at: <https://doi.org/10.1080/09500782.2018.1476527> (last accessed July 7, 2020).

Tellier, M. (2008), "The effect of gestures on second language memorisation by young children," *Gesture*, 8(2), 219-35.

Thorne, S. (2010), "The 'intercultural turn' and language learning in the crucible of new media," in S. Guth and F. Helm (eds.), *Telecollaboration 2.0: Language, Literacies and Intercultural Learning in the 21st Century*, New York: Peter Lang, pp. 139-64.

Tindell, D. R. and R. W. Bohlander (2012), "The use and abuse of cell phones and text messaging in the classroom: a survey of college students," *College Teaching*, 60(1), 1-9.

Tolins, J. (2013), "Assessment and direction through nonlexical vocalizations in music instruction," *Research on Language & Social Interaction*, 46(1), 47-64.

van Compernolle, R. A. (2015), *Interaction and Second Language Development: A Vygotskian Perspective*, Amsterdam and Philadelphia: John Benjamins.

van Compernolle, R. A. and T. Smotrova (2014), "Corrective feedback, gesture, and mediation in classroom language learning," *Language and Sociocultural Theory*, 1(1), 25-47.

van Lier, L. (1984), "Analysing interaction in second language classrooms," *ELT Journal*, 38(3), 160-9.

van Lier, L. (1988), *The Classroom and the Language Learner: Ethnography and Second-Language Classroom Research*, London: Longman.

van Lier, L. (2001), "Constraints and resources in classroom talk: issues of equality and symmetry," in C. Candlin and N. Mercer (eds.), *English Language Teaching in its Social Context*, New York: Routledge, pp. 90–107.

van Lier, L. (2002), "An ecological-semiotic perspective on language and linguistics," in C. Kramsch (ed.), *Language Acquisition and Language Socialization*, New York: Continuum, pp. 140–64.

van Lier, L. (2008), "Agency in the classroom," in J. P. Lantolf and M. E. Poehner (eds.), *Sociocultural Theory and the Teaching of Second Languages*, London: Equinox, pp. 163–86.

Vavrus, F. and K. M. Cole (2002) "'I didn't do nothin': the discursive construction of school suspension," *The Urban Review*, 34(2), 87–111.

Walsh, S. (2003), "Developing interactional awareness in the second language classroom through teacher self-evaluation," *Language Awareness*, 12(2), 124–42.

Walsh, S. (2006), *Investigating Classroom Discourse*, New York: Routledge.

Walsh, S. (2011), *Exploring Classroom Discourse: Language in Action*, New York: Routledge.

Walsh, S. and L. Li (2016), "Classroom talk, interaction and collaboration," in G. Hall (ed.), *The Routledge Handbook of English Language Teaching*, New York: Routledge, pp. 486–98.

Waring, H. Z. (2002), "Displaying substantive recipiency in seminar discussion," *Research on Language and Social Interaction*, 35(4), 453–79.

Waring, H. Z. (2008), "Using explicit positive assessment in the language classroom: IRF, feedback, and learning opportunities," *The Modern Language Journal*, 92(4), 577–94.

Waring, H. Z. (2009), "Moving out of IRF (initiation–response–feedback): a single case analysis," *Language Learning*, 59(4), 796–824.

Waring, H. Z. (2012a), "'Any questions?': investigating the nature of understanding-checks in the language classroom," *TESOL Quarterly*, 46(4), 722–52.

Waring, H. Z. (2012b), "Yes-no questions that convey a critical stance in the language classroom," *Language and Education*, 26(5), 451–69.

Waring, H. Z. (2013a), "Managing Stacy: a case study of turn-taking in the language classroom," *System*, 41, 841–51.

Waring, H. Z. (2013b), "Managing competing voices in the second language classroom," *Discourse Processes*, 50(5), 316–38.

Waring, H. Z. (2016), *Theorizing Pedagogical Interaction*, New York: Routledge.

Waring, H. Z., E. Reddington, and N. Tadic (2016), "Responding artfully to student-initiated departures in the adult ESL classroom," *Linguistics and Education*, 33, 28–39.

Wells, G. (1993), "Reevaluating the IRF sequence: a proposal for the articulation of theories of activity and discourse for the analysis of teaching and learning in the classroom," *Linguistics and Education*, 5, 1–37.

Wells, G. (2000), "Modes of meaning in a science activity," *Linguistics and Education*, 10(3), 307–34.

Wong, J. and H. Z. Waring (2009), "'Very good' as a teacher response," *ELT Journal*, 63(3), 195–203.

Wong, J. and H. Z. Waring (2010), *Conversation Analysis and Second Language Pedagogy: A Guide for ESL/EFL Teachers*, New York: Routledge.

Young, R. F. and E. R. Miller (2004), "Learning as changing participation: discourse roles in ESL writing conferences," *The Modern Language Journal*, 88(4), 519–35.

Zhao, J. (2007), "Metaphors and gestures for abstract concepts in Academic English writing," Unpublished doctoral dissertation, University of Arizona, Tucson.

INDEX

action formation, 8, 27
active listening, 169–70
   embodied, 170
activity shift, 98
activity transition, 97–8, 144–56, 156–8, 169
alignment, 8, 74
   embodied, 112
   interactional, 9, 23, 51, 166, 168
   pedagogical, 9, 23, 51, 166, 168
artifacts, 30, 107, 155, 159
attention, 23, 25, 28, 118, 121, 143

bid for turn, 139, 142, 183
   embodied, 79, 95
body movement, 29, 98, 134–5, 176
byplay, 6, 43, 66
   embodied, 73

catchment, 87
category-bound action, 10, 48–9, 51, 113, 117, 127, 159, 168
checking episode, 19, 52, 70–2, 132, 141–2, 160–1, 169, 187
choral response, 91, 168, 187
   embodied, 94, 96, 140, 169
   verbal, 52–5, 169
claim of insufficient knowledge (CIK), 7, 24, 132
classroom discourse, 15
classroom interaction competence (CIC), 20, 24, 40, 45, 52, 61, 117, 128, 186–7
collaborative completion, 65, 117, 185–6
collections, 31
collusion, 11, 24, 114, 187
common interactional space, 30
confirmation check, 57
conversation analysis, 8, 25
co-presence, 42
Coulthard, 15

designedly-incomplete utterance (DIU), 120
devices, 132, 146–51, 159–64, 171–82

directive, 97
   for multimodal action, 99–102
disengagement, 24, 47, 131–65, 177, 181
   anticipatory, 144
   appearance of *see* display of
   covert, 172–8
   display of, 106–7, 112–14, 161, 163, 177
   domino, 178–82
   performance of *see* display of
   self-presentation as, 159
doing-being-a-listener, 106–7, 115
doing-being-a-student, 1, 10, 12, 21–5, 34, 40, 45–6, 49–50, 51, 116, 129, 130, 131, 136, 160, 163, 165–6, 168, 171, 178, 186–7, 188
doing-listening, 7, 116, 126, 130, 159, 169–70, 186
   demonstration of, 129, 182
   display of *see* demonstration of

ecological huddle, 30, 43, 73, 84, 121, 183
embodied completion, 78, 84, 85, 87
embodied request, 93, 163
embodied response, 95, 140
embodied turn, 26
embodiment, 26
Emdin, 188
emic perspective, 25
encounter, 181
engagement, 1, 7, 11, 23, 25, 26, 45, 47, 49, 51, 74, 76, 85–92, 112–14, 128, 134–5, 140, 141, 142, 144–51, 159, 161, 166–9, 182–6, 187, 188–9
   display of, 116, 189
   embodied, 103–5, 169, 186
   multimodal, 161
   with delayed participation, 77
epistemics, 58, 60–1, 75
   epistemic status check (ESC), 132
explicit positive assessment (EPA), 44, 78, 95, 96

facial expression, 6, 67, 83, 188
F-formation, 30
footing, 128

gaze, 28, 84, 94–5, 102, 113–14, 116–17, 118–30, 176, 185
 aversion, 104
 mutual, 78, 83–4, 103, 132–5, 138, 140, 143, 155, 182
 shift, 92
 to object, 181
 withdrawal, 132–5, 181
Gestalt, complex multimodal, 25, 29–30, 31, 74, 118
gesture, 28, 85–91, 140, 143, 181
 beat, 90
 deictic, 79, 143
 hold, 90
 iconic, 83, 140, 163
 metaphorical, 86
 nod, 91, 185
Goffman, 8, 10, 17, 26, 28, 41–7, 131, 160, 188
Goodwin, C., 8, 10, 26, 27, 29, 74
Goodwin, M. H., 7, 10, 26, 49, 74
Gourlay, 19

hand-raising, 93–5, 136–41
hearership, 106
Heath, 51
Hellermann, 23
Heritage, 25
home position, 29, 86, 93, 116

imitation, 87
incipiency, 95, 129–30, 182–3
increment, 102
initiation-response-evaluation (IRE) *see* initiation-response-feedback (IRF)
initiation-response-feedback (IRF), 16–17, 19–20, 56
institutional talk, 26
interactional awareness, 167
interaction order, 17
invitation
 to bid, 56
 to reply, 56

Jacknick, 11, 22, 57
Jefferson, 26, 129
joint attentional focus, 107, 113, 127, 170

Kendon, 28
Koole, 23, 33, 116, 128

laughter, 143
learning, 12, 68–72, 186, 188
Lerner, 21

letting it pass, 151
listener response, 102–3
listenership, 23, 47, 106, 114
 active, 121

McDermott, 11
McHoul, 16
McNeill, 29
Markee, 22, 27
Mehan, 16, 18, 56
membership categorization, 120
modes, 18, 19, 20, 56
 classroom context mode, 20
 managerial mode, 19, 97, 149–51, 158
 materials mode, 19, 57–58, 70–2, 118, 150
 mode convergence, 20
 mode divergence, 20
 mode side sequences, 20
 mode switching, 20
 skills and system mode, 19, 66, 118
Mondada, 8, 27, 30, 31, 32, 171
monitoring, 1, 11, 28, 42, 51, 90–1, 93, 96–8, 100–4, 128, 133, 141, 142, 164, 166, 167, 168, 171, 176–7, 182, 186, 187
multiactivity, 118, 122, 128, 132, 167, 169
multilogue, 46
multimodal analysis, 26
multimodality, 26
multimodal listening, 106, 169–70
 active, 117–30
 display of, 129
 task-based, 114–17
multimodal response *see* embodied response
multitasking *see* multiactivity

Nevile, 30
nomination, 56, 143
non-participation, 12, 24, 26, 47–9, 51, 69, 100, 121, 131, 138, 141, 151, 165

objects *see* artifacts
off-task, 151, 164, 172
open-floor prompt, 144
open-floor question, 75
other-correction, 118–21, 127–8, 170
other-nomination, 141, 143

parallel activities, 68, 73, 100, 102, 113, 122–9, 130, 132, 164, 168, 170
participation, 1, 7–11, 12, 15, 21–23, 25, 26, 42, 46, 47–9, 51, 112–14, 138, 161, 166
 availability for, 164
 delayed, 140
 disengaged, 113, 135–41
 embodied, 85, 95, 132–59, 141, 186
 engaged, 56–61, 65–6, 130
 grading of, 187, 189

participation framework, 26, 29–30, 35, 42, 43–5, 46, 91, 96, 102, 146, 177
  embodied, 83
participation status, 44
participation structure, 16, 18, 22, 68, 103, 141, 156, 168, 169, 183, 186, 187
performance, 22, 27, 40, 41, 51, 156, 163, 165, 166, 168, 187, 189
performance metaphor, 42, 45–6
performance reading, 121
personal front, 160–3
post-expansion, 59–61
post-mortem, 120, 181
posture, 29, 97, 98, 102, 114, 116–17, 128–9, 156–9, 177, 186, 188
preface, 146
presentation of self as student, 31, 41, 165
pre-sequence, 97, 112
primary activity, 113
progressivity, 114, 121, 128, 130, 143, 158, 161, 172, 186, 187
prompt for embodied action, 77, 96, 102, 135, 138
protective practice, 163
proxemics, 29

rapport, 169
read aloud, 107–14
recipiency, 106, 130, 151, 183
  embodied, 102
  substantive, 118
repair, 118–21, 130, 169
  open-class repair initiation, 63, 83
reproach, 135, 161–3, 177
response pursuit, 163
role, 27, 41, 45
role distance, 45, 188–9
round robin *see* checking episode

Sacks, 26, 29, 74, 106, 129
Sahlström, 95, 130, 138–9, 182
sanction *see* reproach
Sarangi, 18
Sartre, 41
Schegloff, 25, 29, 129
Schwab, 46
Seedhouse, 18, 47
self-correction, 118–20
self-repair, 127–8
self-talk, 146, 181
sequentiality, 27, 74, 169
Sert, 117, 131
shared focus of attention *see* joint attentional focus
side sequence, 140

Sidnell, 8
Sinclair, 15
sleeping, 158–9
smiles, 143
socially-distributed cognition, 12
spatial organization, 182
spatial orientation, 103, 187
studenting, 2, 10, 48, 49, 51, 69, 102, 113–14, 168
  disengaged, 113, 117, 121, 127–9, 130, 159, 168, 170, 188
  embodied, 91–3
  engaged, 61–4, 99
  engaged studenting-cum-learning, 68–72, 168
student initiations, 21, 56–7, 59–61, 100
Stivers, 8
summons turns, 93

teacher-directed *see* teacher-fronted
teacher education, 166
teacher-fronted, 9, 13, 15, 16, 17, 35, 42, 46, 56, 102, 106, 130, 132, 135, 144, 146, 168, 169
teacher-led *see* teacher-fronted
temporality, 27, 74, 96
transcription, 31–4, 52, 170–1
trouble, 117, 118–21, 130, 132, 181
turn-constructional unit (TCU), 120
Tylbor, 11

unwillingness to participate (UTP), 11, 23, 75–9, 84–5, 96, 103, 104, 131, 139–40, 141, 143
  embodied, 132–44

van Compernolle, 23, 47
van Lier, 25

Walsh, 18, 47, 188
Waring, 1, 2, 24
wave, 54
  anticipatory disengagement, 151–6
  delayed engagement, 144–51
  disengagement, 171, 178
  embodied, 93–103, 104, 135, 138–9, 168–9
  engagement, 171
  multimodal *see* embodied
  unwillingness to participate, 133–5
whole-class *see* teacher-fronted
willingness to participate (WTP), 7, 23, 24, 46, 77, 95, 104, 131, 132
writing, 91–3, 98–100, 102, 104, 113, 116–17, 122–9, 138, 172, 188

EU representative:
Easy Access System Europe
Mustamäe tee 50, 10621 Tallinn, Estonia
Gpsr.requests@easproject.com

www.ingramcontent.com/pod-product-compliance
Lightning Source LLC
Chambersburg PA
CBHW071840230426
43671CB00012B/2014